Advance praise for *Connecting to Change the World*

"The Millenial generation's mission is to work together to change the world for the better. *Connecting to Change the World* is destined to become the guidebook for building the generative social networks they will use to accomplish their goal. Everyone interested in making global change happen at the local level will benefit from following the sage advice built on practical experience that permeates the pages of this book."

> — Morley Winograd, coauthor, *Millennial Momentum:*
> *How a New Generation is Remaking America*

"As government leaders steer more and row less, networks become an indispensable tool to solve complex problems and achieve critical public goals. This insightful book will tell you everything you need to know to create and use networks effectively. Beautifully written, with case studies woven throughout, it is as entertaining as it is useful. I wish I had read it twenty-five years ago!"

> — David Osborne, coauthor of *Reinventing Government,*
> *Banishing Bureaucracy, The Reinventor's Fieldbook,* and
> *The Price of Government*

"Whether you're a social entrepreneur, a nonprofit executive, a funder, or a grassroots activist, you'll find strategies, tools, and cases that you can use to power your vision as well as your everyday work. *Connecting to Change the World* is essential reading for anyone who's passionate about using networks to advance social change."

> — Kathy Reich, Director of Organizational Effectiveness
> Grantmaking, David and Lucile Packard Foundation

"*Connecting to Change the World* provides social entrepreneurs with a powerful new tool for organizing change—the creation of generative networks that empower and unleash the complementary energies of large numbers of independent and interdependent actors. Incorporating lessons from dozens of networks in a host of fields—many of which they had a hand in improving—the authors advance the understanding and practice of an important emerging tool for social change, providing specific steps to success and important insights. I highly recommend this book to anyone serious about unleashing social change."

> — Bob Friedman, Founder and Chair, Corporation for
> Enterprise Development (CFED); Board Member,
> Family Independence Initiative, Child and Youth Finance
> International, the Rosenberg Foundation

"Inspiring, practical advice for the most powerful pathway for social impact—the authors bring decades of deep experience in the most dynamic organizing model for creating change. This is a guidebook for twenty-first-century social transformation."

> – Graham Richard, Chief Executive Officer,
> Advanced Energy Economy

"Is there a twenty-first-century blueprint for sustainable social change? If, like me, you've been working in the trenches to grow a new world only to be stumped by the very real barriers of weak tools—foolhardy business models, unimaginative value propositions, and the twentieth-century hangover of scale—then this is the book for you. *Connecting to Change the World* sheds light on why some organizations feel like heavy bricks, whereas others defy gravity. Read on to discover how to situate yourself to grow social change that lives on longer than we do and goes to places we hadn't imagined. "

> – Richard McCarthy, Executive Director for Slow Food USA

"The authors of *Connecting to Change the World* have rightly concluded that pooling talent and resources to address complex social and environmental problems is the only way to go. Their highly readable new book explains the art of creating collaborative solutions. Architecture 2030 is pleased to have worked with the authors when forming a national network of city-based 2030 Districts—local networks focused on carbon emissions, energy, and water reductions. We enthusiastically endorse their approach and recommend their new book to individuals and groups committed to solving problems and ensuring a positive impact."

> – Ed Mazria, Founder and Chief Executive Officer,
> Architecture 2030

"An important contribution to the growing literature on networks, *Connecting to Change the World* offers startlingly useful guidance to those who need to navigate a changing new world increasingly represented by links and nodes. Avoiding the hyperbole and conjecture that sometimes accompany claims on the potential of networks, the authors rely on their research and experience to pinpoint the benefits and limitations of networks. As a person who works with policy makers and is actively engaged in philanthropy, this will become a well-worn reference book."

> –Anita R. Brown-Graham, Director, Institute for
> Emerging Issues, NC State University

About Island Press

Since 1984, the nonprofit organization Island Press has been stimulating, shaping, and communicating ideas that are essential for solving environmental problems worldwide. With more than 800 titles in print and some 40 new releases each year, we are the nation's leading publisher on environmental issues. We identify innovative thinkers and emerging trends in the environmental field. We work with world-renowned experts and authors to develop cross-disciplinary solutions to environmental challenges.

Island Press designs and executes educational campaigns in conjunction with our authors to communicate their critical messages in print, in person, and online using the latest technologies, innovative programs, and the media. Our goal is to reach targeted audiences—scientists, policymakers, environmental advocates, urban planners, the media, and concerned citizens—with information that can be used to create the framework for long-term ecological health and human well-being.

Island Press gratefully acknowledges major support of our work by The Agua Fund, The Andrew W. Mellon Foundation, Betsy & Jesse Fink Foundation, The Bobolink Foundation, The Curtis and Edith Munson Foundation, Forrest C. and Frances H. Lattner Foundation, G.O. Forward Fund of the Saint Paul Foundation, Gordon and Betty Moore Foundation, The Kresge Foundation, The Margaret A. Cargill Foundation, New Mexico Water Initiative, a project of Hanuman Foundation, The Overbrook Foundation, The S.D. Bechtel, Jr. Foundation, The Summit Charitable Foundation, Inc., V. Kann Rasmussen Foundation, The Wallace Alexander Gerbode Foundation, and other generous supporters.

The opinions expressed in this book are those of the author(s) and do not necessarily reflect the views of our supporters.

Connecting to Change the World

CONNECTING TO CHANGE THE WORLD

Harnessing the Power of Networks for Social Impact

Peter Plastrik, Madeleine Taylor,
and John Cleveland

Washington | Covelo | London

Island Press is a trademark of Island Press/The Center for Resource Economics.

Library of Congress Cataloging-in-Publication Data
Plastrik, Peter.
   Connecting to change the world : harnessing the power of networks for social impact / Peter Plastrik, Madeleine Taylor and John Cleveland.
    pages cm
   Includes bibliographical references and index.
   ISBN 978-1-61091-532-8 (hardback) — ISBN 1-61091-532-1 (cloth) — ISBN 978-1-61091-533-5 (ebook) 1. Nonprofit organizations—Management—Technological innovations. 2. Online social networks—Political aspects. 3. Social change. I. Title.
   HD62.6.P635 2014
   '658'.046--dc23

                                                              2014017541

Printed on recycled, acid-free paper ♻

Manufactured in the United States of America
10 9 8 7 6 5 4 3 2

Keywords: networks, social impact networks, social change, network weaving, generative problems

Contents

Introduction   1

Chapter 1.   The Generative Network Difference   13

Chapter 2.   Start Me Up: Designing a Network   39

- Purpose   43

- Membership   46

- Value Propositions   51

- Coordination, Facilitation, and Communication   54

- Resources   59

- Governance   65

- Assessment   69

- Operating Principles   70

Bonus Track—Advice for Funders and Other Network
              Engineers   75

Chapter 3.   Connect the Dots: Weaving a Network's Core   83

Chapter 4.   Network Evolution   103

Chapter 5.   Enable and Adapt: Managing a Network's
              Development   119

- Member Engagement   124

- Network Infrastructure   129

- Provisional Planning   135

- Periphery Relationships   139

Chapter 6.   Know Your Condition: Taking a Network's Pulse   147

Chapter 7.   Back to Basics: Resetting a Network's Design   167

Chapter 8.   Three Rules to Build By   177

             Afterword   187

             Acknowledgments   189

             Notes   191

             Resources for Network Builders   201

             Appendices   209

             About the Authors   231

             Index   233

For our children—

André, David, Emily, Josh, Lauren, Matheus,

Rachel, Sam, Steven—

and the world they are shaping

In memory of Marion Kane,

who helped us start down the network path

If you want to go quickly, go alone.
If you want to go far, go together.

— African proverb

I must confess that I've never trusted the Web. I've always seen it as a coward's tool. Where does it live? How do you hold it personally responsible? Can you put a distributed network of fiber-optic cable "on notice"? And is it male or female? In other words, can I challenge it to a fight?

— Stephen Colbert

The atom is the icon of the twentieth century. The atom whirls alone. It is the metaphor for individuality. But the atom is the past. The symbol for the next century is the net. The net has no center, no orbits, no certainty. It is an indefinite web of causes. The net is the archetype displayed to represent all circuits, all intelligence, all interdependence, all things economic, social, or ecological, all communications, all democracy, all families, all large systems, almost all that we find interesting and important.

Whereas the atom represents clean simplicity, the net channels messy complexity.

— Kevin Kelly

Introduction

Networks are present everywhere. All we need is an eye for them.

— *Albert-László Barabasi*

If you started your first job after 1990, then you missed the heyday of the organization. For much of the twentieth century, the organization was the go-to way to marshal collective energy and get things done. The world was filled with "organization men" toiling in the bowels of business corporations and government bureaucracies. A similar dynamic held when someone caught the social-change bug. They would start an organization, typically a nonprofit, appoint a board of directors that hired an executive director, obtain funds from philanthropic donors, hire staff, and initiate programs. The organization was an extension of the founder's vision and ego. The board and managers at the top made the decisions. Social enterprises became such a large-scale phenomenon that by 2008 the United States alone was home to more than 1.5 million registered nonprofits.

But the stand-alone organization has been losing its sway over how we think about organizing our efforts. Beginning in the 1980s, the corporate business world started to question the effectiveness of its own command-and-control model. The internationally best-selling *In Search of Excellence* offered evidence that better performance can result from decentralized control, in which a business's frontline employees, rather than bosses on high, have authority to make decisions. Tom Peters, Peter Block, Max De Pree, and other employee-empowerment gurus amplified this message in the business-management literature. The 1997 *Fast Company* magazine cover story, "Free Agent Nation," reported that 25 million Americans worked independently—for themselves rather than for a single employer.

Decentralization didn't dethrone the corporate CEO and chain of command, but in the 1990s a new challenger—the network—emerged. A network is a radical version of decentralization that in its most robust form can eliminate altogether the need for an organization. For many people, the network represents an anti-organization worldview; a "net-centric" approach offers a new and better way of dealing with problems and opportunities. In 1994, Jessica Lipnack and Jeffrey Stamps, authors of *The Age of the Network*, declared that "the network is coming of age as a mature, useful, and pervasive form of organization. . . . Life has become too complicated for hierarchy and bureaucracy." A few years later, Kevin Kelly, a cofounder of *Wired* magazine, heralded the rise of networks in *New Rules for the New Economy*: "The dynamic of our society, and particularly our new economy, will increasingly obey the logic of the network." Then the power of social networks drew increasing notice in mass media headlines, from the emergence of Al Qaeda and the far-flung mobilizations of the World Social Forum and Moveon.org to the explosive growth of Howard Dean's Internet-based presidential campaign in 2004, which used a website to grow from 3,000 members to 140,000 members in less than a year. In a blog, Dean's campaign manager, Joe Trippi, put his finger on the difference between a tightly controlled campaign and the peer-to-peer dynamic he was unleashing for the candidate: "Every political campaign I have ever seen was built on the top-down military structure. . . . This kind of structure will suffocate the storm, not fuel it. . . . The important thing is to provide the tools and some of the direction . . . and get the hell out of the way when a big wave is building on its own."

Around the same time, the importance of networks began trending in global thought leadership. Malcolm Gladwell's *The Tipping Point* (2000) described the way that "connectors" help to produce social epidemics. Seth Godin's *Unleashing the Ideavirus* (2001) explained how to turn ideas into epidemics by spreading them through customers' relationships with other customers, and James Surowiecki's *The Wisdom of Crowds* (2004) brought crowdsourcing into the spotlight. *New York Times* columnist Thomas Friedman famously announced in 2005 that "the world is flat":

"We are now connecting all the knowledge centers on the planet together into a single global network." *Linked: The New Science of Networks* (2002) and *Six Degrees: The Science of a Connected Age* (2003) introduced the public to the science of networks—described by physicist/sociologist Duncan Watts as a "world of people, friendships, rumors, disease, fads, firms, and financial crises."

Without anyone planning it, the network thought-wave surged in cyberspace. New Internet-based social-media tools for connecting people with each other—Facebook, LinkedIn, MySpace, Meetup, YouTube, Twitter—met the Millennial Generation. Millennials, born between 1982 and 2003, are the largest generation of Americans ever, and connecting with each other electronically is a defining aspect of their generational culture. They have "a strong group and community orientation and a clear tendency to share their thoughts and activities with others—friends, teachers, and parents," reported Morley Winograd and Michael D. Hais, authors of three books about the generation. Millennials are much less interested in building organizations than their parents were, as Beth Kanter and Allison Fine explained in *The Networked Nonprofit*: "In their world, information sharing and power has shifted toward individuals. This creates a huge distinction in their minds between a cause they're passionate about, such as cancer research, and a stand-alone nonprofit organization they may not care about at all."

Spurred by Millennial adoption, the spread of Web 2.0 tools drove fundamental change in how groups form and work gets done, noted Gabriel Kasper and Diana Scearce: "Social media are engendering new, networked ways of behaving—ways of *working wikily*—that are characterized by principles of openness, transparency, decentralized decision-making, and distributed action." Tom Friedman marveled in April 2013 that, eight years earlier when he wrote *The World Is Flat*, "Facebook, Twitter, 4G, iPhones, iPads . . . the cloud, Big Data, cellphone apps, and Skype did not exist or were in their infancy." Since then, he added, "The combination of these tools of connectivity and creativity has created a global education, commercial, communication, and innovation platform on which more people can start stuff, collaborate on stuff, learn stuff, make stuff (and destroy stuff) with more other people than ever before." The Internet fueled what Yale law professor Yochai Benkler in *The Wealth of Networks* called "the rise of effective, large-scale cooperative efforts—peer production of information, knowledge, and culture." Exhibit A in Benkler's analysis: 50,000 volunteers coauthor *Wikipedia* "and then turn around and give it away for free."

With network-building reaching global scale, it's not surprising to find networks accorded a place on the world stage alongside the nation-state. In a presentation at the TEDGlobal 2012 conference, Beth Noveck, the U.S. federal government's first deputy chief technology officer, declared that "the next great superpower is going to be the one who can successfully combine the hierarchy of institution . . . with the diversity and pulsating life and the chaos and excitement of networks."

What this all adds up to is the Gospel of the Network—spreading the good news that there is another way to organize the future. Claims that the organization-centric model is dead are surely an exaggeration, but the much-heralded birth of the net-centric approach is not. In a remarkably short span of time, Joe Trippi's "big wave . . . building on its own" has arrived, flowing into every community and sector. We have crossed the threshold into what Duncan Watts called "the connected age." The network has become a favored unit of action for people who want to make nearly any sort of difference in the world.

Social-Impact Networks

When we first wrote about networks, in 2004, we were interested in how to use them to more effectively achieve social change. We were veterans in the social-change game—starting our own nonprofits, obtaining grants from major U.S. foundations, guiding foundations and other nonprofits through strategic-planning processes, consulting with start-up social enterprises. We were intrigued by networks. At the time, though, the social-change sector focused mostly on organizations. Foundations provided billions of dollars every year to fuel social change, nearly all of it to organizations. Social entrepreneurs automatically started organizations, in part so they'd be able to obtain foundation funding. We knew Margaret Mead's famous quotation—"Never doubt that a small group of thoughtful, committed citizens can change the world; indeed, it is the only thing that ever has"—but we assumed without thinking that the small groups always started organizations to achieve the change.

After closely examining a handful of social-change networks in the United States, we thought they showed great potential and so we encouraged foundation and nonprofit leaders to pay attention to the emerging phenomenon. Networks, we argued, provide social-change agents with a fundamentally distinct and promising "organizing principle" to achieve ambitious goals. The civil sector was under growing pressure to do more and better. In light of government downsizing and the growing complexity of social problems, civil organizations needed ways to improve their impact, leverage, and return on funders' investments. Nonprofits were expected to be more strategic, entrepreneurial, and high-performing. Growing doubts about the prowess of individual social-change organizations came to a head in a widely read article by John Kania and Mark Kramer that declared, "There is scant evidence that isolated initiatives are the best way to solve many social problems in today's complex and interdependent world. No single organization is responsible for any major social problem, nor can any single organization cure it."

Today the social-change landscape looks quite different. Along with the perfect storm of Millennials meeting the Internet, there has been an upwelling of social entrepreneurship worldwide—of "people who solve problems on a large scale," as David Bornstein described them in *How to Change the World*. "More people today have the freedom, time, wealth, health, exposure, social mobility, and confidence to address social problems in bold new ways." In this new climate for civic problem solving, networks are proliferating. "Civic revolutionaries have networks, and every person in their networks has networks," noted the authors of *Civic Revolutionaries*. "Understanding and mobilizing these networks is the key to driving change."

Generative Networks for Social Impact

People use the word *network* to describe many things, but this book is about something quite specific: networks of individuals or organizations that aim to solve a difficult problem in the society by working together, adapting over time, and generating a sustained flow of activities and impacts. We call these *generative social-impact networks*—"generative" because they are designed to be a platform for generating multiple, ongoing kinds of change, not just accomplishing a single outcome; "social-impact" because they specifically focus on achieving change that results in social good. They are quite different from social-media networks like Facebook and LinkedIn and from other forms of member-based social organizing that usually get tossed into the network basket. Each of these networks is a set of people, typically numbering in the hundreds, whose connections with each other enable them to generate more and more collaborative effort over time. The members don't just connect, share, and collaborate online; they forge powerful, enduring personal relationships based on trust and reciprocity that are supported by face-to-face engagement as well as digital tools for connectivity. Nor do they come together like a coalition to tackle just one thing, like advocating for a specific government policy, and then disband; connecting makes it possible for them to undertake numerous activities, many of which emerge over the years. And they don't just gather to pool their resources to obtain services they all want, like an association; they link to enable themselves, not staff, to do the work.

A generative network is a social-relationship platform—a "human operating system"—for spawning activities. It's a unique and renewable capacity, and this makes it especially useful when taking on complex, unpredictable, large-scale problems like climate change, homelessness, or education system performance, which won't yield to a silver-bullet solution.

In the chapters that follow we'll introduce you to active, long-lived, generative social-impact networks and some of their founders, funders, and coordinators, and explain more about how they're different from other types of collective effort and what makes them tick. These networks include the following:

- The Urban Sustainability Directors Network and eight regional networks of sustainability directors—local government officials—from more than 150 cities in the United States and Canada.
- Three business-driven networks: the Partnership Fund for New York—a network of some 200 corporate and financial-institution executives, started by Henry Kravis, cofounder of the private equity firm Kohlberg Kravis Roberts & Co.; Advanced Energy Economy—a U.S. association of businesses started by Tom

Steyer, founder of Farallon Capital Management; and the West Michigan Manufacturers Council—learning networks that involve dozens of medium to large manufacturers.

- Rural People, Rural Policy—five regional and two national networks of rural-based organizations, initially assembled and funded by the W. K. Kellogg Foundation to promote public policies that benefit rural communities in the United States.
- Reboot—a network of young, Jewish-American "cultural creative" professionals in the arts and media, which explores and redefines Jewish identity and community in the United States and the United Kingdom.
- Lawrence CommunityWorks—a network of thousands of people in Lawrence, Massachusetts, established to revitalize the fading industrial community.
- RE-AMP—more than 165 nonprofit organizations and foundations in eight Midwestern states working together on climate change and energy policy.
- The Learning Network of Greater Kalamazoo—a community collaborative of dozens of local organizations and parents, students, and other individuals who share the vision that every child in the county will be "ready for school, ready for college, and ready for the world"—backed by $11 million in grants from the Kalamazoo Community and Kellogg Foundations.
- The Massachusetts Interagency Council on Housing and Homelessness—a state government initiative using regional networks of state agencies and nonprofit providers to test innovative services for homeless individuals and families and reduce the need for emergency assistance shelters.
- The Network of Korean American Leaders—promoting civic leadership among successful second-generation Korean American professionals, an initiative of the University of Southern California's School of Social Work.
- The Fire Learning Network—a partnership of The Nature Conservancy and U.S. federal government land managers to transform the use of fire in ecological management.

Practice, Practice, Practice

We are network geeks, and proud of it. For more than 10 years we've studied networks, built our own, and helped others build dozens around the world. We talk about networks for hours, only to get more energized. We read the latest academic research to see what theories and models are emerging. We surf the Web to find people as obsessed as we are about understanding and building networks, and we network with them. We've learned how to use network-mapping software and to analyze the fascinating maps it produces. We blog about networks, produce online tools for assessing a network's health, coach network builders, and run workshops about building networks.

We didn't used to be net-aholics. Like everyone else, we had personal networks of friends and colleagues. We dabbled with building a few networks. Madeleine, who's an anthropologist, knew about Social Network Analysis. We had studied complexity theory, which turned out to be useful for understanding networks. When we did start paying serious attention to networks, we studied scientific theories about their unique characteristics and effects, and we got to know some on-the-ground networks. We blogged and posted reports about what we were finding out and why it was important if you wanted to produce large-scale social change. Then the magic of intentionality kicked in: broadcast your intentions to your network and it will provide opportunities to get what you want. That's been our experience. We wanted to work with networks, and a few friends responded, asking for help building new networks or resetting ones already under way. That started the first of dozens of projects in which we advised network builders.

What is there to advise about? After all, most people have networking in their blood. They know instinctively how to connect with each other, make friends, engage with colleagues, break the ice with strangers, and stay in touch. Some are superb at social bonding—"connectors," Malcolm Gladwell calls them, "people with a special gift for bringing the world together. . . . They are the kinds of people who know everyone." But, it turns out, there's much more to network building than the age-old human instinct to link.

Building a network is a *practice*. It involves particular ideas, methods, techniques, and tools—practical knowledge that works. Much has been learned about this practice from the recent experiences of network builders themselves and from the experiments and insights of researchers in mathematics, physics, sociology, biology, computer science, and other disciplines. Knowing how to build a network doesn't require a graduate degree, but it involves a lot more than just going with the flow. This is news to many of the network builders we meet. They love building networks and they just do it. But when we probe a little, they acknowledge that they aren't sure how to handle some of the challenges that have come up during their network building, especially how to boost the network's energy and impact. And their questions come pouring out when we explain that many networks evolve through different stages that can be anticipated; that starting a network involves addressing eight distinct design issues; that developing an ongoing network requires management of four key challenges; that evaluating a network's performance is not nearly the same as evaluating an organization's performance; and that builders of networks play multiple roles, with their success depending on certain skills and a "net-centric" outlook. We also get many questions when we talk with people who are investing in the development of networks, like program officers at foundations: What results can networks produce? How is a *network* different from a *coalition*? Why does a network require so much upfront investment? How can you tell how well a network is doing?

The pages that follow will answer these and other questions and will help you to anticipate—and address—challenges that your network-building efforts are likely to encounter. The practice of building generative social-change networks can be learned and mastered. Practice it thoughtfully and you'll get better at it. That's precisely what this book will help you do, whether you're starting a network or managing one that's already up and kicking.

Eight Insights

What we know about building generative social-impact networks has been field-tested many times by network builders from all walks of life. We tap a portfolio of about 20 networks in this book, started variously by people from business, nonprofits, communities, city and state governments, culture/arts, education, and foundations, nearly all of them clients or colleagues of ours. In our consulting practice we're contacted by network builders from around the world. And we have been fortunate to learn from other thinkers and writers about network building. It has been our privilege to work alongside all of these women and men as they invent and adapt the network way of driving social change. Wrestling with their problems in starting, managing, and resetting networks has sharpened our understanding of the essentials of network building and the powerful social impact that networks can have. (Because network building is inherently a team sport, network builders are reluctant to have their own efforts highlighted without acknowledging others' labors, too. At the risk of creating misperceptions, we've kept the book's stories about networks fairly simple by focusing on just a few of each network's builders.)

This book offers eight orienting insights about network building; each one frames a separate chapter, backed by case studies, illustrations, and how-to information.

1. **Know the Network Difference.** Networks have unique capabilities for achieving social impact that distinguish them from other forms of social organizing, and generative social-impact networks are particularly suited for addressing complex problems.

2. **Design Thoughtfully.** Social-impact networks can be thoughtfully designed from the start; you don't have to fly blind.

3. **Connect, Connect, Connect.** The foundation of generative social-impact networks is the connectivity of its members to each other, which can be cultivated by network weavers.

4. **Anticipate a Network's Evolution.** A generative network's capabilities, complexity, and potential for impact increase as the connectivity of its members deepens and the structure of their connectivity evolves.

5. **Enable and Adapt.** The growth and development of established social-impact networks depend on managing a set of inevitable challenges.

6. **Assess to Improve.** Monitoring and assessing a social-impact network's condition and performance is the basis for improving its impact.

7. **Revisit Design.** Making an existing network more generative, with more engaged members and impact, requires resetting of key design decisions to boost members' connectivity.

8. **Be Network-Centric.** In addition to skills and knowledge, network builders hold a distinct net-centric point of view with its own rules.

The flow of chapters traces the life cycle of network building, from designing start-up networks to managing established networks, assessing their performance, and resetting their design to boost performance. With each chapter building on material in previous chapters, the book is designed to be read from front to back. But we've organized the table of contents so that you can find the particular topics that are on your need-to-know-now list.

Connecting to Change the World moves far beyond our pitch, made a decade ago, for using networks to achieve social change. It is about the knowledge, skills, and attitudes—the deep practice—needed for successful generative network building. Perhaps the fact that there actually *is* a practice, not just concepts and aspirations, will help inspire some readers to take a network path. For readers already on the path, who wonder what to do next and how well they're doing, we offer hard-earned, practical know-how from real-world network building—and our best wishes for your success.

CHAPTER ONE

The Generative Network Difference

Networks have unique capabilities for achieving social impact that distinguish them from other forms of social organizing, and generative social-impact networks are particularly suited for addressing complex problems.

The urgency and scale of social problems, coupled with the limited results to date, cry out for new approaches.
— *Jane Wei-Skillern, Nora Silver, and Eric Heitz,*
"Cracking the Network Code"

Many social-impact networks burst into life out of an unpredictable mash-up of like-minded people who share a problem, get together to see what will happen, and then invent a common path forward. They have an itch to do something, and they share a belief that pooling their resources and collaborating might get them what they want. But they don't know what they'll do together.

Just seven years out of college, Sadhu Johnston had become Chicago's chief environmental officer in 2005, appointed by Mayor Richard Daley to lead the greening of the nation's third-largest city. Two years earlier he'd started working on that goal as an assistant to the mayor, and found himself struggling to find out what other cities were doing. "I was cold-calling people in other cities and Googling to get information. I didn't know anyone in a similar position. It was really a vacuum. For several years this was the primary frustration of my job. What information you did get was largely spin—the positive stuff without any of the challenges.

You learn as much from the failures as from successes, and it was really hard to get that."

Daley had announced that Chicago would become the nation's greenest big city, but no one was sure what that meant and how to make it happen. "Even most environmental groups were not seeing cities as playing a role when it came to climate change and environmental benefits," Johnston recalls. "Cities were still viewed as 'the evil city,' with pollution coming out and resources going in to be consumed." Gradually, though, the idea of urban sustainability, of redesigning urban systems for improved environmental and economic performance, especially reduced production of carbon emissions that triggered climate change, started to catch on. When Daley met with other mayors, Johnston compared notes with their staffers and found they too were frustrated by the lack of useful information. "A number of us thought we needed to be coordinated. But I realized I couldn't do it myself; I had a full-time job." There followed a period of false starts: one organization was interested in helping but didn't follow up; another proposed to help, but wanted far too much money; a gathering of people from a few cities didn't lead to anything. "I was casting about, trying to figure out how to get this done."

In an entirely different context, that of the American Jewish community, Rachel Levin also had an itch to organize something different. In Los Angeles she had helped establish Steven Spielberg's Righteous Persons Foundation and cofounded the Joshua Venture Group, a fellowship program for young social entrepreneurs. The daughter of a rabbi, she was looking for ways to engage young American Jews like herself with Jewish identity and community. Census data had found that a high percentage of Jews were marrying non-Jews, sparking national headlines that the Jewish community was marrying itself out of existence. Other research concluded that the Jewish community was irrelevant to many younger Jews. As a result, renewal and continuity had become a part of the Jewish American agenda. At the foundation, Levin recalls, "We were getting a lot of proposals from more established Jewish organizations, but they were based on how they had organized people in the past. It was not going to work with the majority of young Jews, who didn't want to be forced into a Jewish-only space." There had to be another way.

For Fred Keller, the itch was about securing the future of the

$70-million-a-year manufacturing business he had started at the age of 29. He was worried about global competition. Cascade Engineering, Inc., had three plants in the Grand Rapids, Michigan, area with about 600 employees and a line of products for the office furniture industry. "We were doing well," Keller recalls. "But I was concerned." He had visited Japan a few years earlier, and what he'd learned had blown his mind. "I was in awe of what their manufacturers were doing. We had a lot to learn from these very disciplined Japanese companies. They had figured out how to be incredibly efficient; they focused on quality, and, as a result, they reduced costs." American firms—his and others he knew—hadn't figured out any of this. "Maybe for the first time in the history of manufacturing in the U.S., the competitor was not across town; there was international competition," Keller says. "I had a sense that we're either going to get this right or we're going to lose to them." He turned to his local competitors, talking to fellow CEOs of privately owned manufacturing companies. "I wanted to have a dialogue with some other folks," he says. "I didn't know all of them very well, but we all had a sense that we had to get better fast." So how could they do that?

When Keller, Levin, and Johnston scratched their different itches, each decided to work with peers to build a network.

In 2008, Johnston met Julia Parzen, a Chicago-based consultant, who expressed interest in helping. "We had worked together in developing Chicago's Climate Action Plan, and she seemed like the kind of person who could actually pull together a cohesive effort between cities' sustainability staffers. It would be about the members, not about her and her organization. She was open to listening to others and helping them pull something together. We started to pull in others to make it happen." And what was it? "I didn't want an association, because I knew I didn't want to start a big organization," Johnston says. Someone suggested that they hold an annual conference, but Parzen proposed instead that they form a set of ongoing relationships. "We needed to build relationships among folks in the emerging field of urban sustainability," Johnston says. "A *network* was the right approach." They started with a core group of seven sustainability directors, each of whom invited five peers to join the new network and attend its first gathering in the fall of 2009. "We called it the Urban Sustainability Directors Network."

Rachel Levin also spent time wandering in the wilderness before turning to a network approach. She, Roger Bennett, then of the Andrea & Charles Bronfman Philanthropies, and several colleagues designed an experiment. "We believed that if you bring smart, creative people together, good things will happen." They asked some 30 next-generation Jewish Americans to participate in a weekend retreat in Utah to talk about Jewish identity. "We invited people and were surprised when they said they wanted to come." Most of the participants in the summit didn't know each other, but nearly all were "cultural creatives," people working in the arts and media. "We focused on people who had influence beyond themselves and would come up with ideas we would not come up with." Several rabbis and historians attended as Jewish resource people, but there was no lecturing, just "open space" discussions that took whatever course people wanted. "We thought this was likely a one-time gathering. We were hoping maybe some creative ideas would come out of it." As the retreat came to an end, its organizers weren't sure what to do; they hadn't planned the closing. "We just said, 'Thanks for coming,'" Levin recalls. "And people said, 'What happens next? Are we going to do this next year? Now what happens?' That was the beginning of realizing that this experiment hadn't failed. We had absolutely underestimated what it would mean to people to have this open experience discussing issues of Jewish identity, meaning, and community—that it would have power and meaning for them personally, not just creatively." The next year, 2003, many retreat participants reassembled for a second "summit" weekend. That's when the Reboot network came to life. "We fell into the notion of having an ongoing network as ideas started emerging and we saw people working together from so many creative sectors. We saw how impact was magnified and leveraged in ways we could not have imagined."

Fred Keller had an easier time engaging the five fellow CEOs he linked with; they were in the same community and agreed that collaboration might be useful. "We thought we could learn faster from each other than if we were to go into the textbooks." They formed the West Michigan Manufacturers Council to support the region's manufacturing economy. "It came together because of the energy of the network, not because I did anything special," Keller explains. But it wasn't easy to get going. Learning from each other, from competitors, was not a comfortable process for the group. "It was new," says Keller. "You didn't really know what sharing would lead to. Are you going to be sharing more than the other guy? Are you going to be revealing something you shouldn't? We had to overcome a bias about not sharing information with our competitors. We had to open ourselves up to potential ridicule when they visited our shop floor. What if our plant wasn't as good as the other guy's?"

After an initial burst of energy, a mash-up start-up network's progress can often be slow, because its founders do everything by instinct and trial-and-error; they're feeling their way in the dark. Sometimes the network runs out of energy and fades away or gets stuck doing easier, lower-level activities—meetings, not network building—that don't energize the members for long. Despite the challenges, the three networks we've described built momentum and produced results. Years later—five years for the Urban Sustainability Directors Network, 12 for Reboot, and more than 20 for the West Michigan Manufacturers Council—they are still up and running.

USDN has members in about 120 U.S. and Canadian cities and counties. A network that no one's ever heard of—and can't find out much about on the Web—affects the lives of 53 million city dwellers. More than 400 staffers in local governments participate in many of USDN's activities. The network stages a high-spirited, well-attended three-day annual meeting, operates two funds that have granted about $3 million to members' projects, supports eight regional networks and more than 15 working groups, and has attracted financial support from a dozen foundations. USDN has also started working on climate change with the C40 Cities world network of megacities, including Berlin, Johannesburg, London, Mumbai, Shanghai, and Sydney. Sadhu Johnston, cochair of the USDN Planning Committee and now deputy city manager of Vancouver, British Columbia, has the connections he was looking for: "I can call 120 different cities in North America and get a return call that day. I have access to leaders in each of those cities. I can get on our website and ask a question and get multiple responses. We all have access to each other and to information. This is a game changer for how we do our work."

Reboot members started to act on ideas that had popped up during their annual summit conversations. During the first few years, as new people were invited into the network, innovative products for younger

Jews (and others) emerged and attracted national attention: The National Day of Unplugging, inspired by the Jewish Sabbath, encourages and helps hyper-connected people of all backgrounds to embrace the ancient ritual of a day of rest. A 2007 best-selling book, *The Year of Living Biblically: One Man's Humble Quest to Follow the Bible as Literally as Possible*, is being made into a movie. A 2009 CD, *Mazel Tov, Mis Amigos*, blends traditional Jewish and Latino music. And a 2010 international design competition, "Sukkah City," to reimagine the temporary structures—*sukkahs*—that Israelites lived in during their exodus from Egypt, received more than 600 entries from 70 countries, hosted more than 100,000 people at the display site in New York City, and gathered more than 17,000 votes for best design. A decade after its birth, Reboot has more than 400 members, mostly in Los Angeles, New York City, and San Francisco, as well as the United Kingdom. The network's unique capacity continues to generate innovative products, and members have developed new religious and cultural organizations that also serve non-Rebooters and have started to engage mainstream Jewish organizations, becoming lay leaders or board members, or planning a Reboot-inspired event for younger Jews. "The fact that Reboot still has creative output is incredible," Levin says. "It's totally beyond my expectations."

The members of the West Michigan Manufacturers Council learned to share their problems and expertise with each other. After a few meetings spent talking about various shop-floor problems, Keller says, the CEOs' anxieties about sharing "melted away. The enthusiasm around the table grew. It was more exciting than scary." The excitement proved to be contagious, and during the next six years the Manufacturers Council became a busy hive of activity. Membership grew to 19 local manufacturing firms, ranging in size from 125 to more than 2,000 employees, and the Council sponsored annual conferences on world-class manufacturing. Council members developed a common framework about world-class manufacturing practices. By the end of 1993, more than 150 companies in the region were involved in 18 different Council-driven group-learning processes. "The personal relationships between the members of the network are critical to its maintenance and success," reported a case study; thanks to peer-to-peer learning, the network "combines the introduction of new information with the application to real problems, and learning from each other." In 1995, the Council sponsored an estimated $1.4 million in activities, most of it from member contributions and fees. It settled into an 8,000-square-foot office, training, and demonstration facility. It stimulated development of an Advanced Manufacturing Academy to prepare entry-level employees with the skills needed for world-class manufacturing. Fast-forward nearly 20 years and the Council has some 30 manufacturing members, champions four strategic initiatives, and "remains committed to its founding vision to strengthen the West Michigan manufacturing economy through collaboration."

Fred Keller continues as a member of the network—and points to other impacts. As the network's confidence grew, he says, members developed a proposal to the U.S. Department of Labor that resulted in a $15-million grant to the area for workforce development activities. "After that, we launched 'Talent 2025,' which now has 75 CEOs working as an organized network to hold talent systems [education and personnel] accountable for real results for people and organizations in our 13-county area. I doubt any of this could have happened had we not learned what our network of manufacturers could do together." Meanwhile, Keller's company, still headquartered in Grand Rapids, grew to 1,100 employees located in 15 facilities in North America and Europe. Its annual sales have quadrupled since Keller helped kick off the inter-firm collaboration to learn how to compete successfully.

Managed Start-ups

Other social-impact networks start less impulsively. They are managed carefully into existence, the result of analysis, planning, and negotiation. Usually founders initiate the process because they hope to achieve more impact by getting organizations to collaborate. But to engineer this sort of collective effort, they have to analyze the problem they want to solve and its causes, and determine who should be involved in solving it, what they should do together, and how they should do it.

The Garfield Foundation, led by executive director Jennie Curtis, invested in a year of thinking about the problems of boosting renewable energy use and halting climate change before starting a network was even considered. Garfield was a midsize philanthropy, with about $3 million in grant-making annually, and Curtis wanted to explore new approaches to achieving greater results. She recognized that philanthropies were often not getting the hoped-for impact from their grants to organizations. "There was excellent work being done on the ground, but it was typically fragmented and siloed," she says. "There was not a lot of collaboration among grantees, and there was not a lot of aligned grant-making among foundations."

Curtis's team identified a group of organizations in the Midwest, other philanthropies and nonprofit environmental advocates, which wanted to expand the region's use of clean, renewable energy. "Some of the advocates were frustrated by being bound to the project parameters, defined by funders, about what they could apply for funds for," Curtis says. "We decided to get everyone at the same table so they'd be informed by the same information." In 2004, using consultants and Garfield Foundation grants, the cadre of 24 organizations developed a detailed analysis of the region's electricity system and, to its surprise, concluded that the problem it really wanted to deal with was the potential impact of global warming. "It took a ton of in-person work," Curtis recalls. "Participants were willing to experiment with a systems-thinking approach. In the process, we ended up building a tremendous amount of trust and collegiality. The experience correlated with what is said about network building: it's about relationships, relationships, relationships." The group's continuing analysis identified four interdependent strategies to achieve a massive reduction in carbon emissions within the region's electricity sector: a halt to new coal plant construction, an enormous increase in renewable energy generation, retirement of most existing coal-burning plants, and a steady, incremental reduction in electricity use through efficiency. The system analysis "illuminated what strategic points to focus on," Curtis says, "but it did not tell us what to do." At the group's urging, Garfield initiated and funded a new process. "We switched from systems analysis to multi-stakeholder strategic planning," a way for the organizations to decide how to implement strategies. But, Curtis notes, "We had no idea we were going to build a network."

A similar need to organize new collective capacity drove leaders of The Nature Conservancy (TNC) when they planned the Fire Learning Network with federal land-management-agency officials. By the time Lynn Decker was appointed network director, in 2004, they had been working for about two years on developing an agreement to collaborate, securing funds for the network, running workshops for members, and conducting planning in 25 landscapes—large areas of land—with multiple owners, including federal agencies. The process had begun with a two-day National Fire Roundtable in Flagstaff, Arizona, that brought together more than 60 fire managers and scientists. During the previous three decades, government officials had gradually concluded that their policy of total suppression of wildland fires needed to be revised, because fire was not simply a destructive force but could be used as a tool for ecosystem restoration, reduction of fuel buildup that stoked large blazes, and protection of communities. The number of large wildfires in the United States had increased fourfold compared to the previous two decades, while the cost of federal firefighting had more than doubled to $3 billion in just a decade. However, the revised federal policies had "left unchanged the organizational incentives, budget priorities, and professional practices of agency land managers," explain William Hale Butler and Bruce Evan Goldstein, professors who have studied the network's development. A new approach was needed.

When Juan Olivarez arrived in Kalamazoo, Michigan, in July 2008, to become president of the local community foundation, he heard from his board of directors about the high-priority need for a fresh effort in public education. About three years earlier the city had become nationally known for The Kalamazoo Promise, a scholarship program to stimulate economic development in the city, funded by anonymous donors, which paid up to 100 percent of the college tuition of any student graduating from the Kalamazoo school district and attending a state university or community college. "But," Olivarez says, "Kalamazoo had struggled in making the Promise the reality they wanted, especially in bringing all students up to the level of performance they needed to be college ready and take advantage of the scholarship opportunity." The community had tried several times to assemble and align local entities to boost the performance of minority and low-income students, but it hadn't sustained momentum. "The trustees had a vision for the foundation to support the goal of the Promise; they just didn't know how to get it done."

Olivarez started having one-on-one conversations with key players in the community, including the school superintendent, the mayor, the executive director of the Kalamazoo Promise, and the heads of the local NAACP, chamber of commerce, and Upjohn Institute, which was leading research into the Promise's impact. Eventually he invited these people to meet together, facilitated by a consultant. "The session was absolutely critical," Olivarez recalls. "We got a lot out onto the table. It started our ability to bring our different interests together." Of course, there were tensions and disagreements: "I served as kind of the mediator in between our meetings." At about the same time, at a meeting in Washington, Olivarez met Sterling Speirn, president of the W. K. Kellogg Foundation, a national funder located in Battle Creek, Michigan, just a short drive from Kalamazoo. "We started talking about education and I started telling him about Kalamazoo. He was interested because of the Promise, and we started talking about support for a community-wide effort." The Kellogg Foundation provided the school district with a planning grant—and held out the potential of an even larger grant. "Kellogg was instrumental in getting us to bring together the data different organizations had and getting folks together," Olivarez says. The local group started holding regular meetings, agreeing on strategies, and drafting a plan. "We wrote and we wrote. We were convinced it would take the entire community, not just the schools, to prepare all children to be college-ready. We had to figure out how to coalesce the community."

The Kalamazoo community-building effort, the fire-management planning process, and the Garfield Foundation–supported planning all led to the same conclusion: build networks.

When Garfield's process expanded to include 40 organizations, it became obvious that getting that many, and probably even more, independent entities working at the same time on four distinct but interrelated strategies would require a structure that could be coordinated without centralizing decision making and resources. Then, in 2005, RE-AMP (that is, a Renewable Energy Alignment Mapping Project) came to life, a network with a clear goal—carbon emissions reduction; an initial membership of advocacy and funder organizations committed to the goal; four strategies; a plan for coordinated activities that would implement the strategies; and a budget for building the network infrastructure needed to support the members' activities. By 2014, RE-AMP had 165 nonprofit organizations and 15 foundations as members, spread across eight states. Since 2004, the Garfield Foundation had provided $3.3 million (about $330,000 a year) for building and operating the network, and an additional $8.3 million for projects by organizations pursuing RE-AMP's goals. One impact of these investments was to leverage additional resources for RE-AMP. A set of seven other foundations contributed about $14 million to RE-AMP's internal Global Warming Strategic Action Fund, which supported RE-AMP member projects. Thanks in part to RE-AMP's efforts, the region has seen big increases in renewable energy and investments in energy efficiency, while 20 proposals for new coal-burning power plants were stopped.

The Nature Conservancy and its federal government partners decided to start a national network to stimulate innovation and share lessons learned, in order to enhance the planning and implementation abilities of fire managers and accelerate development of new or revised policies. "When I came on board," says Lynn Decker, "it was a transition period." The initial network of local landscape managers was forming regional networks across the nation. During the next 10 years, the Fire Learning Network involved 650 organizations working in more than 150 landscapes in 39 states. The network operated at local, regional, and national scales that connected to each other. Local members, according to an assessment in 2010, "experiment with new ideas generated within their collaborative group or through interactions at regional and national levels, field-test new practices, and share resources across organizational boundaries." The regional networks brought together participants from multiple landscapes to "exchange ideas on how to overcome barriers to plan implementation." As a result, the report continues, "the network has inspired and informed changes to fire management policies to enable landscape-scale ecological fire restoration." Decker estimates the network has raised some $16 million for its work and leveraged an additional $19 million for on-the-ground landscape-restoration projects. "We have a pretty good reputation," she says. "Our landscapes are seen as highly effective models of collaboration; their processes are open and transparent. We've developed capacity building and training programs to increase the level of the services and address gaps that are keeping people from achieving their overall landscape-management objectives."

In Kalamazoo, Juan Olivarez became, in effect, the planning group's managing partner. As word of the effort got out into the community, he recalls, "People started asking: 'What is it? How do we get involved? Why wasn't I involved?' There were expectations and interests in the community and the group started thinking about how to get more people involved without bringing them into the core design team." Not surprisingly, the process became messier and harder to manage. "It probably happens in a lot of communities," Olivarez reflects. "There's fear about who gets involved and concern about who gets the credit, about 'whose baby is this anyway?' Those are issues we constantly dealt with. We would spend hours talking outside of our meetings to get buy-in, getting some people to let things go, or negotiating about how to spread the credit. It was give-and-take."

In June 2011, the organizing group announced the formation of the Learning Network of Greater Kalamazoo, a long-term effort that would build on the momentum and opportunities created by the Promise to create a comprehensive, countywide educational support system for children from infancy through college. The growing network of community organizations with a shared vision—"every child in Kalamazoo County will be ready for school, ready for college and ready for the world"—was backed by a $6 million grant from the Kellogg Foundation and $5 million from the Kalamazoo Community Foundation.

By 2014, the community-based network had established three action networks of individuals, parents, students, and practitioners to identify and implement practices, and 32 organizations—education systems, hospitals, nonprofit organizations, businesses, and government agencies—were working together in the network's Community Action Team to engage others in network activities, especially people and groups whose participation in the past had been marginalized. "They've been figuring out what work needs to happen in the community to change the system's outcomes," explains Carrie Pickett-Erway, who succeeded Olivarez as the community foundation's president in 2012. Five local organizations were providing a total of 15 people to serve as "backbone" staff for the network. The network had developed and made public a scorecard for its work, with measurable goals and progress reports for seven phases of a young person's educational development.

Generative Social-Impact Networks

"I want my network to be like that"—many people who are starting or managing a network tell us this when they hear about or observe USDN, RE-AMP, Reboot, or the other social-impact networks we've described. They want to get similarly impressive results, of course, but they also recognize that there's something special going on in these networks, something that's hard to attain. It's all the sharing, exchanging, learning, aligning, supporting, inventing, adapting, and collaborating that happens, and keeps happening, among members. Highly energized, productive, and sustained member engagement: how do you bake *that* into the network you're building?

You have to start with a clear understanding of what a generative social-impact network is and isn't. Most simply, it's a set of people who voluntarily organize themselves for collective action to solve a large, complex social problem. These people could be acting as individuals, such as the cultural creatives in Reboot and the sustainability directors in USDN, or on behalf of organizations, such as the advocacy nonprofits of RE-AMP or the Fire Learning Network's federal agencies. The way they organize—as a network—is distinct from other forms of social organizing and has particular advantages. It also has specific requirements, and addressing these effectively is what the practice of network building is all about.

In these networks, decision making is distributed throughout the membership. The members set the agenda and priorities. The networks have minimal formal rules and structure, and their structure may change rapidly. This makes them less stable but more nimbly adaptive than organizations. Most important, in these networks the members are deliberate about building, strengthening, and maintaining ties with each other; over time they forge a renewable collaborative capacity that generates numerous activities simultaneously. Together, they innovate to create new products, services, and programs; learn which practices work, then adopt and spread them; advocate for changes in public policies; provide services, as well as education and training; set up joint purchasing and branding; and organize the use of private, philanthropic, and public investment. Over the years, their networks become robust and adaptive enough to maintain their effectiveness and steadily increase their impact.

The textbooks say that a network is a set of "nodes" connected by "links." This could describe an electricity grid, a highway system between cities, living cells that form tissue, or the neurons in your brain. In a social network, the nodes are people and the links are relationships. The people create value for each other by exchanging information and knowledge, and making available their skills, resources, and connections with still other people. Social networking comes naturally to most people. We make friends, bond with colleagues and neighbors, cultivate allies, and join clubs and associations; we make contacts, stay in touch, gossip, mingle, meet online, go to parties, and hang out. This was true long before Facebook made it easy to "befriend" with just a click. Some 2,300 years ago, when a mere 50 million humans inhabited the planet, Aristotle observed that "Man is by nature a social animal. Anyone who either cannot lead the common life or is so self-sufficient as not to need to, and therefore does not partake of society, is either a beast or a god." Now, with more than 7 billion of us around and the Internet a part of common life, it's easier than ever to socialize, to forge ties with many others.

People network with each other for many different purposes. Often, we network for personal benefit. Consider one of the most extensive personal networks in the modern world: the Friends of Bill Clinton, a lengthy roster of the president's boyhood pals, celebrities, billionaires, donors, political allies, and even some political rivals. Clinton's famous network, like anyone's personal network, is an extension of his personality, interests, and needs. He is at its center, a hub from which many spokes emanate to connect to everyone else. He decides who is in the network and who is out. He activates and cultivates the network; it serves him. We also network for professional or collegial reasons—to improve our knowledge or status, or to share camaraderie. We link to make money: business supply chains produce goods and conquer markets, while investment networks share opportunities and risks.

But networking for *social impact* originates from another motivation. Look at the Urban Sustainability Directors Network that Sadhu Johnston helped to start. Its purpose is to advance cities' efforts to address climate change, urban quality of life, and sustainable economic development. Of course, each USDN member may benefit professionally and personally from participating in the network. But engagement is also an opportunity for members to serve a bigger purpose than just their own well-being. Social-impact networks use their resources to tackle practically any social problem in new ways. In addition to urban sustainability, the networks described in this book address economic development, education, poverty, climate change, manufacturing competitiveness, business development, homelessness, renewable energy, grassroots community leadership, cultural revival, rural community well-being, mercury poisoning, and management of wildlands.

Notice, though, that these social problems are complex. They are large in scale, not fully understood, and resistant to predetermined, simple, quick, or one-time solutions. A complex problem, explain the authors of *Getting to Maybe*, is much more difficult to address than a simple problem— or even a complicated problem, which is different from a complex problem. Baking a cake, they say, is a simple problem, and requires a recipe that can be easily replicated. Sending a rocket to the moon is a complicated problem that requires rigid protocols and high levels of expertise; success depends on having a blueprint that specifies how all the different players and parts relate to each other. Raising a child, though, doesn't depend just on protocols, expertise, a blueprint, or even experience; it's a complex problem. Complex social problems—the AIDS epidemic, nuclear waste disposal—are what social policy scholars call "wicked"—meaning that they require many people to change their minds and behaviors, and often the people involved are polarized according to their radically different ways of understanding the problem.

Complex, wicked problems are dynamic. As Adam Kahane, a world-class facilitator of high-stakes conflict resolution, observes, they unfold in unpredictable and unfamiliar ways. They change over time and last a long while. As you come to understand more about such a problem, you have to adapt your approach to solving it. In a word, these social problems are *generative*.

Generative social problems require generative responses—learning, innovation, and adaptation over long periods of time. That's precisely what generative social-impact networks are designed and managed to do. USDN, RE-AMP, the Fire Learning Network, and the other networks we've described: they, too, are complex and unpredictable. They change as they go along, issuing a flow of experiments and organizing ways to scale up what proves to work. They reinvent themselves, adjusting their own dynamics as they go along, even as they sustain themselves. They are particularly well suited to take on complex, wicked social problems that have proven to be far beyond the grasp of top-down, centralized, command-and-control approaches.

Of course, not every social problem is a generative problem. Some are well defined, and solutions can be implemented by one or two organizations, as John Kania and Mark Kramer explain, offering several examples: funding college scholarships, building a hospital, or installing inventory controls at a food bank. Other problems may require unprecedented coordination and cooperation among organizations, but they don't call for the propagative dynamics of a generative network. It's also true that generative problems don't usually yield just to network approaches alone. Complex, large-scale solutions typically require an array of organizations and other forms of social organizing. But generative social-impact networks can play a special role in the mix because of their distinct capabilities.

Distinctions

In addition to creating an organization, there are several ways to organize for social impact: social media, coalitions or alliances of organizations, associations with members, even large-scale social movements. But these are quite different from networks.

Facebook, LinkedIn, Twitter, and the other social media have become emblematic of networking in the Information Age. "In just a short time," notes Randi Zuckerberg, director of marketing for Facebook, "a large number of people can come together around a common interest in a truly global conversation." But the millions of users of these online services don't all share a desire for specific social impact. They enter and exit the online services willy-nilly. They connect with some, but not nearly all, of the other members in the service. And it's the service providers, not the members, who make the rules (e.g., no hate speech) that regulate activities. This doesn't look anything like the USDN, Reboot, or RE-AMP networks, in which the members embrace and enact a collective purpose, set the mission and goals, and make the rules. More and more people are using social media as tools to help their organizations, associations, movements, and networks to share their passions for a cause and raise awareness and money. In November 2013, for instance, comedian Stephen Colbert asked his Internet and TV audiences to out-donate the nation of China, which had pledged only $100,000 in disaster relief for the recent typhoon in the Philippines. Within a few days, the so-called Colbert Nation had donated more than $250,000, and Colbert offered his congratulations: "Folks, you did it. . . . I'd say China is out and the Colbert Nation now gets your slot as a world superpower." Social media are remarkably powerful tools, but they're not social-impact networks.

Nor are coalitions or alliances like generative networks. They are temporary alignments of organizations formed to achieve a specific objective, such as electing someone or securing adoption of a new law. They usually disband when the campaign is completed. "The most successful coalitions are much more narrow in scope and membership than networks," explains June Holley in *Network Weaver Handbook*. "Coalitions operate by controlling the actions and agenda of those involved." Indeed, some alliances find that as their work winds down they want to become longer-lived social-impact networks—a phenomenon we call *morphing*.

Associations may look like social-impact networks because they are member based, but they are organized mainly to pool resources and provide their members with various services. The members don't necessarily develop powerful, enduring relationships and collaborations, and it's the association staff, not the members, who do most of the work.

Finally, social-impact networks are not the same as social movements in which large numbers of people become aligned around a cause, such as gay rights or environmental protection, their passion ignited by a personal desire to right a wrong. Networks may help a movement to form, and movement adherents may start networks, as well as other organizing vehicles. But movements are big, sprawling affairs, much less coherent and focused than a social-impact network.

With all of these options available, why choose to build a social-impact network? One good reason is that because a network can provide an adaptive and sustainable capacity with unique advantages, something no other organizing method can fully achieve.

Morphing into a Network

Morphing occurs when the participants in or funders of a coalition or campaign feel, once its purpose has been completed, that they want to keep working together. They have built relationships that they value and have seen how working together amplifies their strength. But the purpose and dynamics of their collaboration don't have generative power. For that, their purpose would have to be broader, their relationships stronger, their collaboration more extensive. What they need is a transformation, a morphing—something that Josh Karliner and his colleagues at Health Care Without Harm (HCWH) recognized.

Karliner, international team coordinator for HCWH, won't easily forget the morning of January 19, 2013. An environmental activist with an international portfolio, he was packing his bags at 6:00 a.m. to fly home from Geneva, following an all-night negotiating session in a United Nations conference room. The international delegates and advocates like Karliner had been meeting for a week to wrap up three years of bargaining over restricting the use of mercury, a hazardous substance accumulating in the atmosphere, soils, lakes, streams, and oceans. Early that morning, before the final gavel came down, the world's governments had agreed to eliminate the use of mercury-based devices in health care, the focus of HCWH's efforts.

It had taken HCWH and its allies 15 years to get this done, part of a broader effort involving numerous organizations and coalitions, especially the Zero Mercury Working Group, to secure the first global, legally binding treaty to prevent mercury emissions and releases into the environment. Starting in one place, HCWH had helped build a global coalition of nurses and doctors, hospital and health system administrators in dozens of countries, ministers of health and the environment on every continent, global health federations, international nonprofit organizations, and UN agencies. "The collective impact of this constellation of actors," Karliner explains, "began with a few health advocates working in one hospital in Boston, spread virally to thousands around the world, growing in momentum and inevitability." In 1998 HCWH, then a new organization of grassroots environmental health groups, had decided to get health systems to shift demand for mercury-based thermometers and blood-pressure monitoring devices to non-mercury alternatives. In the United States it gradually found allies in the nation's hospital and nurses associations, pharmacies, the federal Environmental Protection Agency, and socially responsible investors. In Europe, nonprofits joined the campaign, and the European Union took action. HCWH linked with the World Health Organization for a global initiative that recruited three global health associations to the cause. In Buenos Aires, one hospital ward went mercury-free, which triggered citywide change, then the involvement of several provinces, and finally national action throughout Argentina. This helped catalyze efforts in Mexico, Chile, Brazil, and elsewhere in Latin America. In the Philippines, Taiwan, and India, hospitals and government agencies committed to phase out mercury thermometers. Hospitals in South Africa, Senegal, and Tanzania moved toward mercury-free health care. Then came the years of treaty negotiations, and an agreement to end by 2020 the production, export, and import of mercury-based medical devices.*

But even as a powerful coalition against mercury emerged, HCWH's leaders had the start of something else in mind. "We saw the mercury advocacy work as a base-building exercise," Karliner says. "We went in to win the issue and to build our base of relationships with health sectors around the world. We were laying the groundwork for what we hope will be much more engaged advocacy on key issues, especially climate change, the most pressing issue of our time. That's our longer-term vision. We're hoping the health sector will put its moral, political, and economic clout on the line to address environmental health issues in their communities and global issues." What Health Care Without Harm wanted was a linked global capacity that, on a sustained basis, would mobilize over and over again in different ways to improve environmental health. In other words, it wanted its coalition to become a generative network.

---

*Joshua Karliner, Gary Cohen, and Peter Orris, with Veronica Odriozola and Merci Ferrer, "Mercury as Messenger: The Anatomy of a Fifteen-Year Global Campaign," unpublished manuscript, May 2013. A version was subsequently published, authored by Karliner, Cohen, and Orris, "Lessons in Forging Global Change," *Stanford Social Innovation Review* (Winter 2013).

Advantages

A social-impact network can assemble novel and flexible combinations of human talent that would be difficult or impossible to pull together in a single organization. This aggregation can come from organizations or individuals. When multiple organizations identify a shared goal and then align their capacities and coordinate their efforts to achieve it, they create a new, more powerful ability embedded in a network. This is precisely what the builders of RE-AMP and Kalamazoo's Learning Network were after. When the Garfield Foundation launched the process that led to RE-AMP, this sort of network building was rare, but this is no longer the case. Now some funders are insisting that their grantees work together, and social-impact organizations, especially those that deliver education and other services within a community, are also turning to collective action as a way to solve intractable problems. "Examples suggest that substantially greater progress could be made in alleviating many of our more serious and complex social problems if nonprofits, governments, businesses, and the public were brought together around a common agenda to create collective impact," say Kania and Kramer in an article in the *Stanford Social Innovation Review*. They cite, as successful examples, Strive, a collaboration of more than 300 leaders in greater Cincinnati working on improving education, and the Elizabeth River restoration project in Virginia, which engaged more than 100 stakeholders from four local governments, the state and federal governments, the U.S. Navy, universities, businesses, community and environmental organizations, and schools.

As we saw in the cases of Reboot and USDN, individuals also network to build capabilities that are highly innovative. They bring together a fresh diversity of people and ideas, and they can be highly responsive to changes, because they assemble only small increments of people's time for episodic use, rather than locking their members into full-time, stable work. Reboot's Rachel Levin wanted hundreds of creative people to interact and then make innovative products relevant to young Jewish Americans. It wasn't just about making movies, playing music, writing books, or holding events; it was all of the above—and whatever else might be invented along the way. The effort needed more than a few employees. It was episodic work, not continuous. It was risky, not certain.

The need for flexible capacity was also evident in the Partnership Fund for New York, a generative network (originally called the New York City Investment Fund) started by financier Henry Kravis in 1996 to help diversify and grow the New York City economy. The Fund was an experiment to combine the capabilities of a private investment firm with the purpose of a place-based government economic development agency. But to successfully invest millions of dollars in business start-ups, the Fund needed a capacity to analyze, negotiate, and follow up on complicated financing deals with scores of entrepreneurs in many different types of industries. It needed talented people who would interact occasionally, but not continuously, to do work that was not highly predictable. Kravis built a volunteer network that quickly attracted the energy of nearly 250 business and finance leaders and entrepreneurs, who in their first few years together labored over more than 400 investment proposals and provided financing for 46 businesses.

A social-impact network can also create what's called "small-world reach," the ability of members to connect efficiently with many people—network members and *their* networks—and thus gain access to information and other resources. For instance, each of the 100 or so members in USDN connects to hundreds of other city staffers and, through them, to other networks. When a member searches for help, as cofounder Sadhu Johnston appreciates, it's just a connection or two away. Thanks to this multiplier effect, a network can potentially provide its members with efficient access to thousands of other people.

Another network advantage lies in its ability to grow rapidly because of what's called the Law of Increasing Returns. In a nutshell, it's naturally in members' interests to have more members with whom to connect and transact. "The overall value of the network [increases] with the addition of each new member," explain *The Starfish and the Spider* authors Ori Brafman and Rod Beckstrom. A network may expand explosively when its members bring some or all of *their* networks into the network—an instant infusion of many new members. This growth potential is one reason that foundations investing in the development of large-scale capacities for public-policy advocacy favor a network model. For instance, the RE-AMP network grew to more than 165 organization-members after starting with several dozen. When the W. K. Kellogg Foundation launched a "Rural People, Rural Policy" initiative to develop a national critical mass of advocates for public policies that supported rural communities, it chose to build networks of rural organizations, hoping that they would greatly expand their connections.

Finally, a network can move information quickly and widely. Information flows between members through the numerous links they have established, instead of having to go through a central hub or the top of an organization chain of command before being sent out to the troops. This unmediated exchange facilitates the swift dissemination of ideas and the collection of feedback across a large and potentially diverse number of nodes. The Fire Learning Network uses its members' information flows for "the generation and dissemination of innovative fire planning and management techniques," according to its evaluators. As Beth Kanter and Allison Fine note, a network's "collective intelligence creates a 'cloud' of information that many people can distribute for use." USDN, for example, surveys members regularly to find out what its more than 100 cities are doing to improve their sustainability and what their priority needs are, and then shares the aggregated information with all members.

These effects—flexible capacity, small-world reach, the Law of Increasing Return, and more—are due to a network's distributed capacity and decentralized, nonhierarchical organizing structure, which can't be fully replicated in other forms of social organizing. But there's still more to understand about what social-impact networks can do and how they work.

Which Kind of Network?

Builders of social-impact networks must choose which of three kinds of networks to create: a connectivity, alignment, or production network. Each of these has a different capability and, therefore, can have different impacts.

A *connectivity* network links people to allow them to exchange information easily and, often, to learn as a result of the interchange. It doesn't try to do more than that. Such networks can be important to social-change agents concerned about the isolation of particular individuals or groups from other people. Schools in segregated urban or isolated rural areas, for example, might connect students with adults in workplaces who act as mentors and guide student projects—a way of exposing the kids to new information about how the world works. Foundations and other institutions provide resources to leaders from scores of communities in a geographic region to spend time with each other at retreats or summits and gain new information about what their neighbors are thinking and doing. In 2006, for instance, Je Hoon Lee, an associate research professor at the University of Southern California, started the Network of Korean American Leaders, bringing together second-generation Korean American professionals to connect them to each other and to first-generation leaders in the Korean American community. The purpose: "to create a powerful pipeline of Korean American leaders that crosses political, economic, social, and cultural 'silos.'"

An *alignment* network links people for a different purpose: to help them to create and share a set of ideas, goals, and strategies. This allows them to more efficiently exchange information and coordinate with each other as a group. Alignment is the principle purpose of networks of organizations like RE-AMP and the Learning Network of Greater Kalamazoo. Their members align around an overarching goal, such as reducing carbon emissions or improving the local education system's results, and then coordinate or revise their activities to achieve that goal. Many of the growing number of "collective impact" community collaboratives are alignments of local organizations designed to improve a local system. In 2013, the Garfield Foundation focused on the power of alignment when it launched a new collaborative-networks program to emulate its experience building the RE-AMP Network. It circulated a request for Letters of Inquiry to see what might emerge from the field and to gauge interest in collaborative network approaches to solving complex problems. The foundation was looking for collaborators who "are inspired by opportunities to create collective impact" and would align around "shared insights and strategies." More than 800 organizations responded, grouped in 64 submissions—another indication, says Garfield's Jennie Curtis, that "there is huge interest in network approaches to solving complex problems."

Builders of a *production* network foster collective action by members to produce innovative practices, public-policy proposals, and other outputs for social impact. Reboot is a production network; its members create movies, books, new cultural and religious organizations, and more. Members of the Fire Learning Network invent and test ways of using fire to support a landscape's environmental health. In 2008, the Massachusetts Interagency Council on Housing and Homelessness established 10 regional networks of public and nonprofit organizations to test proven best practices and develop innovations for delivering services for homeless people. "Five Regional Networks tested innovations to prevent individuals from becoming homeless," reported a 2011 evaluation of the program. "Two Networks tested triage models to ensure appropriate rapid rehousing and stabilization services for individuals. In addition, eight Networks developed plans to pursue low-threshold housing strategies for unaccompanied chronically homeless adults in their region." They were production networks.

These different types of social-impact networks accomplish different things, so deciding which kind you want to build depends in part on what you're trying to do. But each kind poses different requirements, and this should be factored into your approach, too.

Must Dos

Connectivity is the foundation of a successful social-impact network. Develop strong connections among members and, at a minimum, you'll have a connectivity network. But if you want to construct an alignment network, you still have to start with connections and then build on them. And if you want to build a production network, here too you start by developing connections. Whatever the objective, the starting point is to forge connections, and this involves much more than introducing members to each other. Making connections is such an important topic that we devote chapter 3 to how it's done.

Creating alignment and production networks requires members—organizations or individuals—to align around common goals; they must come to shared understandings about definitions, ideas, and even language. This usually takes facilitation, time, and patience, especially if the members have little experience working together or if they have been rivals for funding or other resources. For a network's members to attain production, after they have been able to connect and then align, they must collaborate in and manage production processes that are rarely easy to pull off.

Many network builders want to create a production network. Given the complex nature of the social problems they tackle, they see a need for a network to produce more than just connections and alignment. But conducting joint production by network members takes collaboration to a new level of complexity, because it requires members to specify the product or service, assemble the right set of capacities to perform the production, agree to responsibilities, and establish a production process with schedules, inputs, and coordination that have to be enforced. The network builder's challenge, then, is to navigate through a developmental sequence that builds connectivity, then alignment, and then production capabilities. We don't know if the connect-align-produce sequence is an iron law of network building, but it's definitely a pathway to success.

Some network organizers start with a connectivity network in mind, and then find that, as connections are made, the potential for members to align emerges, and after that members start to undertake collective projects. We saw this, for instance, in the West Michigan Manufacturers Council, which started by connecting company CEOs for peer-to-peer exchange, then aligned them around creating a framework for world-class manufacturing. After that, the members produced training programs for other manufacturing companies. Other networks aim for alignment, but shift into production when they find that coordinating their members' efforts isn't going to be enough to reach the goals they've set; they need more powerful impact. Some network builders find that, although they want to build a production network, their efforts get stuck at the connectivity or the alignment stage—and collaborative projects don't emerge. They can't get to the next level of network development. In chapter 4 we discuss how network builders take a network through the connectivity, alignment, and production stages.

Whatever type of social-impact network you're building, it won't automatically become generative and able to sustain a high level of member engagement, activity, and adaptation. How do you ensure that your network members continue to learn, grow, and take action together? You make a social-impact network generative by building on the basic human desire to connect, share, belong, and make a difference. Essentially, you add powerful social dynamics to the unique, decentralized network structure that unleashes the advantages we discussed earlier. In a network, two social forces are set into motion: the generosity with which members treat each other and the shared sense of identity they develop. A network's members give to each other. "The net rewards generosity," says former *Wired* executive editor Kevin Kelly; a network, he says, is "a gift economy." It's a splendid description. Members give away their knowledge, skills, connections, and resources. They give in the expectation that giving to others will be rewarded by getting from others, that mutual exchange—reciprocity between members—will occur in the network. (Anthropologists call this phenomenon "generalized reciprocity.") When this member-to-member exchange happens, the network's structural advantages magnify the value of the gifts, efficiently spreading the benefit to other members who, in turn, enhance it and spread it even further. As a result, members don't just bond with the members with whom they have engaged; they develop a feeling for, a loyalty toward, and a willingness to support the network as a whole. The network is a gift that keeps them giving. Being a "good citizen" of the network becomes highly personal and important.

When you successfully take a network down these developmental paths toward greater capability and generativity, what you get is what you saw in our earlier descriptions of networks: members who freely contribute their skills and talent to a unique capacity they own together; who efficiently reach whomever they need to reach in order to obtain the information and resources they need; who readily attract new members to add their value to the network; who act independently *and* in alignment, even though no one is in charge; and who, when their collective actions achieve impact, are eager to increase their contributions to and aspirations for the network—in a virtuous cycle that feeds the network's momentum.

Initiating these developmental processes is the principal task of starting a generative social-impact network.

CHAPTER TWO

Start Me Up: Designing a Network

Social-impact networks can be thoughtfully designed from the start; you don't have to fly blind.

All beginnings require exceptional care if they are to result in great harvest.

— *The I-Ching*

Whatever your reason for starting a social-impact network, whether yours is a mashed-up, managed, or morphed beginning, the launch process can be exhilarating and nerve-wracking at the same time. Excitement comes from several sources: tackling a problem you care about, meeting new people, starting a journey. The jitters come from the uncertainty. Will it work? Will others join and contribute? Will they get along with each other? Will they see the potential value of the network? How long will it take to get going? There's also the anxiety that comes with not being quite sure about what you're doing.

When Bill Traynor, an experienced community developer, returned to his hometown of Lawrence, Massachusetts, in 1998, he hoped to engage community residents in efforts to reverse the city's steep economic and civic decline. Mobilizing a cadre of urban planning graduates from the Massachusetts Institute of Technology and a handful of seasoned organizers, the goal was to create a new grassroots leadership capacity that would rally around, implement, and sustain a vision for the city's future. To achieve this, they had to get thousands of residents to talk about and work on local issues, come together to build their leadership skills, and connect locally in ways that would shape and advance a shared vision. Traynor suspected that no organization could pull this off; instead, he says, he and his colleagues wanted to develop "something that creates a different contract between and among people and between people and us [the organizers] that is not so territorial, not based on position, but based on action." This called for building a network, so they launched Lawrence CommunityWorks—but from the outset it wasn't entirely clear what to do to ensure a healthy birth and robust growth.

In Asheville, North Carolina, Maggie Ullman knew she wanted to build a network because of the network she was already in. The city's sustainability manager, Ullman had been a member of the Urban Sustainability Directors Network since its first meeting. "I had access to an amazing national network. But a lot more people were starting to do this kind of work in cities in North Carolina and Tennessee and across the South. I felt a responsibility to help them the way I'd been helped. What I wanted was to give to others in my region what I was getting from USDN—learning and sharing ideas, time to just hang out together." She'd participated in a national organization's effort to start up a network in the Southeast, but it had failed. "They facilitated some conference calls with some of us. But it was a waste of time. They weren't really member driven. They had an agenda, *their* agenda. When no one responded, they had to cancel calls. What I wanted was a peer-to-peer network." When Ullman set out to start a network in 2012, she had many questions: Who should she ask to join? What should she tell them they'd get out of participating? How many people should she ask? How could she make them feel that it was *their* network, not just hers? She started to think about inviting people to join and holding their first meeting.

Network founders like Traynor and Ullman, as well as funders of networks, may have different starting points for building networks, but whether what's intended is a network of organizations or individuals, their start-up tasks are much the same.

Designing a Network

A network's purpose, membership makeup, size, and value propositions are matters of network design. These are some of the key elements of a

Are You Network-Ready?

Some people and organizations can't handle the demands of collaborating with others. To adapt a phrase used by the teachers of young children, to build a generative network you have to be able to "play well with others." In a network, you have to share decision making, resources, and credit. This requires "a different mindset," according to John Hagel III and John Seeley Brown, authors of "Creation Nets"—"one that recognizes that flows of knowledge across institutional boundaries are the key to generating the new knowledge and new practices required to succeed in a rapidly changing world."[1] In the social-change arena, the typical "egocentric" organization "becomes the hero of its own story, the central character in a drama where peer organizations inevitably are bit players," lament Jed Miller and Rob Stuart in their online article, "Network-Centric Thinking." Funding proposals and appeal letters portray the organization's work as indispensable to making progress and social change. Its programs are heralded for their superiority to the programs of other organizations with similar strategies (and success rates). The organization's work is described as a model for the field, while the contributions of others go unmentioned.[2]

Another challenge for organizations is to make networking a sustained priority. Some organizations have "short attention spans for activities like networks unless the work is well integrated into the organizational priorities," cautions Heather Creech, director of global connectivity at the International Institute for Sustainable Development and a veteran network builder. "Institutional priorities may well clash with network priorities unless they are proactively aligned."[3]

1. John Hagel III and John Seely Brown, "Creation Nets: Harnessing the Potential of Open Innovation," *McKinsey Quarterly* (May 2006), www.mckinsey.com/insights/innovation /creation_nets_getting_the_most_from_open_innovation, accessed December 1, 2013.

2. Jed Miller and Rob Stuart, "Network-Centric Thinking: The Internet's Challenge to Ego-Centric Institutions," www.compasspoint.org/sites/default/files/images/NonprofitDay /NetworkCentricThinking.pdf, accessed December 1, 2013.

3. Heather Creech, "Form Follows Function: Management and Governance of a Formal Knowledge Network," version 1.0 (Winnipeg, MB: International Institute for Sustainable Development, 2001), 33, www.iisd.org/pdf/2001/networks_structure.pdf.

network that largely determine how well the network will take off and perform. For each element, there are choices to be made, and each choice has consequences. The West Michigan Manufacturers Council decided, for instance, to invite manufacturing CEOs only. This kept the companies' other top managers out of the network, but allowed the CEOs to get comfortable in dealing with each other because they were peers with similar concerns and responsibilities. USDN decided to have no more than 120 or so members in North America. It could have opened its doors to sustainability directors in many other cities or to cities around the world, but it rejected membership expansion in favor of the sense of closeness and trust that members valued and did not want to risk losing by growing too large and impersonal. Reboot, on the other hand, decided to add as many as 30–40 new members a year, rather than capping its membership, because it hoped that infusions of "fresh blood" would spur more innovation.

Successful networks are designed—they don't just happen. Network builders must know which elements of a network can be designed, what design choices are available, and the different potential implications of each choice. This is true whether you are starting up a network or managing an existing network. Some design choices present themselves right at start-up, others emerge later in a network's life. A few persist from start to finish, and network designers may decide to revise their previous decisions in response to the network's needs. This is especially true if the network is just limping along and needs to be reenergized. For each design element, there's no one right choice—there's the choice that is right for the network. Network-building practice isn't based on applying a one-size-fits-all formula. It involves selecting from a repertoire of possible decisions and actions, based on an understanding of the situation. And once you've designed and started a generative network, you have to continue to develop it, being alert to changes in the network and knowing how to adapt to them.

In our work with network builders we've identified eight design issues that should be addressed during start-up or readdressed during any time of significant transition or trouble in a network's life:

1. *Purpose*: What is the network's reason for being?
2. *Membership*: Who is eligible to become a member, what are the membership requirements, and how many members will there be?

3. *Value Propositions*: What will be the benefits of membership—for individuals and collectively?

4. *Coordination, Facilitation, and Communication*: How will network members link and work with each other?

5. *Resources*: What is the network's funding model?

6. *Governance*: Who decides what the network will do, and how do they decide?

7. *Assessment*: How will the network monitor its condition and performance?

8. *Operating Principles*: What rules will guide the network's culture?

The point of the many decisions you make about a network's initial design is to attract and mobilize resources and create momentum, fanning the spark that instigated the network in the first place and putting into motion the connect-align-produce sequence described in the previous chapter.

In offering practical advice for starting up networks, we'll also address particular challenges faced in starting what we call "engineered" networks, in which foundations, government agencies, or nonprofits, instead of network members, are the catalysts. And we'll describe how one network engineer, a foundation's executive director, helped to start and fund a network, participating in its activities and decision making for years without being a controlling force. (See Bonus Track—Advice for Funders and Other Network Engineers, page 75.)

Purpose: A Reason for Being

In the beginning, network builders have to translate their personal passion for creating a network into a clear statement of network purpose that potential members will also find compelling. You have to explain what the network will be about in a way that helps others see themselves taking part in it. Making your intentions explicit often helps to clarify your own thinking about your initiating instinct and the network's reason for being. A network statement of purpose should address three topics:

- Who is the network for?
- What problem is it working on?
- What type of collaborative activities will the network undertake?

If that sounds like a mission statement, it is—just like organizations, networks have missions.

When Lawrence CommunityWorks (LCW), now a network of thousands of people, describes its purpose, it covers all three topics. It specifies that its members are community residents and stakeholders and that its purpose is "to transform and revitalize the physical, economic, and social landscape of Lawrence." It goes on to depict what network members do with and for each other: they engage in "building family and community assets, providing each other with caring and mutual support, building leadership and civic engagement skills, and engaging in collective action for positive growth and change."

The founders of the Urban Sustainability Directors Network also addressed these three elements of a network's mission:

> USDN's purpose is to be an active and engaged network of North American city sustainability directors who exchange information, collaborate to enhance our practice, and work together to advance the field of urban sustainability.

Clearly the network's members would be city sustainability directors. They would connect to exchange information and also do something more than that, described generally as "collaborate to enhance our practice." And the network would take on the generative problem of "advancing the field of urban sustainability." The clarity and broad scope of this mission statement has held up with the network's membership ever since. Note that USDN, like LCW in its statement, declares that network members will create value for each other, not just for themselves.

Probably the biggest challenge in drafting a network purpose statement is achieving clarity about what kinds of activities the network will do. The LCW and USDN statements signaled that members would do more than exchange information; they would collaborate to enhance their practice, build leadership skills, and so on. Having members share information is a natural starting point for a new network, because it builds a necessary base of connections among members and is relatively easy to do. Ultimately, though, a generative social-impact network's members must do more than exchange information, since doing that alone won't be enough to achieve the network's goals. But what precisely they *will* do may be difficult to foresee at the outset—activities emerge over time as members decide what they want to do. In USDN's five years of existence, for instance, activities have included development of more than a score of working groups, some with as many as 40–50 participating members, to discuss and learn about topics they selected; organizing an Innovation Fund that has raised more than $1 million and awarded it to members for projects; and supporting the emergence of regional networks of sustainability directors, like the one Maggie Ullman started. None of these activities was anticipated at the network's inception; they all grew out of the members' emerging priorities.

For some networks, a general statement of purpose is not enough of a starting point; the members must agree on measurable goals that they will seek to achieve. RE-AMP declares that it "brings environmental, labor, faith, youth, energy, conservation and other groups together to share one audacious goal: to reduce regional global warming emissions 80 percent (from 2005 levels) by 2050." This sort of shared performance measurement is the key to initiating the "collective impact" model that some foundations and nonprofit organizations have started to favor. It allows a set of organizations to align with each other in a collective sense of purpose, and it obliges each of them to specify its role in achieving the goal. For instance, the many organizations in the Cincinnati, Ohio, region that are working together as Strive partners to improve education adopted a single set of goals with success indicators that would be monitored. Aligning who will do what allows for unprecedented coordination of the organizations' efforts and creates a benchmark against which collective performance can be measured over time. Shared measurement, say Kania and Kramer, "enables the participants to hold each other accountable and learn from each other's successes and failures."

It's smart for a founder to find one or more partners, people who might join the network, to help with formulating the network's purpose. It will probably improve your thinking and ensures that your thinking resonates with at least one other person. Maggie Ullman turned to friend Susanna Sutherland, then sustainability manager for Knoxville, Tennessee, who also wanted to start a regional network in the Southeast, to fashion the network's first purpose statement. Their collaboration had another advantage: when it came time to share thinking about the network with potential members, there were two founders to spread the word.

Membership: Who's In, Who's Not

Whatever their purpose, generative social-impact networks have boundaries and here, too, there are design choices. The borders may be soft or hard, easy or difficult to penetrate. In an *open* network most anyone can become a member—the more the merrier. In a *closed* network the membership is more tightly controlled and limited. Generative social-impact networks lean toward having a closed membership, often handpicked by other members, and keep themselves relatively small so members can develop strong generative relationships with each other. Lawrence CommunityWorks has many times more members than most of the generative social-impact networks we know. Five years after birth, it had about 700 members, and the count reached 3,000 active members by 2014. Nonetheless, it's a closed network—only Lawrence residents can become members.

When it comes to designing a membership model, network builders have to address four basic questions:

- Eligibility: who is eligible to become a member and what criteria must a potential member meet?
- Size: how many members should there be?
- Categories: should all members have the same benefits and responsibilities, or should there be different categories of members?
- Requirements: what requirements for participation should there be for members?

Choices about member eligibility are many. You can see some of this range in the different eligibility decisions made by four networks with the same type of member, a sustainability director. USDN, the North American network, decided that its members had to be city-government sustainability directors. But three regional networks started by USDN members took different approaches. The Heartland Local Government Sustainability Network, covering seven states in the central United

States, identified "local-government sustainability staff" as its members, which opened the network to county officials as well as cities. (After a few years, USDN also accepted urban county sustainability directors.) The Southeast Sustainability Directors Network, started by Ullman and Sutherland, found that few of its region's cities had a government-appointed sustainability director, so it started with a broader definition of who could become a member—any local government staff. And while USDN invites individuals—not cities—to join the network, the New England Municipal Sustainability Network defines its members as communities whose mayor/manager designates a representative to participate in the network.

Like the New England sustainability directors network, many networks have organizations as members, and typically the organizations appoint representatives to participate in the network. This doesn't change the need for clear eligibility criteria—identifying which organizations may participate in the network and, perhaps, what position in the organization a representative in the network must have. (In chapter 3 we discuss some of the challenges involved when it comes to building strong relationships among network members who represent organizations.)

The design of member eligibility hinges on what assumptions you make about the affinities that network members will share and that will help to bind them together. In USDN's case, the affinity was the work and challenges of being a local-government sustainability director, a new kind of job in a new field of practice. Many other people work on urban sustainability—consultants, nonprofit staff, academics, federal government officials, corporate sustainability officers—but they are not eligible to join USDN. In Reboot, the affinity had nothing to do with the jobs people had. It was about their interest in engaging with and reinventing Judaism, as well as the creative talent they brought to the network. And, as Reboot members testified in surveys of the network, one of the network's most important attractions was the opportunity to spend time with "people like me." In the case of collective-action initiatives of organizations, a desire to pursue a shared, measurable goal is a strong affinity. Thus, an organization that wants to join RE-AMP must commit to the network's specific goals for addressing climate change.

The fact that network members share an affinity doesn't mean that the members will all be the same; the network inevitably will have some diversity. For instance, some local sustainability directors have experience working in the private sector, others don't; some are at early or late stages in their careers; some come from cities with millions of people, but many work in cities of fewer than 100,000 residents. In Reboot, members had very different childhood experiences being raised Jewish; some had visited Israel, some had not; some belonged to Jewish community organizations, some did not; a few members were converts to Judaism.

Another eligibility hurdle some networks use is more personal: a requirement that new members be recommended by someone already in the network. This has the benefit of creating some assurance that new members will be compatible with the network. But it has the potential disadvantage of limiting the network's diversity, as people will tend to know and recommend people much like themselves. The more similar a network's members, the more likely it will be for them to find common ground for learning and working together; they tend to have had common experiences, concerns, ideas, and language. But there's a potential trade-off: greater diversity in a network helps to promote new ideas, because diverse people bring different perspectives to the network, and mixing them together can spur innovative thinking. Still, it may take longer for a group of highly diverse people to figure out how to relate and talk with each other, and sometimes they don't connect at all.

Heather Creech, director of global connectivity at the International Institute for Sustainable Development, has worked with many policy- and knowledge-creation networks, and identified additional criteria that can be used for membership: acknowledged expertise or competence in the network's work, connections that matter, capacity to collaborate and be a good network citizen. In addition, some networks use a so-called market test—the willingness of potential members to pay a membership fee or dues, even a small amount. USDN started with no dues, but after several years it gained confidence that members recognized and cared about the network's value, so it introduced relatively low dues on a sliding scale (according to the size of a member's city), while allowing members to ask for a scholarship to cover the fee.

Whatever the network's eligibility criteria, the question of rightsizing the network has to be tackled: How many members will be enough? How many will be too many? Rightsizing is an art, involving judgment calls that are likely to change as the network matures and its situation changes. But at start-up there are two initial concerns. First, how many members are needed to develop an initial critical mass, a sense of momentum, in the network? Typically, the network founder, whether a single person or a small group, identifies a list of prospective members (based on eligibility criteria), recruits them, and then gathers them at a kickoff meeting. You need enough members to bring sufficient initial energy and resources to the network, and to impress other potential members that something worthwhile is getting started. But you don't want so many members at the outset that it's difficult for people to build connections with each other and agree on what the network is about. Based on our experiences, an admittedly broad rule of thumb for sizing a network's *initial* critical mass would be to have at least 10 to 15 members and probably no more than 75 to 100.

A second sizing concern is how many members the network will need to achieve its purpose. Lawrence CommunityWorks set out to build grassroots leadership for a city of more than 70,000 inhabitants, so it wanted thousands of members; it made sense to make any resident eligible for membership. Although most of the members of the Reboot network live in the three cities where most American Jews live—Los Angeles, New York, and San Francisco—the network had its eye on expanding into other U.S. cities with smaller Jewish populations. This would allow the network to reach a broader audience while also drawing into it additional members with different perspectives.

A network's right size can also be a function of its maturity. As an early-stage generative network's activities become more ambitious and complex, it may naturally involve—and need—more members. Whatever the starting size, the network can grow quickly, if that's what you want. For instance, RE-AMP, which began with about 20 member-organizations and now has about 165 members, uses an annual membership renewal and application process to manage the network's size.

Although most networks begin with just one category of members, some expand by creating one or more additional categories with different eligibility and participation requirements. After USDN capped its core membership at 70, it responded to demand by creating a class of associate members who may participate in many network activities, but not the annual meeting, and who pay only a nominal membership fee. RE-AMP allows each member-organization to have more than one person in the network, but one of them has to be the lead member and holds the organization's voting rights for selecting the network's steering committee members. Some networks establish a class of "learning members"—individuals or organizations who participate in the network's learning activities but not in other network activities. The Climate Change Knowledge Network established an observer category to accommodate other organizations working on climate change. "Observer members may attend [network] meetings, offer suggestions for projects, and will have access to the network members," Creech reports. "As observers, they are not asked to participate directly in projects but are encouraged to share relevant work. Observers are asked to cover their own costs of participation." When researcher Bonnie Shepard looked at 13 regional and national networks of nonprofit organizations in Latin America that advocate for women's rights, she found a diversity of membership arrangements, including two networks that institutionalized different levels of membership to recognize different levels of commitment to the network's activities.

A network can expand its number of participants without growing its membership. USDN, for instance, allows members to bring other people in their city government's staff into USDN activities and its website. As a result, the network of about 120 core and associate members engages roughly 300 other sustainability professionals from municipal governments.

Whether a network has one or several categories of members, designers have to decide what will be required of its members. Must they attend conference calls and meetings, respond to network surveys, share information with other members, and do presentations on their relevant work? In short, what must members give? At the outset, network builders are probably just grateful that anyone at all participates in the network; they worry that imposing too many or too stringent participation requirements could scare people away. It's a reasonable anxiety, because a start-up's members can't be sure at first that participation will be worthwhile, and they may not want to make a big commitment right away. Still, it's wise to set some minimum participation standards from the beginning. This signals that there are expectations, that the network's culture includes having members making upfront commitments about how they will behave in the network. And it sets the stage for increasing the participation standards as the network evolves and members find that their value propositions are being met. USDN has increased its standards for members, adding an annual membership fee and increasing participation requirements—contributing to network working groups, attending the annual meeting, posting to the USDN website—to be a member in good standing.

(For an example of a detailed network membership model that covers most of the bases, see Appendix A.)

Value Propositions: Benefits of Membership

Knowing a network's purpose and membership sets the stage for spelling out its value propositions, the specific benefits that network members will realize by participating in the network. Doing this well is crucial. "If there's no value, people will start to exit," says LCW's Bill Traynor, an astute network builder. "It's a self-regulating system."

Most people join a network with the idea that participating will get them something that helps them or their organization do their work. They may not have thought much about working with other members on a common goal. They have an *individual* value proposition, but not a *collective* value proposition that they share with others and that requires the collaboration of a network. But, as Creech points out, "If the network serves only as an umbrella for a collection of individual projects, it is not realizing its added-value potential." It's up to network builders to cultivate the collective value that will bring members together in common cause and allow them to give to, as well as get from, each other.

Network members may care about different value propositions, and many members may have multiple value propositions. When Je Hoon Lee started the Network for Korean American Leaders (NetKAL) in 2006, he asked its first 24 members—young, successful, second-generation Korean American professionals from around the United States—what motivated them to join the network. Their combined responses formed a list of eight distinct propositions they valued:

- Develop projects that help the community
- Fuel my passion to lead, build my skills to lead
- Learn from Korean American leaders
- Develop the capacity to be a leader in the Korean American community
- Connect with interesting people and make friends
- Exchange ideas with people
- Make good contacts for professional/business work
- Develop an Asian American perspective on leadership

For Wall Street financier Henry Kravis, raising money to start the New York City Investment Fund (now the Partnership Fund for New York) was the easy part. He turned to his personal and professional network, calling on corporate CEOs, financial institution heads, and other friends to join him in putting up $1 million each. His pitch attracted $67 million. Along with the funding, Kravis asked for and received an influx of more than 200 volunteer venture capitalists and investment bankers ready to help. Early in the Fund's life it became evident that for some members the entrepreneurial excitement of working on the network's business-finance deals was a powerful attractor. Other members found value in engaging in civic responsibility—giving their time and expertise to help their community. Some liked rubbing elbows with Wall Street players, and still others found that the network generated private business opportunities for them.

Network builders who recognize that members hold multiple value propositions will offer members a menu of potential benefits rather than just one way to get value out of participation. When Traynor and his colleagues designed Lawrence CommunityWorks, they offered members a variety of programs to take part in and contribute to. "They were designed to draw people into the network," Traynor explains. "Having many different doors is critical," he says, because it increases the chance that someone will find value and, therefore, a reason to join and stay in the network.

Network members create value for each other by sharing the assets they bring to the network: their knowledge, connections, skills and other competencies, and resources. USDN members share what they know in workshops and online, answering each other's questions. Partnership

Exchanging Value in a Network	
Connections	Can you connect others in the network to people who may be able and willing to help them?
Knowledge	Do you know something that may be valuable to others in the network?
Competencies	Do you have a skill that may be of value to others in the network?
Resources	Do you have access to funds or other resources that may be useful to others in the network?

Fund members share their connections to others with specific business expertise so entrepreneurs can get the help they need. Reboot members share their skills—journalism, filmmaking, musicianship—to develop projects with others in the network. West Michigan Manufacturers Council members share their workplaces as settings for learning together.

There are two ways to develop a network's collective value propositions. One is to identify an overarching value proposition, a big goal that *all* members of the network share and are motivated to achieve. This is the method often used in the managed start-ups described in chapter 1. Organizations or individuals work together to reach a goal they know they can't get to by themselves. Each may bring other value propositions to the process—the hope that they'll gain resources or status, for instance—but the collective proposition is in the shared goal. This sort of value proposition may be articulated, even before the network starts, as a compelling reason to form a network. The second way is to be alert to opportunities within the network—members sharing an interest in a topic, for instance—to identify and test the members' appetite for collaboration. Instead of organizing value around a single major value proposition, the network will engage with multiple value propositions, each of which attracts some, but not necessarily all, of the members.

As a network's members develop collective value propositions, they also create a sense of shared identity, of belonging to something. This may sound touchy-feely, but don't discount it. The collegiality that members experience in a network, the sense that they share a "safe space" with people who are like them, understand them, and have relevant experiences and similar aspirations—this value can help to develop the intangible social effect that we described in chapter 1 as critical to building a generative network. For instance, the Fire Learning Network, according to a 2011 evaluators' report, "has fostered a collective identity among fire professionals, allowing them to speak and act autonomously but with a coherent purpose and set of practices."

In a 2011 survey, NetKAL member Patrick Chung, a principal at an investment firm, described how this sense of shared identity had grown on him: "NetKAL gave me permission to be more outgoing, bold, and aggressive. Now I think, why not do more? You have potential, so they give you tools to do your thing, which then helps the community. You're a part of a larger mission. NetKAL is a very big part of my life and always will be." At USDN, membership surveys probe for this collective value creation, asking members to what extent they agree that participating in USDN "makes me feel a part of something big and important" and that the network's other members "should feel proud of what we have built together."

As a network builder you can't escape an essential fact of life: more than any other factor, value creation for members drives a network's success, and the real nature of the value being created—and whether it's sufficient—is in the eyes of the members, not the network founders, funders, or coordinators. To find out what your network's members value, just ask them. But ask in ways that give them room to say what's meaningful to *them*, not just their response to *your* ideas. Since members' value propositions, or the importance of a particular value proposition, may change, you have to ask members regularly what's most meaningful for their continuing participation. Never stop worrying about your members' value propositions and whether or not they're being satisfied.

Coordination, Facilitation, and Communication: Linking Members

Almost nothing will slow down a network's value creation and development more than the failure to coordinate and facilitate the members' work, which includes helping them communicate with each other. When fledgling network builders tell us they haven't been able to schedule face-to-face meetings or conference calls among members, or figure out what members want to do together, or how to keep members in touch with each other, or follow up on something network members decided—take your pick—these are the sorts of problems that can cripple a network.

We've seen three coordination roles in network building: logistics, operations, and strategic management.

- *Logistics* involves setting up meetings, conference calls, and other ways members can engage with each other; tracking and documenting network activities, decisions, revenues, and expenditures; creating and distributing essential information such as a directory of members and contact information.
- *Operations* typically involves other duties, such as running a website and other external communications; facilitating group processes of members; documenting network decisions and activities and managing an archive of network documents; administering the network's finances; helping members to draft proposals for funding; and orienting or onboarding new members of the network.
- *Strategic management* is a higher level of responsibility focused on helping network members, especially those with governance duties, make and implement decisions about the network's development. This could include managing relationships with outside partners and funders, supporting members who are undertaking initiatives for the network, and creating and modifying network plans.

It's rare for a network to need all three of these roles filled right out of the starting gate. But from the beginning someone has to do the logistical work, and it's not unusual for a network's founders—whether an individual or an organization—to volunteer for this; it's absolutely necessary and it's not too difficult or time consuming. Sometimes volunteers rotate the responsibility (running the risk that some may not perform as diligently or as well as others). But before long, as network membership and activities expand, logistical coordination starts to require more time and additional skills; it graduates to the operations level and becomes a part-time or even full-time job. Network members themselves usually don't have that kind of time, and some don't have the skills either.

What a Network Strategic Manager Does

In 2013, when USDN started searching for someone to succeed Julia Parzen, the position description it circulated identified more than eight primary duties, including the following:

- Help members set USDN direction together, working with the Planning Committee to develop an annual strategic plan based on members' priorities.
- Sustain and increase member connectivity and value creation, facilitating peer-to-peer exchange, nurturing member-leaders, overseeing two annual surveys of members, helping to establish and support user groups of members.
- Broker member collaborations, in part by identifying topics ripe for collaborations, helping to develop project proposals, helping to identify and choose consultants and overseeing their work.
- Support the expansion in size and capacity of regional networks supported by USDN, as well as collaborations among the regional networks, and continuously assess the relationship between national USDN and regional networks.
- Liaison to two funds established by USDN, reviewing all plans, participating in meetings, and seeking ways to increase the funds' impacts.
- Plan the USDN annual meeting, choosing the site, designing the agenda, choosing speakers and preparing them, and managing the hired meeting planner.
- Manage USDN operations by staffing the Planning Committee, hiring and managing USDN staff, managing the budget and grant reporting to funders, overseeing new member recruitment, ensuring that member requirements are met, and being an ambassador for USDN.
- Build relationships with funders and fundraise for USDN.

Drawn from several internal USDN documents regarding "Planning for Future Staffing and Succession within USDN." Several of the authors served as advisors to the USDN coordinator search process.

Strategic management of a network requires even more time and skill. In 2013, RE-AMP—an extremely active and relatively well-resourced eight-year-old network (with 23 full- and part-time staff and a $4.5-million annual operating budget)—decided it needed a chief network executive officer (CNEO) to whom an operations coordinator would report. The CNEO would be responsible primarily for development of network strategy, structural adaptations, and fundraising, while the coordinator was responsible for network operations and external communications. In effect, RE-AMP divided network management into two jobs, one with an external focus, the other with an internal focus. At USDN, Julia Parzen had the title of managing director, and performed both the strategic management and operations roles, with a small staff taking on the logistical work and some of the operational work.

As with any job, an effective network coordinator should have certain skills and experiences, such as the ability to communicate, manage budgets and projects, and solve problems. But networks looking for a top-level manager also want someone who understands that it's their job to *enable* the network, not to tell it what to do. This can be a matter of personality and style. RE-AMP, for instance, described the ideal CNEO as having "knowledge of network structures and operations" and being "experienced at creating 'community' among geographically dispersed and diverse staff and members." Its job description called for someone "who is comfortable playing a pivotal role in a broad network without being the team leader in charge." Likewise, USDN said it was looking for a managing director who was "able not to own projects and to let go of projects that don't have member leadership and support." In chapter 8 we'll have more to say about the characteristics of people playing these roles in networks.

Coordination helps network members get together to work. But in the start-up stage, it takes facilitation to help them do the work once they are together. A facilitator helps things run more smoothly and effectively, and that's usually what's needed by network members unfamiliar with each other and probably not used to working as volunteers and with other volunteers. Collaboration can be difficult to do; for some people it doesn't come naturally, and much of our work life inside organizations is more about coordination and cooperation than collaboration. It's not unusual for network members to launch working groups in order to organize their work together, but to help the working groups get going you should provide them with facilitation. This can be an additional role of a network coordinator, or it can be provided by a member of the network with the appropriate skills, or you can bring in someone to do the job.

We should note that, as staffing grows, some networks of organizations decide to have several member-organizations provide staff for the network, rather than have network support come from a single entity. The idea behind this decentralized model is to help spread a sense of ownership around the network and also to prevent a centralized staff from becoming too strong a force in the network. As the network's staff continues to expand, however, decentralization can lead to weak communication and cohesion within the staff.

Facilitation and coordination at any of the levels we've described also require tools for supporting communication among members. A network's communication infrastructure is essential to the network's success because it will enable or impede collaboration. Networks must provide for effective, speedy, flexible, affordable, and diverse communication among members, as well as informational databases for members to tap into with ease. A network must be able to move information quickly to the right places. "All members should have equal access to network information and the tools to participate effectively," recommends Creech. "In the early stages of network development, technology assessments should be undertaken for all members and infrastructure development funded and implemented for those who may not have the same ready access to e-mail and the Web." Marty Kearns, executive director of Green Media Toolshed, points out that a network communication system should enable "cheap, long-distance collaboration" and the use of hardware and software across the network. Effective networks "usually have significant capability to use information and communications technology (ICT) to facilitate rapid and broad-based interaction among members and with key stakeholders," report Suzanne Taschereau and Joe Bolger in a 2006 paper for the European Centre for Development Policy Management. In most cases, they add, this means using the Internet. "Examples from large decentralized networks in big countries such as Brazil suggest that an electronic communications infrastructure—and especially the Internet— have been very important to network growth and development."

Whether it's using e-mail, Listservs, or scheduling and collaboration software, there has to be a human touch to help things along. We've seen start-up networks in which members had access to communications software but almost none used it. Some members didn't want to deal with having yet another website to go to and another password to enter. Some weren't comfortable with learning how to use the new site. Some tried the site and didn't find anyone else there, so they dropped it. The lesson seems to be that you can't just provide everyone with an online communications tool and expect they will start to use it. You have to encourage and support them.

Networks often ask us which of the many available online tools are best. A valuable assessment was done by Hershey/Cause Communications, which identified 11 different uses for collaborative communications tools, provided examples, and identified which of them had any of eight features, from minimum cost and ease of use to the fostering of personal relationships. (See Appendix B; the information won't tell you what to use, but it will help you figure out what you need the software to do for you and where to start looking.) Some networks end up developing their own communications site for members, designing it to their own specifications.

Resources: Funding Model

A coordinator, communications software, conference calls, and meetings—all of this can cost money. But most social-impact networks start with hope, not with a budget, or at least not with an adequate budget. Unless the network has sufficient outside funding, getting started requires "sweat equity"—volunteer labor—from its members. In addition, you can usually count on members to cover their costs, paying for their travel and lodging at meetings or access to conference calls—unless the travel costs are quite high, or members' organizations have severely restricted employee travel to save money.

The network's goal, of course, is to secure a sustainable financial base for supporting ongoing collaborative activity. But there's no magic formula for funding a network start-up, and no standard business model, either. The model is opportunistic: you look for funds here, there, and everywhere, tapping different types of sources, and shifting the sources over time. To succeed you have to figure out what it might cost to operate the network, what blend of revenue sources the network might pursue, and how to make the case for the philanthropic funding that most social-impact networks hope to raise.

A network has both operational and project costs. The operational costs are what it takes to run the network, such as paying for coordination, meetings, and conference calls, as well as accounting systems. These are your fixed costs—they are inescapable, not optional. Project costs are what it takes to fund the network's various collaborative activities, such as implementing RE-AMP's strategies for policy change or Reboot's innovative projects. These are variable, or optional, costs—you don't have to take them on. Most important at the outset are the fixed operational costs. Typically, these fall into three categories:

- *Convening* includes the travel expenses, meeting space, food and lodging, meeting facilitation, and materials involved in bringing members together. Members can absorb much, but not necessarily all, of this cost. However, these costs can get high enough that they become prohibitive for some members. This is especially true during the network's start-up phase, when members can see what the cost of participating will be, but can't be sure what benefits they will get.

- *Staffing* involves the coordination of network logistics and, ultimately, the more difficult, higher-skill operational and strategic management tasks, as well as accounting and other necessary services. Sooner or later this cost must be addressed, and it is sure to rise as the network becomes bigger and more ambitious.

- *Communicating* includes the various conference calls, websites, software, and more that enable members to engage with each other. As discussed previously, there are many options for communications, and for a time you can manage so there's no cost by using e-mail and "free" conference calling services that charge each caller. But here, too, as the network grows and becomes more active, real money will have to be spent to ensure effective communications. Doing this on the cheap could hamstring member-to-member connections.

A social-impact network usually needs a blend of funding sources, and where it gets funding probably will evolve over time. Whether the starting source is mostly from the members or from a single outside funder, most networks seek to diversify their funding base as quickly as they can. They can't depend on a single funder to stay the course for the long run, and they probably can't lean on members alone to pay all of the bills. Still, the members will probably have to contribute a substantial portion of the resources. "In every truly needle-moving collaborative we studied," reports the Bridgespan Group, "there was at least a modest investment in staff and infrastructure. This investment often included in-kind contributions of staff and other resources from partners."

Fundraising at the outset of network building is particularly difficult, because the network has no track record of delivering results. Also, much of the early cost is for building the network's capacity, not producing impact.

No matter what the network's potential sources of revenue may be, the case for obtaining funding usually hinges on the value—the results, the impact—that will be created by the network. Some potential funders may be intrigued by the idea of supporting a network, but most will be wary since they have little experience with supporting networks and will wonder how a network, as opposed to an organization, could produce the desired impacts. Although every pitch to a funder should be customized, taking into account the funder's expressed interests, we have a few tips about making the case to potential funders.

- *Pitch the potential impacts of your network, not its network-building processes.* In presenting anticipated impacts, stress what the network members can achieve as a collective that is beyond the reach of a single organization or individual. In other words, show them the car, not the factory floor. Collective impact is the network's comparative advantage in seeking funding. The network may, for instance, enhance opportunities for learning and knowledge creation through the exchanges among and innovations by its members; exercise more influence on public-policy decision makers thanks to its size and connections; or generate capacity for long-term mobilization—advocacy and

Sources of Social-Impact Network Revenue

Philanthropic funders—individual donors, corporate foundations, private foundations, family foundations, and community foundations

Much has been written by others about how to raise money from foundations. In general, it's easier to obtain funding from philanthropists for projects rather than operations, because they want to have impact, not just build capacity. However, as noted in chapter 1, more and more foundations are looking to networks to produce a collective impact that cannot be matched by the single organizations they traditionally fund. This makes them more willing to pay for operations.

Member dues or fees

Asking members to pay dues tests how much importance they place on being in the network. This can be a high hurdle early on, when it's not yet obvious to members that being in the network will generate value for them or their organization. It makes sense, though, that at least a small portion of a network's budget should come from its members, instead of relying entirely on outside funding. (USDN targeted 25 percent of its annual operational budget to come from dues.) Having member dues also shows potential funders that the members "have some skin in the game." Some networks start off with dues (sometimes on a sliding scale), while others introduce dues only after the network's value has been established. When the Funders' Network for Smart Growth and Livable Communities found its membership growth slowing, it reduced the dues for a new member's first year in the network.

Sponsorships

Some networks turn to outside entities, particularly corporations, to sponsor some of their activities, such as annual meetings, websites, and publications. A potential sponsor is interested in obtaining favorable visibility with network members (and their networks) or enhancing its public brand by associating with the network. For some networks, sponsorships may be problematic because of the potential perception that the network has been co-opted—"bought"—by the sponsor.

Partnering

Developing projects with outside entities allows a network to tap the outsiders' expertise and in-kind services. If the project is funded, the network can share in the resources.

Government grants or contracts

Some government agencies will fund network development or projects if the network's efforts are aligned with the agency's goals and programs. As with foundations, most agencies will want their funding to achieve impact, not just build capacity.

Crowdfunding

Fundraising websites such as Kickstarter.com or NationBuilder.com can be used to promote your cause and raise donations from online communities. These new tools are drawing more and more attention, but Kanter and Fine caution that "using social media channels alone for fundraising will not be as effective as making them a part of a multichannel strategy that includes the traditional fundraising techniques."*

Earned income for services and products

We haven't seen many social-impact networks tap this source, especially in the start-up stage when a network is still organizing itself and not likely to be able to deliver services or products. But in theory, a social-impact network can produce value for customers and collect revenue.

---

* Kanter and Fine, The Networked Nonprofit, 140.

action—that won't become exhausted. In proposing projects with potential impacts, you can build a reasonable portion of the network's operating costs into the project budget.

- *Anticipate funders' many questions about networks—and be ready to answer them.* They are likely to ask: Who can be held accountable for producing results, when so many organizations or people are involved? Why do so much time and so many resources have to be spent up front in developing the network instead of having an immediate impact? How will the network capture what it is learning and share it with others? How can the network's performance be evaluated? You get the drift: most funders aren't familiar with networks, and the idea of funding one may make them uneasy. Answering their questions before they are asked—displaying your network-building sophistication—may help to develop confidence in the network.

- *Show funders the value of the network members' voluntary efforts.*
  The major "cost" of operating a network is the time of its members. It's free, but if you monetize this, it usually dwarfs the cost of everything else. Do the math: Imagine a network with 100 members who have an average annual income of $50,000, with each member spending an average of one week a year on network activities, or about 2 percent of their work time. The annual cost of that time, if it were being paid by the network, would be $1,000 per member. Multiply that by 100, and you have a total "in kind" value of $100,000 a year being contributed to the network's purpose by its members. This is worth figuring out and making visible in the network's budget as both a cost and an in-kind revenue item—so that potential funders recognize the commitment and financial value their investment would leverage.

When a network pursues funding from foundations, it has to consider whether or not it may be competing with some of its own organization-members who could be going to the same source. This problem comes up often. A network that is an energetic fundraiser will usually coordinate its efforts with the fundraising efforts of its members, ensuring that they

Strictly Legal

Social-impact networks may choose from at least three different models when it comes to being a legal entity:

- **Established NGO.** Reboot and Lawrence CommunityWorks are non-profit organizations with boards of directors made up of network members.
- **Fiscal Sponsor.** Neither RE-AMP nor the Urban Sustainability Directors Network has established a legal entity; both use nonprofits as fiscal sponsors and each of them has a committee of members who take responsibility for guiding the network.
- **Program within a Nonprofit Organization.** The West Michigan Manufacturers Council is a program within a nonprofit, The Right Place, and the Fire Learning Network is a cooperative program of the U.S. Forest Service and Department of the Interior agencies and The Nature Conservancy.

"divide and conquer" or jointly seek funding, rather than compete for funders' affections.

Governance: Making Decisions

As a network takes shape, it's natural to think about how it will be governed, especially since the usual top-down command model of organizations is not an option in a decentralized world.

We usually urge network designers to keep network governance informal for as long as possible. In a network's early days the founders are its government, and there's nothing wrong with that. Most other network members aren't ready to take responsibility; they're still wondering if the network will be worth participating in; they want to get something out of the network, not invest time in building it. So they're inclined to let the organizers be the deciders. There's another reason to hold off on formalizing governance: the purpose of network governance is not to tell members what to do, but to enable them to do what they want to do—and it usually takes some time before members know what they want to do together. An early-stage network just doesn't need a lot of enabling governance and should take its time to figure out what governance it will need. "In networks," notes Creech, "it may take some time for network members to work through how a network will operate, what its goals and objectives should be, and how to achieve those most effectively. In the process of operationalizing the network, the governance arrangements will become clearer, and can be codified in a governance agreement."

Sooner or later, though, authority should shift from a network's founders to its members, which will expand the number of deciders and, inevitably, make network decision making more complicated. There's no one best model for network governance; so much depends on the particulars of the network's purpose, membership, size, and other design elements. The seven organizations of the Massachusetts Smart Growth Alliance, a network focused on public policy development and advocacy, tailored its governance to their network's specifics. They decided in 2003 that all network members would have equal power to make network decisions; it was a relatively small network, so this wouldn't be difficult to implement. The most important decisions facing the network involved taking positions on public policies the network would work to enact.

Because network members had different interests and competencies in policy making, the Alliance required the unanimous consent of the members for it to take a policy position. If unanimity was not reached, the Alliance would not take a position, but individual members were free to promote the policy on their own. On other Alliance decisions, such as the network's work plan and budget, if there was no consensus, then a majority vote would rule. The Alliance's scheme illuminates the three basic elements of governance design: who decides, what is decided, and how it is decided.

Which network members have governing authority and which don't? In the Smart Growth Alliance all members had equal authority. This is typical of a network with a small number of tightly connected members that depend on each other to achieve results. But it's impractical in a large, more loosely connected network. In contrast, the thousands of members of the Lawrence CommunityWorks network regularly elect representatives to a steering group that governs the network. At USDN, a planning committee of 10 members, about 10 percent of the membership, acts as an informal governing body. It's not elected; instead, every year members may volunteer to join the committee, and the committee selects at least two volunteers to replace sitting committee members. This allows the committee to maintain institutional memory—founder Sadhu Johnston is still a committee member—and to bring in fresh blood. And the committee can select members with particular aims in mind: to cultivate an active network member for leadership, for instance, or to fill a gap in the size of cities present on the committee. In USDN and other networks with more than one class of member, it's usually the core members who have a say in governance, while less-engaged members do not.

What exactly do network members have to decide? The answer ranges from "everything" to "as little as possible." Some networks assign to governance a big list of decisions that resembles the elements of a strategic plan for an organization, including goals, values, membership responsibilities, activities, and budget. Other networks are less inclined to make such plans; they try to minimize formal governance in favor of maximizing the freedom of network members to decide on their own. Not all decisions have to be subject to the same governance arrangements. As we've seen, the Massachusetts Smart Growth Alliance made an important distinction between decisions about policy positions it would take and all other decisions. It created a higher standard—unanimity—for taking policy positions, because these decisions were more important for the network. As it turned out, the Alliance didn't take formal votes; consensus prevailed even though it was not required for all decisions.

Network builders sometimes fall into the trap of thinking that a network's decisions should be made by all members and apply to all members, but that's not the case. Sometimes—quite often in some networks—a group of members wants to work on something that others don't care about. Do they need the approval of others or are they free to act as they wish? In fact, in a generative network it's highly unlikely that all members will want to do the same thing all the time. They won't march in lockstep, and you probably don't want them to, because requiring everyone's agreement could reduce the number of opportunities that members could have to engage in and, therefore, would lower the energy and commitment of members.

Networks use any or combinations of four different methods to make their decisions:

- Some make decisions *by community*—a consensus of the members or their representatives. All of the members with governing authority discuss, deliberate, and decide, and—as the Massachusetts Smart Growth Alliance required—only when 100 percent agree is a decision considered made. The Alliance found that requiring unanimous consent "has proven critical to maintaining trust and encouraging the development of solutions that serve all interests," concluded a self-assessment by the network. A Bridgespan Group study found that many community collaboratives make decisions by "relying on a strong culture of trust among participants. . . . Unity is achieved through common purpose and trust (enhanced by effective communication and clear decision-making rules), rather than a highly formalized governance structure." However, many users of consensus arrangements find that this method can bog down when there are enduring disagreements among members. Some networks start with consensus governance, but when they run into trouble they add rules for deciding by majority vote when consensus cannot be reached.

- Other networks make decisions *by emergence*—through the actions of members. Sometimes networks decide by letting groups of members collaborate as they wish, rather than making a formal decision through consensus or by majority of the network. If, for instance, a group of members wants to start sharing information about a certain topic or to initiate a project together, they can go right ahead—they don't need the network's permission. In other words, "decisions" emerge as the aggregated actions taken by members, an approach that might be called "coalitions of the willing."

- Still others make decisions *by democracy*—using a majority vote of members or representatives. A time-honored governance mechanism, this has potential risks in networks since it may mean that members whose positions lose in the voting may become alienated from the winning members; this risks leading to network fragmentation. The Massachusetts Smart Growth Alliance decided that such a risk was a serious matter for its network; one assessment concluded that "It is likely that if the Alliance made regular use of these voting policies [rather than consensus-building] the Alliance would cease to operate as effectively because trust, a key determinant of effective, long-term collaboration, would begin to erode."

- And some networks make decisions *by imposition*—complying with conditions set by others. The network founder or a big funder of the network simply makes some or all of the decisions. A funder might, for instance, decide who will be members of the network at the outset and which network activities will be supported. These decisions might be embedded in the funding agreement for the network. A founder might decide what the value proposition of the network is or what the rules of communication among members might be, and these would be built into the initial network design.

Given the many different options, there's no governance model that works best. You have to tailor governance to the purpose, membership, size of the network, and other factors, recognizing that as the network's activities and resources grow—as there is more to decide—you will probably have to adapt governance to fit the conditions.

Assessment: Monitoring Network Health

As your network starts making decisions and taking action, how will you know how well the network building is going? Far too many network organizers don't ask this question until long after the network has matured, so in the early stages, as the network gets going, they don't really know how it's doing. They may have anecdotal evidence—a member says she likes the network; several members collaborate on a project—but the organizers have no substantial information, no baseline data, about the network. Yet it's quite easy to establish some initial measurement of the network's health—and this can set up in-depth assessments later on that will influence the network's strategic direction. We'll have much more to say about how to evaluate a network in chapter 6.

At the outset, though, two types of evaluative information should be gathered. One is the degree to which the network is satisfying its members' value propositions. You're flying blind if you don't know which value propositions your members care about and how well they feel the network is doing in delivering on them. All you have to do is ask the members and then keep asking them, using a survey. The other assessment information that matters is the degree to which members are connecting with and relating to each other—the network's connectivity. Connections are the foundation for a generative network; they are so crucial that we've devoted the next chapter entirely to the topic. (Of course, once network members start working together on projects, you should also start to assess the impact the network is having.)

You can start monitoring your network's connectivity even before it meets for the first time, as Laura Bartsch, a network builder for the national nonprofit Advanced Energy Economy, did when she was organizing a network focused on state government policies. She asked every founding member to identify which of the other 14 members they knew

and how well they knew them, offering five gradations of potential connectivity, from "I have not met this person yet" to "I can reliably count
on this person for information and a quick response." It turned out, she
reports, that "most did not know each other or did not know each other
well enough to work with each other comfortably," and this finding reinforced the need to allot some time in their first meeting together for them
to exchange personal information and build stronger connections with
each other. As the network matures, Bartsch can continue to survey the
members' connectivity and assess how it is changing.

Operating Principles: Guiding the Culture

- Make the network do the work.
- Do everything with someone, not alone.
- Let connections flow to value.
- Keep network information and decision making open and
  transparent.
- Keep plans flexible.

Starting a network doesn't end with designing its purpose, membership, value propositions, resources, coordination, and governance. You
also have to guide development of the network's culture, the way members will conduct the network's business and express their expectations.
Because a network doesn't work like an organization, it's not always immediately obvious what the guidelines should be. From our experiences
with building networks, we've developed several operating principles to
help network organizers get things going and avoid defaulting to the "organization-centric" habits so deeply fixed in all of us. You can use these
principles, and others that feel right to you, to help members establish a
consistent and net-centric "way we do things here."

- **Make the network do the work.** The steering group of an economic development network in western rural Maine wanted to
  get several projects going as soon as possible. Some members
  thought the best way to do this would be to hire a staff person
  to do the work. Others, including Bruce Hazard, who had started the network, argued that that was the way an organization

would do things. The network way, they said, would be to get the network members—not a staff person—to do the work together, using their connections, knowledge, competencies, and resources. The point of a network is for the members of the network to collaborate to produce value for each other. "Members don't increase their influence and reach by calling up staff," says Rick Reed, a senior consultant to the Garfield Foundation who was instrumental in developing the RE-AMP network. As USDN's Parzen puts it, "A network is not a service organization—we require that members do the work." Of course a network may hire staff—a coordinator, for instance—but those people are there to support the network members, not perform their work and produce their results.

- *Do everything with someone, not alone.* Network consultant June Holley gets this just right: "Make your motto, 'No one works alone.'" When a member wants to pursue an idea, help him connect to others who might want to join the effort. Establish working groups of members to explore possibilities for collective action. Make sure that decision making is collective.

- *Let connections flow to value.* The developers of Lawrence CommunityWorks used a variety of programs to attract people to the network. In 2005, it had about a dozen of these working clusters. But network developers noticed that one of them—a program for youth interested in architecture—was not attracting many network members. What should they do about that? Some network organizers argue that a network should keep supporting weaker activities, while others say they should be allowed to die. We hold the latter view. Network members link to working groups or clusters because they perceive they might derive value. It's inevitable that some activities and groups will have more participants than others and that some will attract only a few members. This uneven distribution poses challenges for network developers. "Popular" clusters attract more resources and can come to dominate a network, while "unpopular" ones struggle along at the margin. Should a network builder try to override these signals—continuing to invest, for instance, in the capacity of a working group with few members? If so, how will this change the nature of the network and affect its development? We said earlier, in the discussion of collective value propositions, what members value is what should drive networks. At USDN, says Parzen, "If no one's showing up for something, we end it." Network organizers and funders should not insist on having the network continue to do things that members don't find valuable.

- **Keep network information and decision making open and transparent.** No secrets, no information hoarding: this principle honors the decentralization model in which no member is more powerful than any other. And it's essential for building trust among members and stimulating collaboration. "When we share what we are doing," explains Holley, "others can join with us and improve what we do or support our work in some way. We *want* people to 'steal' what we are doing because that way good ideas and practices go viral and really make a difference."

- **Keep plans flexible.** Most of the networks we know make plans that are inherently short term and temporary, a year or two at the most. "All our programs and committees have to be seen as provisional—useful only in that they get us where we need to go," state Bill Traynor and Jessica Andors of Lawrence CommunityWorks. At USDN, members identify their priorities for the network every year at their annual meeting; existing processes continue only if they have enough support, and proposed new efforts don't start if they don't attract sufficient member support. Networks are unlikely to create the sort of three- to five-year strategic plans that organizations do. Because they don't start with the sense of permanence that organizations do, expecting instead to adapt their plans as they go along, their planning horizons are relatively short. They tend to plan two things: projects they will undertake and the development of the network as a whole. But neither of these usually requires or lends itself to long-term planning.

Picture the aggregate impact of grounding the network's culture in these sorts of operating principles: what the network undertakes only happens when and because members step up to make it happen, and what happens can be changed quickly by the members without having to dismantle long-term commitments. If these are characteristics you want in your network, then you should build them in from the beginning.

More Than a Balancing Act

Designing a network start-up, from purpose to principles, involves a balancing act of choices and trade-offs. Some design choices pose extremes—too big or too small, too closed or too open, too top-down or too bottom-up. Often the right answer lies somewhere in the middle. As Kevin Kelly notes about network governance, "Without some element of governance from the top, bottom-up control will freeze when options are many. Without some element of leadership, the many at the bottom will be paralyzed with choices." Finding the best answers when designing a decentralized system, say the authors of *The Starfish and The Spider*, is "like Goldilocks eating the various bowls of porridge. This one is too hot, this one is too cold, but this one is just right."

The point of the balancing act is not just to get the network going. It's also to get it started in a way that will create the conditions that support the connect-align-produce sequence of network evolution and unleash the network effects and social effects that make generative networks special and worth building. Above all else, the network's start-up design should fuel the development of a strong core of well-connected members. Without a core in place, little else will happen to drive the network's development forward. A network builder's design decisions could hinder the development of a strong core if, for instance, they result in starting with too many members or weak collective value propositions, or they allow haphazard coordination of members, or they create governance that divides members.

But building a strong core of members doesn't just depend on the network builder's choices about network design. It depends crucially on how well network builders practice the weaver's art of connecting members to each other.

Advice for Funders and Other Network Engineers

W e've worked with foundations, government agencies, nonprofits, and high-net-worth individuals that decided to assemble organizations, grantees, or contractors to form a social-impact network. As outsider-engineers, catalysts but not founders of the network, they must address most of the same design issues as any network builder. But they face a significant risk of failure due to the possibility that they will exercise excessive control over what's supposed to be a decentralized, member-driven arrangement. There is nothing wrong with engineers exerting strong influence over a network's design, but if they are too heavy-handed or persist in controlling things for too long, their networks may never become highly engaged or generative; the members will just wait to find out what the engineer wants. To avoid this, engineers must be clear about how much control they must have and for how long—with as much control as possible passing to network members as quickly as possible.

A funder's money is a powerful force for control. When a single source of funds invests in a network, there's a natural tendency for network members to defer to that source. So the funder may have the power to design the network in whatever way the funder thinks best—and this may be reinforced by the funder's desire to claim credit for whatever the network achieves. But sooner or later, control and credit have to become more distributed among the network's members. "Funders succeed with networks by providing sufficient resources to support the network without overpowering it," advise the authors of "Cracking the Network Code: Four Principles for Grantmakers." And "they let go of control by allowing the network members latitude to make decisions and manage operations for themselves."

This challenge confronted Jennie Curtis, executive director of the Garfield Foundation, when the foundation funded and helped to create and develop the RE-AMP network, which has about 165 organization members. Since RE-AMP's birth in 2005, Curtis has served as a network member and participated actively in network decision-making processes. Garfield's positioning as a network engineer and leading funder raised the potential that Curtis's team could use its power to dominate network decision making, a risk that Curtis readily acknowledges and has tried to diminish. "From the get-go," she says, "we tried to neutralize the power balance. Sometimes it worked, sometimes it didn't. Dealing with these power dynamics is an ongoing challenge." Curtis's work with RE-AMP and our engagements with other engineers offer lessons about how engineers might best shape their intentions and behaviors to start generative social-impact networks.

10 Lessons for Network Engineers

1. Don't dictate the network's purpose; co-create it with potential start-up partners.
2. Be open to surprises; don't try to pin everything down.
3. Lead, but allow others to co-lead in organizing the network.
4. Let network membership expand naturally through members' connections, not through the engineer's dictates.
5. Intentionally dilute your power over time.
6. Entice other funders into the game.
7. Make sure you know what other network members think about your ideas, and don't override their concerns or objections.
8. Step up to support the monitoring of network health.
9. Recognize that having anyone in the network exercise dominance erodes, rather than builds, the network.
10. Patience is essential and will be rewarded.

1. Don't dictate the network's purpose; co-create it with potential start-up partners. If the engineer hands potential members a purpose that they don't understand or care about, they won't feel committed to the network. They may participate, but it's only an act of compliance and won't be generative. The best way for network engineers to manage this risk is not to design the network's purpose in a vacuum and then give it to the members they've selected. Instead, in consultation with the potential members of the network, they should figure out the network's purpose and craft it to meet members' needs, too.

The Garfield Foundation used a consultant's scan to conclude that shifting the electricity system in the Midwest toward renewable energy and away from fossil fuels was the potential purpose the foundation wanted to explore. The scanning process identified several dozen organizations, mostly environmental advocates, and foundations in the region that were working on the problem. The next step the foundation took, after it confirmed the organizations' willingness to participate, was to get all the potential partners together for discussions and systems mapping, so that everyone had the same information and knew what was going on. "A core principle of our model," says Curtis, "was that foundations had to be at the table as authentic and equitable partners."

When a government agency in the United Kingdom discussed with us its plan to start a network of some 25 cities to which it was going to provide planning grants, we stressed the importance of consulting with the prospective members, instead of mandating their participation. But consultation has to be done with a genuine openness to having the network's purpose develop as the members see fit, and a recognition that it's probably too early in the network's life to insist on highly specific outcomes. If engineers cannot take this approach, then whatever they design isn't likely to become a generative network.

As with a network's purpose, so with its value propositions. Engineers bring *their* value proposition to the start-up of the network—and may assume that the network members they select and recruit will also embrace that value proposition, and that it will be sustained as the network matures. But this is a risky assumption. We've seen engineers decide to build a network to create value they care about—increasing the impact of their programs and grants, for example, or helping to develop knowledge of best practices that will help others in a field—without worrying about whether it's a value proposition that ranks highly with network members. But in donor-driven networks, the impetus is much less sustainable than if the members also have their hands on the steering wheel. Network engineers should take the time to fully explore and validate their value proposition with potential members of the network they are building—and be open to having the network pursue other value propositions prized by the members.

An additional caution for engineers: Beware of starting a network in which the members' main value proposition is that they will receive funding for their projects if they join. The lure of funding will get members to sign up and come to meetings, but it's not a value proposition that is likely to motivate members to do more than submit to the engineer's requirements to get their money. "I'll do what I have to do" is not the basis for launching a generative network.

2. Be open to surprises; don't try to pin everything down. In engineered start-ups there's also a risk of overemphasizing the funders' desired outcomes for the network. Many networks start with a general, not specific, end in mind. For instance, the Urban Sustainability Directors Network wanted to "advance the field." That purpose attracted substantial funding, but it might not be nearly specific enough to meet the needs of outside funders who want to be sure that money they provide to the network will lead to the results *they* desire. Early in a generative network's life, it is unwise to put its development on a production schedule and to commit the network to specific outcomes and timelines. It's hard to know how a network will evolve; surprises emerge, and that's a good thing. Funders have to be patient enough with the network to invest in its front-end collaborative capacity and allow it to forge its own direction, rather than trying to impose a plan and targets.

The discussions that the Garfield Foundation initiated with environmental advocates and regional climate-change funders were in person and in depth—and, to everyone's surprise, led to a different problem focus that Garfield subsequently embraced. "It wasn't just the electricity system that the group wanted to work on collaboratively; it was global warming," says Curtis. "This was a big realization for the group."

3. Lead, but allow others to co-lead in organizing the network. Early on, the RE-AMP group didn't know it would build a network. Its discussions and additional analysis identified four potential strategies for affecting climate change in the Midwest. "Through our collective, year-long systems analysis, we had a lot of information, but the foundation was not attached to any particular next step," Curtis recalls. "We said, 'Maybe you guys can use this information to inform your work as independent operators or to work in a new way.'" Presented with the option of stopping or moving forward, the group of nonprofits and funders decided to continue the work, with several of them taking the lead to flesh out each strategy and bring additional organizations into the effort. The Garfield Foundation paid for most of this next phase of work, with other foundations chipping in, but it didn't dictate what the work should be.

4. Let network membership expand naturally through members' connections, not through the engineer's dictates. When the engineer determines a network's membership, several things can go wrong. The engineer may bring together members who are not personally committed to the network but are complying with the engineer's wishes, or are not ready and able to collaborate effectively in a decentralized structure that depends on connecting and sharing. Because members have their primary relationship with the engineer who selected them, that will tend to dominate—and can stifle—the network's development. "Funder-driven relationships may lack the trust and goodwill among partners that helps collaborations succeed," offers "Cracking the Network Code" in advice to funders. "Many well-intentioned joint initiatives have failed because partners have been selected by others (rather than coalescing via self-selection) and because a key motivation to come to the table is the potential for funding."

In an effort to promote diversity of membership in the network, the engineer may assemble members whose differences are much greater than what they have in common. Such diversity may result in benefits as members engage with and adapt to each other's points of view, but having to work toward a "meeting of the minds" will likely slow the crucial process of building strong connections among members.

The engineer may manage the addition of members to suit the engineer's needs, rather than allowing expansion to occur naturally based on the desire of members to add connections that create value. For instance, the engineer may have set up a multiple-year budget and plan for the network's development and insist on following that predetermined scenario no matter how the network is actually evolving. And if the engineer maintains tight control over the selection of additional members, the effect could be to stymie existing members' natural desire to bring *their* connections into the network.

Grantmakers for Effective Organizations advises foundations working with networks to "help make connections, but don't force them." Instead of selecting members, says Lois Savage, president of the Lodestar Foundation, "What a funder can do is create an environment that maximizes the opportunities for nonprofits to get together and develop relationships of trust that lead to collaboration."

5. Intentionally dilute your power over time. As the RE-AMP network started to form, the Garfield Foundation recognized that it was beginning to have a vested interest in keeping the process moving, but also appreciated that if it did not share power the effort would fall flat. In 2005, the network founders established a steering committee selected from the original systems-analysis group. Within a year, the steering committee was reformed into a body democratically elected by the growing network's members. "We wanted to empower a governance structure in which Garfield was just one voting member, but could still provide leadership," Curtis says. "There's a difference between leadership and dominance. We're very careful about just being one vote."

A network may want to incorporate funders as members and also into its governance structure, Heather Creech notes, since it can "interact more closely with donors as part of engaging their interest in and contribution to the projects." She describes the way the Sustainable Development Communications Network (SDCN) handled this. "Donors are considered members of the network and are encouraged to actively learn from the SDCN's experiences by participating in network meetings and on the network extranet. Donors are invited to review and advise on network projects but not asked to take the lead on a network project."

6. Entice other funders into the game. Getting other funders involved helps to diminish the potential power of any single funder, while adding to the network's resources. The Garfield Foundation paid nearly all of the costs of the analysis and network design process and committed to provide substantial funding to support RE-AMP's operations and related project grants. Curtis says, "Our promise to other potential funders was that, not only would we pay for the process, but we would bring $500,000 of grant funding for each of five years." This was a significant commitment for a midsize foundation to offer, and it helped other foundations to perceive Garfield as a serious funding partner, gain confidence that the initiative would be well resourced, and recognize that their investments could be spent on issues they cared deeply about. During the following years, 15 foundations contributed to RE-AMP operations and projects, and some became active in network decision-making processes.

7. Make sure you know what other network members think about your ideas, and don't override their concerns or objections. It's natural for other members to defer to a funder, especially when the funder is being insistent about something. So when funders think there's something worth insisting on, Curtis says, they should curb their power. Instead of preempting challenges to their thinking, they should participate in the decision-making process and learn what others are thinking. And although they should strongly voice what they think is right, they should do this without forcing others to acquiesce. Curtis recalls that she advocated RE-AMP investment in ways for the network to learn from its mistakes. "But making this learning system work has been hugely challenging. We're the voice behind the necessity of this." But, she adds, Garfield's insistence came with the knowledge that others in the network "agree in principle that we should learn from our mistakes and get smarter over time. It's just that putting it into place has been so hard. No one has outwardly objected to trying."

8. Step up to support the monitoring of network health. Engineers can play an important constructive role when it comes to early-stage network assessment. They should support assessment of the network's condition at the start-up stage, instead of regarding it as an unnecessary cost. But they should focus assessment on network health, not on impact, since so much of the start-up is about building the network's capacities.

9. Recognize that having anyone in the network exercise dominance erodes, rather than builds, the network. "Is a network a network if you've got some dominant players?" Curtis asks, and then answers her own question:

"It is counter to what you're trying to engender. If whatever governance structure you set up can't call the dominant character on that kind of behavior, then there's a design flaw. You want to create a set-up that doesn't allow that type of behavior."

10. *Patience is essential and will be rewarded.* Building a generative social-impact network is a marathon, not a sprint. It takes time to get started well, to build the base of connections and then align, even before there is production over the long run. Funders and other engineers have to be willing to support relationship building before expecting impacts.

CHAPTER THREE

Connect the Dots: Weaving
a Network's Core

The foundation of generative social-impact networks is the connectivity of its members to each other, which can be cultivated by network weavers.

Connectors . . . are extraordinarily powerful. We rely on them to give us access to opportunities and worlds to which we don't belong.

— *Malcolm Gladwell*

In May 2006, Kathy Moxon found herself sitting with four strangers in a conference center in Scottsdale, Arizona. She was, in network terms, an unconnected node. The director of Redwood Coastal Rural Action, a small network of organizations in northern California, Moxon had responded to an invitation from the W. K. Kellogg Foundation, which aimed to build networks of rural-policy advocates across the United States. The foundation's staff had decided who would attend the first session of its "Rural People, Rural Policy" initiative. "They brought together organizations who wanted to expand their policy work," Moxon says. The foundation had committed to create a critical mass of advocates—rural nonprofit organizations—to voice rural communities' concerns in government arenas. "But 'policy' was undefined," recalls Moxon, "and we had little else in common. We weren't geographically linked or programmatically linked. We didn't know each other." Somehow these unconnected people were supposed to find common purpose and work together.

That's precisely what happened—the individuals connected, clicked, and started to work on projects together. "We bonded, even in that first meeting. We committed to each other that we would find our way through the confusion—and do it in a way that made sense to us and our organizations and communities," says Moxon. "We actually stayed up all night and created a video about what we hoped the network would be and what our intention was." They named their collaboration Networks United for a Rural Voice (NURV). Seven years later they were still at it, working together as an even larger network of rural advocates. "We glued together out of stubbornness and mutual respect," Moxon says. "We said, 'We're going to figure out what this opportunity really is.' We found that we liked each other and respected the work each of us was doing. So we thought we'd muddle around until we could figure something out." The muddling lasted awhile. During each of the next two years the foundation assigned additional sets of organizations to join NURV; the arrival of new members disrupted the network's development. "The last group that came in wanted an executive committee and rules," Moxon recalls, "but we hadn't been operating that way. We weren't clear why the newest group felt it was necessary for the network's development."

Gradually, though, the expanding body of NURV members identified potential rural-policy issues that seemed ripe for advocacy efforts. "We asked ourselves, where is there a 'window' open for policy change and do we have a champion in the group willing to push an effort?" Moxon says. "We ended up with different people in the network picking up the lead. I agreed to champion an issue that I knew nothing about—federal transportation legislation that was up for renewal in the Congress—because the window of opportunity was clear to me and it would give me the experience of pulling people together." Other working groups formed—addressing immigration, youth and education, entrepreneurship, workforce development—and some of the policy efforts scored victories: articulating a set of rural-friendly principles for federal transportation programs and securing changes in legislation; designing and implementing a new program to increase the number of Native American doctors; producing and disseminating information materials about the impact of the federal Affordable Care Act on rural immigrant communities.

Moxon could see that the far-flung network had become a valuable asset: "It helps you make your case to policymakers because you can say that all these different people, from different geographies and different sectors, agree. When we went to Washington to talk about rural transportation, they said, 'Why would an education program, a youth development organization, and a disability advocate be here to talk about transportation? Why are you guys together? There's no commonality.' And we said, 'We all believe in these principles for transportation.'" Over time NURV became 15 organizations strong, engaged with other networks on policy issues, and started to take on new concerns. "We've stayed together," Moxon explains, "because we like working together." In December 2013, Moxon underscored this point. She had just returned from a trek along Nepal's Annapurna Circuit, taken with three other members of NURV. "The network," she reflected, "*is* all about the relationships."

NURV's biography demonstrates the essentialness of connectivity in network building—complete strangers have worked together successfully for years because they developed and maintained strong, enduring relationships with each other. As they learned more about each other, personally and professionally, they decided to try to collaborate. Knowing each other made it possible for some of them to take the risk of offering to lead shared work. Unless they had connected, nothing more could have happened.

Levels of Connectivity

Connecting people in a network involves more than just introducing them and then letting nature take its course. Introductions are only a first step toward building the trust that is the basis for strong, enduring relationships. When network members become confident that they can rely on each other's intentions, integrity, judgment, and abilities, they will act in new ways toward each other—sharing secrets, making commitments, providing help, taking care, being accountable. Trust facilitates the quality of information and efficiency of transactions that flow between network members; it allows the network's gift economy to emerge.

Connectivity among network members has different degrees of intensity; the greater the trust, the more intense the relationship. You can see this in the four-level connectivity scale we developed for several networks to measure their members' connectivity. At level 1, introductions have

Measuring Intensity of Member Connections

Level	Definition
1	I have been introduced to this person, but do not exchange information with them on a regular basis (at least once per month).
2	I exchange useful information with this person on a regular basis (at least once per month) but have not worked/do not work directly with them on a project.
3	I exchange useful information with this person on a regular basis and have worked or am working directly with this person on one or more projects.
4	I depend on this person regularly for important advice and have worked with him/her on more than one project.

occurred but no trust has been built. In levels 2 and 3, exchanges of information and working together on a project have led to more trust and a deeper relationship. (We'll say more in this chapter about how to build trust among network members.) At level 4, members have built enough trust that they are comfortable seeking important advice from each other. The value of a scale, whatever indicators of connectivity you use, is that you can see how connectivity changes (moves up or down the scale) over time.

It takes time to build trust. Some of the smaller networks we know—like NURV, with only a dozen or so organizations in the mix—have taken a year or more to launch themselves. What they're doing during that time is meeting and talking, sharing their stories and values, checking to see if there's a good fit among them, and deciding if they want to work together.

Making strong connections among members is a step that should not be skipped in network building. This is true even when a start-up network's members or its funders/engineers are eager to get to the substance of their work—to organize collaborative projects and produce results. They may be impatient with relationship building, because it seems less essential than figuring out what to do together, and because it takes time (and money) for people to gel. But connectivity is the foundation of a generative network.

Building a Strong Core

When more and more people in a network connect and build trust, a core of robust and resilient connections forms; scattered, unconnected individuals become a cohesive group. The emerging core doesn't necessarily include everyone in the network; some members may develop connections more slowly or not at all. And it doesn't include all of the same people over the years; some members depart, others step in, some become more or less active. But a network core has enough members who, because they are sufficiently connected with each other, want to start transacting with each other—not just sharing information, but also collaborating, taking time and risks to work together and taking responsibility for the health of the network. June Holley, in *Network Weaver Handbook*, describes this effect as "a tipping point where the community starts operating in a qualitatively different way: people working together to co-create a community that is healthy for all becomes the norm."

The Urban Sustainability Directors Network built a large, healthy, and sustained core out of a few initial connections and many intentional efforts to connect members with each other. Sadhu Johnston and Amanda Eichel, sustainability directors in Chicago and Seattle, respectively, knew each other, and Johnston had connected with Julia Parzen, who became the network's managing director. Then the original pair multiplied: Johnston and Eichel contacted five other sustainability directors they had met. The seven of them contacted five more each. The 35 members of the embryonic network made additional connections, and the membership grew to 70. That's when a meeting room came into play; most of the members turned up at the network's first annual gathering in 2009 in Chicago. "Maybe half of them were pretty well networked, but the others weren't," Parzen recalls. Data from a member survey at the time shows that most connections in the network were superficial, based on people having been introduced to each other, but not having exchanged much information or undertaken any collaborative activity. The meeting substantially boosted the network's connectivity. Afterward, more than half of the participants reported they felt "strongly connected" to seven or more network members and felt they would get a quick response from 10 or more members they might contact for information. During the next five

Weaving Networks of Organizations

When organizations form a network, they assign people to participate in the network on the organization's behalf. These people represent their organizations' value propositions—the benefits the organizations are seeking. When they connect with each other in the network, their primary interest is in presenting their organization's interests, concerns, and constraints, and in learning about those of the other organizations in the network. They may also have personal value propositions, but as representatives they are accountable for what their organization gets out of the network and what it has to give to get it. This can pose something of a barrier to establishing a generative network's gift-economy dynamics, especially if, as Paul Vandeventer and Myrna Mandell note in *Networks That Work*, the organizations are worried about "loss of turf, power, prestige, even money."*

A key to weaving a network of organizations is this: even as the organization's representatives discuss their organizational value propositions and search for common ground with other organizations, you have to help them share their personal value propositions and find common ground there, too. Connecting at a personal level can ease the often bumpy and winding journey of a multi-organization negotiation. It's where trust gets built. And having organization representatives who trust each other will also help smooth the way when the organizations in the network start to implement their agreements. Rick Reed, who helped to weave RE-AMP, recalls that the early network building "was entirely personal. I formed one-on-one relationships with the individuals who were going to be in the network core. For the first years I never thought about the organizations behind these people. Even as RE-AMP built out to 65 organizations, it was really more like 65 people, something you could still manage with a lot of personal engagement."

Even when organizations in a network share a common goal, it's important to do more to build trust between the people representing them. Just getting organizations in a community collaborative to share and use data to inform their decisions requires trust, says Carrie Pickett-Erway, who helped develop the Learning Network of Greater Kalamazoo. "Using shared data, how hard can that be? The truth is it requires relationships of trust. It takes years to create that."

---

*Paul Vandeventer and Myrna Mandell, *Networks That Work* (Los Angeles: Community Partners, 2007), 7.

years, USDN's overall connectivity soared, even though some members departed and new members joined. In 2009 the average USDN member had only one connection in the network, but by 2013 the average member's number of links had reached 10. Even more telling, data showed that for the first time the average member either knew or knew someone who knew every other member. The "path" that members had to follow to connect with each other through other members had become quite short.

However, the most important network-building advance in USDN was the forging of a network core. Early on, about a dozen of the original members became well connected with each other; they grew comfortable sharing, discussing, and brainstorming together, and readily volunteered to undertake network-building activities—helping to plan annual meetings, presenting at network workshops, and more—as well as participating in the network's initial activities. "People interested in leading USDN, that was the core," says Parzen. The core grew to about 30 highly connected and engaged members; most had been in the network for at least two years and had championed one or more network activities. Nearly all were well connected with many other network members; a few linked strongly to nearly half of the network's more than 100 members. This core of members populated the major working structures of USDN, its planning committee, and the Innovation Fund's Steering Committee, and it chaired many of the learning work groups.

Creating a core of connectivity is the first big step in a network's evolution, and, as Holley notes, network builders constantly fret over the condition of the network's core: "Does the core have enough people? Enough energy? Enough diversity of perspective? Is it too dependent on one group or individual? How could the core be improved? Who is missing from the core?" But a strong core at USDN didn't just happen because members met together or e-mailed back and forth. Like Kathy Moxon's NURV network, forging deep connections required attention and nurturing, patience and risk-taking. A network core has to be woven.

The Art of Weaving

Connecting network members with one another is called *weaving*. Network founders do it and so do funders and other engineers. Network members do it and so do network coordinators and other staff. Some people are naturals at it, others not so much—but they can learn. A network's need for weaving never ends, but especially in its early days someone has to be weaving connections and doing it well. The weaver could be anybody in the network, but you can't leave it to chance. The work has to be done.

Weavers don't just introduce people to each other. They serve as the "on-the-ground eyes and ears" of the network, picking up information as they connect with people. They are, notes Holley, "skilled at discovering the needs of people in their networks, and then linking them to others in the network who can work with them to have those needs met." A weaver helps network members to develop new knowledge and skills that will allow *them* to connect with others more easily. Weaving, says Lawrence CommunityWorks' Bill Traynor, "requires curiosity, caring, the ability to get information and then share it, the ability to hook people up to opportunities that you know exist." In 2004, he notes, LCW started to "recognize weaving as the principal and highest form of leadership in the network." It created the annual Reviviendo Weaver Award that it presented to a member at the annual meeting.

Network weavers must understand their networks—what connections the members have with each other, what members think they need, and what they are good at doing. And they have to know how to build networks—making connections that enhance trust and understanding among members—as well as the specific context and subject matter of the network that's being built. If, for instance, it is a network of organizations that advocate for rural-friendly policies, the weaver must know something about rural policy, since that is the "currency" of the members. A weaver must step completely into the world of those who are to be connected—and this means knowing about that world.

People build trust with each other on the basis of the information and experiences they have. Most people don't trust strangers, and just getting information about a stranger, even a full profile, is usually not enough to build trust. It takes more—shared experiences that allow you to see how someone acts in a situation, letting you "look them in the eye" and make a judgment about them. To build trust among a network's members, you have to increase the bandwidth of information they have about each other—its quantity, quality, and diversity. Don't just focus on sharing

Successful Network Weavers . . .

- Unearth other people's dreams and visions.
- Model an approach to relationships that is positive, appreciative, and focused on strengths and gifts.
- Treat everyone as a peer.
- Encourage reciprocity—you share information and resources with another without expecting something in return from that person because you know that others will share with you.
- Point out the value of knowing people with different perspectives and from different backgrounds.
- Encourage people to see conflicts as opportunities to develop breakthroughs.
- Encourage people to listen deeply to each other.
- Encourage people to identify shared or overlapping interests or values.
- Help people make accurate and realistic assessments of others.
- Show people how to build trust through small, low-risk collaborations with others.

Adapted from June Holley's *Network Weaver Checklist*

information relevant to the network's purpose. Ties between people are stronger when they are multidimensional, involving personal interests such as family and hobbies, workplace successes and problems, career trajectory and aspirations, and more.

When it comes to building bandwidth, social science research emphasizes that you cannot overestimate the power of in-person information sharing. "There is no substitute for meeting face-to-face," summarizes researcher Bonnie Shepard. "Regular membership meetings serve the important function of building interpersonal trust. Such exchanges can begin or continue via email, but face-to-face conversations produce resolutions and decisions more efficiently when dealing with complex issues and diverse opinions." Sometimes it is useful to have an outsider facilitate meetings of members when sensitive subjects, such as racial differences or a history of conflict, are being explored. A facilitator can ensure that the conversation doesn't break down and that members reflect carefully about what they are learning about each other.

Along with information, experiences of reciprocity build trust between network members. Reciprocity refers to episodes of give-and-take and mutual support among members of the network. Karen Stevenson, a network analyst, describes the power of reciprocity as "the alchemy of mutual give and take over time turning to a golden trust." When members do something together, they inevitably have to work through differences and build on the commonalities they discover. They may develop more respect and understanding for each other. The same may happen when one member volunteers to help another member get something done, even without being asked.

Through trust, people build strong ties to each other, relationships in which they have more regular contact, exchange more information, and do more together than in weak-tie relationships. Strong ties allow you to take more risks in collaborating with each other, but maintaining these ties takes more effort. Most people have fewer strong ties than weak ties, since they have only so much energy available to maintain close relationships. As the Internet has made it easier to communicate and stay in touch, people have been able to increase greatly the number of weak ties they maintain. "Reciprocity online is incredibly easy and inexpensive," explain Beth Kanter and Allison Fine. "Sending a thank-you e-mail can be done for free in seconds. Posting a thank-you note on Facebook for your community to see is just as easy and even more powerful because it's public."

There are two ways to help network members build strong relationships: *Mass* weaving turns the network into an information-rich environment that any member can contribute to and draw from. *Customized* weaving creates specific value for specific people by bringing them together. Together these methods form the weaver's toolkit.

Mass Weaving

Mass weaving creates a milieu in which people can efficiently find out about and contact each other. It's like a never-ending mixer that uses different tools—publications, meetings, conference calls—to give network members useful information and numerous opportunities to connect informally.

When Kathy Moxon's NURV network first met in Arizona, the Kellogg Foundation also brought together representatives from other

---

Weaver's Toolkit

Mass Weaving
- Produce member directories.
- Spread the news—who's doing what.
- Use many information sharing methods.
- Use ice breakers.

Customized Weaving
- Build triads.
- Activate hubs.
- Build and support "bridgers."
- Engage the unconnected.

---

organizations to start other rural-policy networks. Few of these people knew each other, since the foundation had deliberately selected a diversity of types of organizations with little experience working together. Naturally, they decided to share with each other information about their organization's mission, priorities, and capacities by providing website material, brochures, and other documents. They also shared information about which other organizations each of them was connected to. They created Listservs to facilitate communication and explored the use of blogs and collaborative websites that allow members to post documents, share calendars, alert each other, and build databases and document archives. (The emphasis on electronic communications was easier for some members than others, because they already had experience using the relevant software and the technology.)

Mass weaving is all about helping network members "bump into each other" and decide to build relationships. Networks like NURV and USDN use a typical set of tools and methods for mass weaving:

- *Produce member directories.* Publish online and/or hardcopy profiles—short and sweet or quite detailed—of network members. They may include photos of members and lots of optional background information, along the lines of a LinkedIn profile. Network directories contain personal as well as professional information. Typically network members fill out their own profiles. For members slow to do so, we've seen network builders use a little peer pressure, letting them know that their name will appear on a list of "camera shy" members who did not share information with others. For its 2013 annual meeting, USDN published a Participant Directory—a framed slide for each member, funder, partner, advisor, and consultant attending. It included a photo of the member, their description of an exciting project they'd been involved in, and their "urgent question." At the meeting, the slides were projected on a screen in a continuous loop.

- *Spread the news—who's doing what.* Regularly provide network members with information and updates about member-driven activities in the network, and alert them to opportunities to work with other members. Make sure to highlight the people behind the activities, not just the activities, and how to contact them. This is easy to do by e-mail and you can monitor who's opening the e-mails and who's not.

- *Use many information-sharing methods.* Use conference calls and workshops to identify which members are interested in which topics and who has relevant expertise or experiences. Before USDN's first annual meeting, when members still knew little about each other, Parzen initiated monthly conference calls of a small number of members: "We had five people on the call talking about what was important to them. It was a really good, easy starting point. They would talk about something and sometimes someone else would say they were really interested in that topic." At the beginning of the many topical workshops that USDN conducts at its annual meetings, all participants are asked to introduce themselves and explain why they are attending—a sharing of personal and professional information.

- *Use ice breakers.* Start any gathering (in person, telephonic, online) with an exercise or two that allows participants to reveal their interests, experiences, successes, and challenges relevant to the meeting topic. This gives others information they can use to forge deeper connections later.

Customized Weaving

Customized weaving involves directly connecting members to each other. A weaver notices what's happening in the network in order to identify opportunities to connect members with each other in ways that meet their needs. Parzen incorporates this approach into practically everything she does with network members. "I look at every person and ask myself, how would we create an 'aha moment' for them, when making a connection benefits them?" says Parzen. When a member does make such a connection, she adds, it has a generative effect: the member starts making connections on her own, to see what value can be created.

Mia Arter, USDN's associate coordinator, provides an example of how tailored weaving works: "USDN members frequently use the internal network website to ask questions of each other. Staff pays attention to questions that are answered by several members, as they may be opportunities for collaborative work." In 2013, the staff noticed several questions about solar energy programs and saw that 18 members had responded to the questions. "Given this amount of interest," Arter says, "staff e-mailed these members to see if they would be interested in a call to discuss their solar programs. More than half were, and quickly responded to a scheduling request." These members came together around a shared interest—so they could explore opportunities to work together and increase their collective impact.

Noticing members' common interest is one way to bring specific network members together. Another is to leverage connections among members:

- *Build triads.* Find a network member who knows two other members who don't know each other, and get that member to introduce them to each other. It's called "closing the triangle" and it works well, because members will be more receptive to an introduction made by someone they already know.

- *Activate hubs.* Every network, even at the start-up stage, contains some members who are natural connectors; they are "hubs" who may already know others in the network or they are eager and able to make connections quickly. You can find a network's hubs by mapping the members' connections and, often, by simply observing members' behaviors, looking for extroverts and members who seem to get involved easily. For a weaver, a hub is an opportunity—a way to connect efficiently with many other nodes. Hubs can close the triangle with many of their connections and are likely to be good at reaching out to and connecting with other members. Although hubs are well connected in the network, some may not be very engaged in network activities. If that's the case, then invite them to join one of the network's activities. If they participate and find value, they may influence their connections to become more active.

- *Build and support "bridgers."* Within a network, even in the start-up phase, there may be a set of people who are connected to each other, forming a cluster of members, but are not well connected to others in the network. Look for members who are in more than one cluster; they are bridgers who can connect people from different clusters to each other.

- *Engage the unconnected.* Just as the network may have some well-connected hubs, it probably will have some relatively unconnected members. Ask hubs to connect with them. Ask unengaged members to join a network group or project, or to help another member. As Holley notes, "Asking someone to help another person is a very powerful way to draw him into your network. Almost all people truly enjoy helping others." Find out if they face barriers to connecting. For instance, Holley points out, "When people are from different cultures or backgrounds, they may need help clearing up assumptions they made about each other." Don't try only once to connect network outliers; try a number of times in different ways and follow up to assist with connections they do make. Holley, again, offers good advice: "Sometimes people just need a reminder to keep the relationship on track."

A network can also designate some members to serve as weavers. For instance, the 10 members of USDN's Planning Committee who play a role in guiding the network also take responsibility for checking in regularly

Connectivity Watch

An important element in the art of weaving is to notice a network's connectivity. In chapter 6 we explain the uses and benefits of connectivity mapping. For now, though, here are questions that weavers should be asking about connectivity in their network:

- Who is connected to whom? Who's not connected?
- Where are the hubs—members with more connections to other members?
- Where are the clusters—small groups of members connected to each other?
- Are new connections forming?
- Are new patterns of connectivity forming?
- What's the overall connectivity of the network?

with a "circle" of a handful of designated members—asking how they are doing and, if possible, connecting them to opportunities and others in the network. Every month they get a report on how active their circle's members have been—are they participating in working groups and the website, have they taken on new activities? And they report to each other on what their circle is up to. "On every monthly call we take 10 minutes and one committee member reports on their circle," Parzen explains. "They bring up specific things that people in the circle have said, and we talk about it. They seem to really care about their circle. It's very affirming for them, because a large part of the circle will be happy with the network, and so they get to share that someone said they love what the network is doing. But they also bring specific criticisms for the committee to consider."

Laura Bartsch was sitting in her network's first organizing meeting in July 2013 in Boulder, Colorado, when she realized that it was going well. The dozen or so founding members from organizations and associations around the United States were energetically discussing how to add members, how often and when they should meet, and how to structure their work together. They debated names for the network and settled on SPIN (State Policy Innovation Network). Bartsch was pleased and surprised. "They were all very open to talking about what this network might be.

Designing F2F Meetings: Mass Customization

- Make increasing connectivity an explicit objective of the meeting.
- Make enough time for members to connect, not just work together.
- Leave room for network members to invent what they want to do on the spot.
- Promote what members are doing and what they know; don't over-rely on outside experts.
- Increase members' awareness of the network.
- Find out how much connecting has happened.

I had thought they'd just want to talk about the content of their work." She had prepared for the session for months, inviting and surveying the initial members and designing the meeting. She worked for the national nonprofit Advanced Energy Economy (AEE), which wanted to start a network of people working on state government policies to support clean energy. AEE covered the costs of the meeting. Bartsch was not a member of the network; she was its catalyst from the outside, what we call a *network engineer*—and she made this clear to the members from the beginning. By the end of the session, a long day sandwiched between a dinner the night before and a hike the morning after, Bartsch had a strong indicator that the network had built momentum. "In the post-meeting evaluation, they all said, 'I met people I want to continue to engage with and it will help my work.' They found value that mattered to them and that they don't get another way."

Meeting in person, with or without dinner and a hike, creates the opportunity for dialogue and shared experiences that allow people to understand and bond with each other. In a network's early meetings, especially, members need time to talk and hear about each other's passions, interests, and concerns for the network. Finding time to meet together can be difficult, but it is essential. Julia Parzen noted this in addressing the 2013 annual meeting of USDN, held at a baseball stadium in Memphis: "The network is never more palpable than when we are all in this room together."

Given the importance of using face-to-face time for building relation-ships, don't squander meetings—in person or electronically—by working exclusively on topics, content, substance. Instead, as Holley urges, "Make sure every meeting and phone call includes relationship-building activi-ties." As USDN's first annual meeting approached, Parzen recalls, "People started saying, 'We're coming to your annual conference,' and I'd get re-ally annoyed and say, 'We don't have an annual conference. We have an annual networking meeting and the purpose of it is to help people get to know each other and find people with common interests.'"

Although the art of designing meetings is well understood, we have tips for designing meetings of *networks* to increase connectivity:

- *Make increasing connectivity an explicit objective of the meeting.* Acknowledging the importance of connecting in this way can ensure that meeting planners build in efforts to increase con-nectivity and to assess whether or not this goal was achieved.

- *Make enough time for members to connect, not just work together.* Schedule a blend of time focused on the content members care about and time for making and strengthening connections among members. Don't assume that when members are study-ing or discussing a topic together they are getting enough of the information about each other that is so essential to build-ing trust. It's probably not enough to let members connect over meals or after hours; build connecting time right into the agen-da—to signal its importance for the network and to make sure it happens. For its annual meetings, USDN added tours of the host city's prominent sustainability achievements—during, not just before or after, the meeting—because it's a great way for members to spend time together and get to know each other, while also seeing examples of relevant, substantive work. You don't have to always separate connecting time from content time—just ensure that when members are working they are do-ing it in ways that help them make connections, too.

- *Leave room for network members to invent on the spot what they want to do together.* However well the meeting is planned, a network's members will bubble up new ideas and surprises when they are with each other. Leave "open space" time in the formal agenda for members to pitch their ideas for small group discussions.

- *Promote what members are doing and what they know; don't over-rely on outside experts.* As much as possible, have members lead meeting sessions and talk with each other, peer-to-peer; don't just throw one expert after another at them.

- *Increase members' awareness of the network.* Make the network's condition visible to the members, even briefly. Remind them of the early-stage network-design decisions and the role every member can play in making the network work. Show them maps of members' connections in the network and the results from surveys of network members. Tell them about opportunities to participate in the network. Help them understand what they are a part of and how they can contribute. Get some members to share stories about how connecting to others resulted in benefits. "From the beginning," says Parzen, "we've wanted members to understand the network." At USDN's first annual meeting, consultants did a short presentation on the results of member connectivity mapping and satisfaction surveys. "The reaction was, 'Why are you wasting our time on this?'" Parzen remembers. "We said, 'You have to know how this is different from being in an organization.' And then in the second year, we had another presentation and people not only internalized the information, they saw how the network was different."

- *Find out how much connecting has happened.* Use meeting evaluations to find out more about connecting activities among members. This, too, signals to members that connecting matters, and it also helps to assess how well the meeting went. This doesn't have to be complicated. For instance, at its first annual meeting USDN asked participants how many strong connections they had made with other members. Forty-three respondents said they felt strongly connected to four or more other members.

It's not easy for networks to convene often, due to distance, cost, or lack of time. Members of USDN and the rural policy networks like NURV look for conferences they plan to attend to see if they can add a day to get some face time together at relatively little extra cost and inconvenience. And they schedule network meetings months ahead of time to make sure the sessions get on everyone's calendar.

Beyond a Connected Core

Weaving builds a critical mass of relationships early in a network's life, a core of strongly connected members who know each other well, exchange information, respond to the network's needs, and begin to form a shared identity and invent collaborative projects. The core won't become an insiders' club if weavers constantly work on connecting all members and if opportunities for taking responsibility for network activities are distributed throughout the network. Instead, the core can be inclusive, which is a key to the network's staying power or resilience over the long run.

But connecting to build a core is only the first phase of a network's development. The point in building a social-impact network is for members to collaborate and have impact, not just to build happy relationships with each other. Weaving members into a strong network core sets the stage for two essential evolutionary processes of network building.

CHAPTER FOUR

Network Evolution

A generative network's capabilities, complexity, and potential for impact increase as the connectivity of its members deepens and the structure of their connectivity evolves.

Begin with the end in mind.
— *Steven Covey*

Social relationships evolve. Some friends become best friends, some become enemies. People drift apart from each other. Casual acquaintances become staunch allies. Clusters of people—think of your high school or college crowd—stick together for years or become separated by distance and experience. Sports and workplace teams meld into high performers, but they don't stay that way forever.

What's true in society is true in social-impact networks. They evolve, and network builders can and should be highly intentional about guiding their network's evolution. Recognizing a network's potential evolutionary patterns can help you to anticipate and manage opportunities and challenges likely to come your way. And comparing your network to an idealized model of network development can help you assess just how your network is doing and what you might want to do next. By "evolution" we mean that networks undergo a process of change in which they develop better capability, more complex structure, and greater impact. These changes don't happen automatically. Many networks stagnate and disband before their potential has been achieved. Networks aren't going to live forever, but they can become disabled or die prematurely. We're not saying that networks have entirely predictable evolutionary patterns validated by scientific experimentation. But when we've closely examined how robust generative social-impact networks became successful and sustained, and when we've studied the research on social networks, two fairly consistent patterns were evident:

- The development of a network's capability, what its members are able to do together, progresses from connectivity to alignment to production.
- The development of a network's connectivity structure, which channels flows of information and resources among members, progresses toward greater intricacy and decentralization.

The "C-A-P" Sequence

We briefly described the first evolutionary pattern in chapter 1, the connect-to-align-to-produce sequence that develops a network's capability for collective action and impact. In each phase the nature of member connectivity builds on and becomes more advanced than in the previous phase. In the connection phase, members exchange information and build trust. You can see this in the story of Kathy Moxon and the Networks United for a Rural Voice described in chapter 3. NURV's strangers started by sharing information, getting to know each other, at the Scottsdale encounter. In the connecting phase, a network builder's principal task is to weave members together.

In the alignment phase, members capitalize on their connections to discover, explore, and define goals, strategies, and opportunities that they share. As they do this, their connections deepen, and their appetite grows for taking collective action related to what they align around. As NURV's members became connected and built trust in each other, they developed a shared identity and agenda as a network. Other social-impact networks, such as RE-AMP and the Learning Network of Greater Kalamazoo, aligned around ambitious goals. During alignment, the principal task of network builders is to facilitate members' efforts to reach common ground.

Alignment sets the stage for the production phase in which members organize to take joint action. Organizing production adds new dimensions to members' relationships, since they must go through the process of agreeing on, designing, and implementing projects. This requires members to make decisions and commitments that are far more demanding and consequential than connecting and aligning. In NURV's evolution, as members developed a collective sense of who they were and what they wanted to do, they began to collaborate on policy-change projects to create impact. Similarly, Reboot members began to produce films, music CDs, publications, and other products for Jewish American audiences—processes that employed their talents, but required substantial effort and dedication. In this phase, the network builder focuses on helping members to organize and implement collective performance of projects.

Although we've presented this unfolding as an orderly sequence, in many networks it occurs in much messier fashion. Imagine a network in which some members are connecting, while others are aligning, and others are producing; some are engaged in clusters of members that are moving through the phases of the sequence; some have completed a production phase and are starting the sequence again by connecting with other members to align and then produce something else. This is the look of a generative social-impact network of evolving social relationships, a robust platform for sustained production and impact.

We've worked with networks that didn't start by investing intensely in building connections among members. They jumped right to alignment and collaboration. This is often the case with coalitions and alliances, whose members come together for a campaign or other action to achieve a particular public-policy change or other specific result. There's nothing wrong with that one-time approach—unless what you have in mind is to build a generative network with the staying power to tackle a generative problem. As we mentioned in chapter 1, some alliances realize that they want to keep working together and become generative. This happened in the Western Adaptation Alliance, which for two years successfully brought together eight communities spread across the western United States to learn how to plan their cities' adaptations to climate change, using similar methods and shared data. In the process, the group met twice, focusing almost exclusively on the content of their work and coached by outside experts. And the Alliance held a two-day "leadership academy" attended by teams from each community. The project was going well, but in 2013 Vicki Bennett, Salt Lake City's director of the Office of Sustainability, and a few other members were concerned about the Alliance. Some founding members had changed jobs and left the network, and their replacements were still getting up to speed. So were the new members from four additional communities. Meanwhile, members had moved ahead with adaptation planning at different speeds; some were at a beginning stage, some were in the middle of planning, and some were implementing plans. "We've been so busy collaborating that now we have to look at how to keep this network going," Bennett explains. Conditions were changing, and the Alliance, once concentrated on getting its chosen work done, needed to become more generative. Our advice: start by strengthening the foundation of connections that a generative network must have.

Early in a social-impact network's life, thinking about the connect-align-produce sequence allows network builders to ask themselves this crucial question: are network members forging the quality of connections—building the extensive bandwidth of shared information and the sense of trust—that will lead them to be willing and able to undertake the more difficult work of aligning around specific goals and ideas or producing new products and services? If the answer is no, then you have to focus seriously on deepening member connectivity. If it's yes, then you can start to introduce into the network opportunities for alignment or production.

Aligning and Producing

How does connectivity become alignment? How does alignment become production? What can a network builder do to push these development processes forward?

Alignment is a process in which members reach shared understandings. In RE-AMP, the Learning Network of Greater Kalamazoo, or Strive in Greater Cincinnati, alignment was around shared goals and measurable indicators of success embraced by organizations in the networks. But you can't agree on goals and measures without first agreeing on definitions of words and ideas. In the West Michigan Manufacturers Council, the most crucial member alignment was around a framework of what they meant by "world-class manufacturing." It had nine categories of practice, including Planning, Systems Thinking, Core Business Processes, Measurement, and Process Improvement. For USDN, one alignment the members pursued was around an agenda of federal government policies that could help cities advance their sustainability. Getting to agreements of this sort involves analyzing, comparing, and synthesizing the many differing points of view that members may have, and then having members formally endorse the result. This process involves managing group dynamics and almost always includes members having to make adjustments in their thinking, so it's usually best done with skilled facilitation that enables the process without having a stake in a particular point of view. The process typically takes much more of the members' time, and it may require research to learn more about the topic for which alignment's being sought. As a result, alignment requires more of members and involves more risk of disappointment than just connecting and exchanging information.

In many networks, the primary mechanism for alignment is the formation of working groups of members, usually set up around particular topics. Working groups often start out as settings in which members build connections with each other by sharing their experiences and knowledge. But once this has been done, they become settings in which to dive more deeply into a topic and explore the potential of alignment. "Collaboratives with a narrow focus also tend to have a few working groups," reports the Bridgespan Group, "but those tackling more than one issue (for instance 'cradle-to-career' collaboratives such as Strive Cincinnati) often maintain many separate subgroups or committees. Strive's 30-member executive committee oversees five strategy teams focused on the five core priorities of the partnership." Each year, USDN operates 15–20 working groups that reflect members' priority interests. The Kalamazoo learning network set up three working groups, called "action teams," to align organizations in the community around improving kindergarten readiness, college and career readiness, and adult learning.

Working groups can also serve as bridges to the production stage in a network, in which collaborating members develop and implement projects based on alignment they have achieved. USDN created an internal fund that provides grants of up to $100,000 to collaborating members who are developing or spreading an innovative practice or policy for urban sustainability. The Innovation Fund is directed by a 15-member steering committee, and all projects must have at least four collaborating members, although most have many more than that. The fund could not have been established in USDN's early years when members were connecting but hadn't yet aligned around any particular interest. But the idea of a fund that supported collaboration and innovation took hold, and the steering committee—a working group—became the setting in which agreements were reached about the fund's purpose, goals, and grant programs, such as periodic Requests for Proposals. The committee also scores all proposals and decides which ones to fund.

The working-group model was particularly important in the evolution of the Partnership Fund for New York. Once Henry Kravis had persuaded hundreds of corporate and financial-institution officials to volunteer to help the Fund invest millions of dollars in business start-ups to help diversify the New York City economy, the next step was to figure out how to organize the network's production. To provide guidance, Kravis says, "We invited a lot of creative thinkers, to see where the ball would land." It landed everywhere—one advisor focused on education, another on retailing, and yet another on health care. "We shook our heads," Kravis recalls. He had to cancel the Fund's first scheduled meeting because there was no course of action to recommend. Kravis turned to Kathryn Wylde, an expert in housing and neighborhood development, to organize the network, and she created "sector groups" to bring together people with expertise or interest in different economic sectors—Media and Entertainment, Health Care and Sciences, and others—to look for, develop, and vet possible investment deals for new or expanding businesses. The brainpower and experience amassed in just one sector group, Media and Entertainment, led one Wall Street veteran to call it "the best media investment bank in the world." The Fund's sector groups provided a way for some, but not necessarily all, network members to start to work together to achieve a particular aspect of the network's purpose.

In the Fund's case, working groups were based on economic sectors, since the Fund was looking for business investment opportunities. But the logic of what working groups work on depends on the purpose and nature of the network. In RE-AMP, the main working groups were based on the network's four strategies for achieving its climate-change goals. At Lawrence CommunityWorks, working groups formed around various programs the network offered, such as a sewing club, community revitalization committees, a financial literacy course, and leadership development classes. USDN organizes working groups around the priority interests of members and their willingness to sign up for and engage in the groups. A working group has a focus—a topic or a task. It may be porous: network members can join and also may drop out as they choose. It has a champion, one or more network members who organize the group's efforts, setting meeting agendas and facilitating the sessions. USDN appoints cochairs for working groups, so if one chair is not available or leaves the network, the working group can continue without disruption. The working group may also have network staff that supports its work.

Shifting into production further ups the ante on members' commitment. It creates a level of member interdependence that is much deeper than connecting and aligning. It requires detailed agreements about who will do what when and coordination and management of production processes. The collaborating producers must have time together to make decisions and ways to hold each other accountable for delivering what they committed to do.

Because production can be so demanding for a network, if often makes sense to start with experiments or pilots. "Encourage initial collaborations to be 'small acts' or projects," recommends Holley, and then "help small projects move to scale." The USDN Innovation Fund started with $100,000 to provide in grants; several years later, after members had demonstrated a strong interest in developing and implementing innovation projects, the Fund had more than $800,000 to invest, and USDN had established several other grant funds for its members to access.

Shape Shifting

The second evolutionary process in network development involves the shape or structure of a network's connectivity. A core of members forms the initial shape of connectivity in a developing network. To explain where things go from there, we examine a case in which a network's shape has evolved substantially in a fairly short time.

In September 2013, USDN members in their fifth annual meeting viewed a slide of what looked like schematic drawings of the unfinished Death Star in *Star Wars* movies. Julia Parzen, USDN's managing director, announced that "connections among members are deepening and

Three of the Annual Maps of All USDN Connections

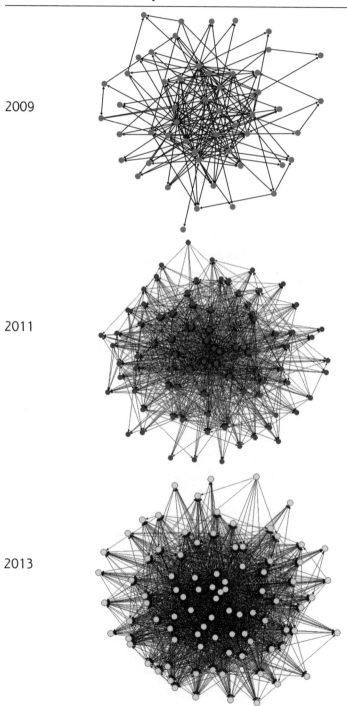

2009

2011

2013

collaborations are increasing more than ever before." Some of the evidence was in the pictures—circular masses with thick interiors and spiky exteriors. These were maps, produced by mapping software, of the connections among network members: each dot was a member, each line a link. They showed who was linked to whom, with what strength of relationship. These and other connectivity maps for each of the network's five years showed how USDN's connectivity had evolved. Every year members had answered a survey in which they identified their ties to other members. The strength of members' connections was measured on a sliding scale that progressed from "exchange useful information with this person on a regular basis" to "work directly with this person on one or more projects" to "depend on this person regularly for important advice." The aggregated data were used to produce the intriguing maps and a mathematical analysis of the network's overall connectivity. Other color-coded maps that Parzen displayed depicted factors that might affect the number and strength of members' ties: how long they'd been in the network; how active they were; how often they used UDSN's website; the size of their city and the region it was in. Every year the maps and analyses were shared with USDN members and used to develop strategies for increasing members' connectivity. (Chapter 6 explains the use of network maps.)

As a network's members connect, align, and produce with each other over and over, new patterns of linkage appear; the network takes on different shapes. Perhaps the most familiar network structure is the Hub-and-Spoke, in which one node in the network connects to many other nodes unconnected to each other. That hub node becomes the network's "connectivity center" through which information and value flow to the other nodes. But quite different shapes also commonly arise in networks:

- *Cluster:* Every node is connected to every other node; there is no hub that everyone goes through.
- *Multiple-Hubs:* Two or more hubs (with their many spokes) are connected to each other.
- *Many-Channels:* Many members connect directly with each other, typically in addition to their connections with hubs and in clusters.

Hub and Spoke

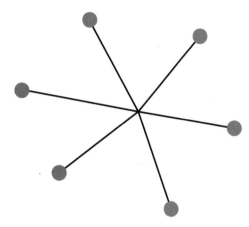

Cluster

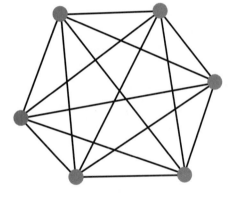

Multiple-Hubs

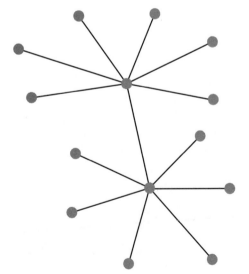

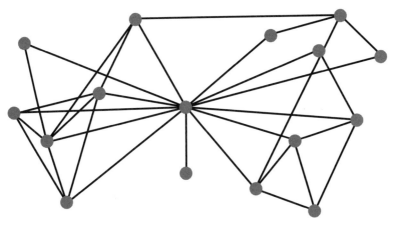

Many Channels

Each structure enables connectivity among nodes in different ways and affects the flows in a network. For instance, a hub-and-spoke structure may be a great starting structure for your network, since the hub can be a source of energy and coherent direction, but many network organizers find that a central hub can eventually become a bottleneck that slows down information flows and gets in the way of relationship building among the other network members. A cluster of tight relationships can do well at combining organizational competencies into a disciplined production process, but it's not necessarily the best structure for rapidly growing a network, since new members may find it difficult to break into a close-knit set of members. A multiple-hub structure can readily serve the task of mobilizing many people, because it takes only a relatively few nodes to connect to all nodes. And the many-channels shape tends to support rapid diffusion of information and responses through its numerous connections among members.

In 2004, Valdis Krebs, an expert network analyst, and June Holley, an avid network builder, depicted what a robust generative network's structural progression might look like, based on the evolution of the Appalachian Center for Economic Networks (ACEnet), a network of food, wood, and technology entrepreneurs in 29 counties in southeastern Ohio. Their multistage model, which we've revised slightly, is instructive because each connectivity structure in the evolution poses benefits and risks for the network's development.

The starting point, of course, is unconnected nodes, scattered people and organizations and their networks.

When someone weaves these nodes together, typically a single hub-and-spoke structure emerges, with the founder/weaver as the hub connected to a set of other nodes, most of which are not connected to each other. Where things go from there matters; a dominant hub is a network's friend—and can also be its enemy. Whoever organizes a network becomes, for a little while at least, its hub. Hubs can become very influential in a network, and they tend to get more powerful over time, because new members tend to prefer to link to more-connected members. As a network expands, network researchers say, the "rich get richer," meaning the

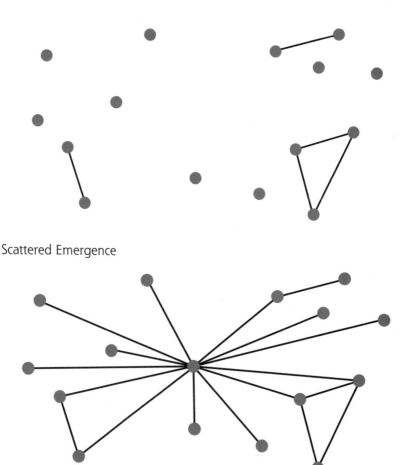

Scattered Emergence

Hub-and-Spoke

more-connected nodes tend to attract more new connections. There's a point in a network's early life when a dominant hub-and-spoke structure is extremely useful, perhaps essential.

But, as noted earlier, the same structure can become a problem. Two networks started by the International Institute for Sustainable Development (IISD)—a Sustainable Development Communications Network and Trade Knowledge Network—started as hub-and-spoke structures with IISD serving as the hub for the network. IISD connected to all the network members, but the members did not connect much with each other, except through the IISD hub. Members had no real opportunities to exchange experiences and work with each other, and they were not accountable to each other for their work on projects the network undertook. The structure did not promote collaboration. "We realized," write IISD's Heather Creech and Terri Willard, "that more-collaborative models support sharing and creation of new knowledge, better linkages to policy processes and extended relationships, and capacity development across the network." In short, if a network remains in a hub-and-spoke configuration, then its growth and development will probably be limited. And if a network's dominant hub should "fail" for any reason, the network members could be left unconnected.

When a network's early hubs promote evolution, instead of trying to extend their dominance, then more and more nodes become connected with each other, and a many-channels structure emerges in which nodes connect with each other directly, rather than just through hubs, to share information and resources. This can be an exciting development, as all of the connecting creates new opportunities for network members. But it also can be a confusing and frustrating time; if the flow of possibilities outpaces the network's capacity for taking advantage of them, the network will be more chaotic than orderly. As this evolution occurs, a new order emerges structurally: as some nodes build stronger connections with each other and/or bring their connections into the network, a multiple-hubs and multiple-clusters structure develops.

In ACEnet, both of these changes happened. Several of the nodes—businesses and nonprofit organizations—began to build their own networks within the larger network. Eventually multiple hubs emerged: a Mexican restaurant became the hub of other restaurants, while a bakery

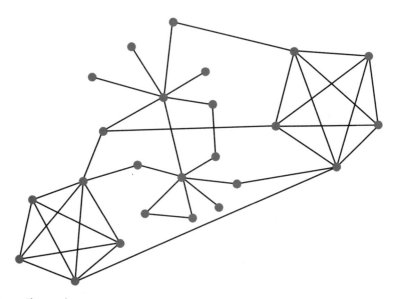

Many Channels

became a hub that helped food entrepreneurs develop new recipes. A few years later, a farmers market brought together some 90 farmers and local food vendors—another ACEnet hub adding even more nodes to the network. Even as a network develops multiple hubs and clusters, it may also maintain a many-channels structure, through which nodes connect with each other outside of their hubs and clusters, and within which hubs connect to each other.

USDN's 2013 connectivity maps showed that it had become a many-channels network with a high level of connections among nearly all members, a large number of hubs connected with many other members, and an emerging set of clusters of tightly connected members who together were aligning and, in some cases, producing. Within this larger pattern, as we described earlier, a core of members had strongly connected with each other and taken active roles in developing the network. Quite a few of these core members served as "bridgers" between clusters. We also saw this bridging phenomenon when we mapped the Reboot network—identifying a set of members who connected across the network's three main geographic clusters of members in Los Angeles, New York, and San Francisco.

In a final evolutionary development, when a network has established a core structured of multiple hubs and clusters and many-channel

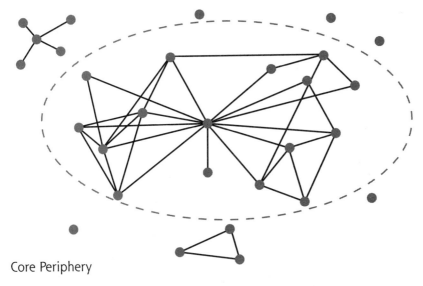

Core Periphery

connections, it can start to focus outside of its structure, on the potential of entering into mutually beneficial relationships with other organizations or individuals at its periphery. "The periphery allows us to reach ideas and information not currently prevalent in the network," explain Krebs and Holley, "while the core allows us to act on those ideas and information." When a network starts to engage with entities outside of its own membership, seeking to draw their energy into the network's influence, then it has very likely developed a complex but relatively stable core.

Using Foresight

The two paths of network evolution—the shift of capability from connecting to aligning and producing, and the shift of structure from single hub to many channels and multiple hubs and clusters—are entwined. Increasing connections among members requires a structure that enables much more connecting than a single hub will allow. Aligning members involves hubs that help to bring nodes together around ideas and goals. Organizing production—designing and implementing collective work— requires clusters, because nodes have to enter into and sustain close, disciplined interaction.

You can use these evolutionary models to anticipate what your network may need in the future and, therefore, what might be useful to do in the present.

At the start-up stage, for instance, you can anticipate the need to ensure that the initial organizing hub or hubs don't remain dominant and stifle the emergence of many-channels and multiple-hubs connectivity. That could mean helping the organizing hubs (perhaps including yourself) to shape evolution-friendly intentions, and, if necessary, helping them let go of their dominant position. It might also mean helping other nodes in the network develop into hubs. At the same time, you can anticipate that, as the network shifts from a single-hub shape into a many-channels or multiple-hubs shape, members' communications with each other will become more frequent and complicated, and therefore the network will need better communications tools to support connectivity.

As the network develops, clusters that want to align and produce will need different types of support than they did at the connectivity stage; for instance, facilitation of group processes and organization of collective work. At the same time, as clusters emerge in a network, there's some risk that the network could pull apart, if members feel their connections and work in clusters are much more valuable than their connections and work in the broader network. So you can anticipate the need to continue to revise the overall network's collective value proposition so it is different from the value created by clustering and still engages the interest of members.

Finally, network builders should recognize that the periphery can be useful as a source of connections that members don't have or as a partner in production. "The network should not work in a vacuum from other groups interested and involved in similar work," says one network researcher. But—and this shouldn't be ignored—it takes energy to engage organizations and individuals at the network's periphery, and unless the network's evolution has gotten far enough along, it may not be able to do a good job of managing periphery relationships.

In these ways, considering the implications of your network's potential evolutionary paths can allow you to prepare for the big challenges of managing an ongoing network.

CHAPTER FIVE

Enable and Adapt: Managing a Network's Development

The growth and development of established generative social-impact networks depends on managing a set of inevitable challenges.

The balance point—often called the edge of chaos—is where
. . . life has enough stability to sustain itself and enough
creativity to deserve the name of life.

— *Mitchell Waldrop*

"I was running around so fast I couldn't breathe," Lynn Decker recalls. It was early in the life of the Fire Learning Network, a collaboration of The Nature Conservancy (TNC) and federal government land managers established in 2001–2002 to generate and spread new practices in landscape management. Decker was its director, but the network had grown rapidly across the United States; it contained members from hundreds of organizations and there was so much to do. "The first three years," she says, "it was me alone" when it came to coordinating the network.

It took about five or six years for the network to stabilize. "Things got pretty smooth," reports Decker. "The network gelled." Its structure of more than a dozen regional clusters of practitioners in many landscapes allowed it to add new local-level members easily. Members in regions met several times a year, and, when the network's budget permitted, an annual national-scale gathering took place. There were standards and expectations for members, an informal governance process, and an annual planning process. The network's federal funders were firmly committed. "Now," Decker says, "they want to know if we can start another network if they give us money. We got them to believe it's like a Swiss Army knife—you're deploying a multi-faceted tool to get the outcomes you want." Financial accountability systems were in place. A shared brand promoted the network's seven government agencies and TNC. A national director's office with six staff people enabled landscape- and regional-level meetings and planning, and a continuous-improvement process. National staff gathered lessons learned in the network and coordinated communication to share information. "The members see us as highly effective rats running around and enabling them to do their work," Decker says. Over time, the regional networks have grown more resilient, carrying on even as some members come and go. "They are so durable they can easily change out people, have new people come in. They have identity." When some members left to take jobs in other landscapes, they rejoined the network from their new locales.

The Fire Learning Network's purpose has evolved. It started with an orientation toward managing fire in the landscape, but it now addresses issues of biodiversity and the economies of the landscape areas. "If you dig into any of the landscapes," Decker observes, "they're working on everything." Recently the network started to build capacity in communities so that local people could collaborate effectively with land-management agencies before, during, and after fires.

Adaptive Management

After start-up, generative social-impact networks like the Fire Learning Network evolve, mature, and become more complex. Their membership changes, as people join or leave the network, and other design features—even their purpose—may change as well. Their capabilities—connecting, aligning, and producing—evolve. The journey takes at least a few years. Heather Creech and Terri Willard observe that networks of organizations may take as long as five years to become established and produce concrete work. Many networks of organizations don't even get that far. "The private sector literature on strategic alliances and networks reveals that over 60 percent of these relationships fail outright or underperform."

Along the way, building the connectivity of members remains essential. Although the Fire Learning Network is more than 10 years old, Decker explains, "I spend most of my time network weaving, making sure that information and knowledge are moving back and forth through the network." That's because, she adds, "The whole thing about a network is that it's a constant job of figuring out what to do, figuring out how to get the cross-pollination going among members." As generative networks succeed, they become more secure, with satisfied members and confident funders. But they also become busier and more demanding: many activities take place, some unconnected to each other; much more information flows; new ideas and opportunities emerge; and the attention of potential partners and funders outside the network grows.

Network builders invariably describe these developments as heartening, but also difficult to keep up with. "It's managed chaos," says Rachel Levin, cofounder of the 11-year-old Reboot network. At the same moment, the network may seem fragile and robust, ready to fall apart and to take off. This uncertainty keeps network builders on their toes. You constantly wonder if you are doing the right thing. The condition is what scientists of complexity call an "edge of chaos" phenomenon: networks, like other complex, self-organizing systems, continuously balance and rebalance themselves between order and chaos. In the case of a radically decentralized system like a network, chaos is what happens when individual members exercise their autonomy and each goes in a different direction; order is established when members engage in collective action and come to share an identity. While organizations tend to strongly favor order and regard chaos as a crisis to be avoided, networks have to respect and maintain member autonomy—and the chaos it may bring. Members have to find their own reasons to choose to work with other members. Instead of squelching chaos, network builders have to recognize it as a source of network vitality. Out of the chaos comes order, but the order is not permanent; collective actions end, shared identity fades, what members value changes, new members join the network. And when order erodes, it's out of the chaos of autonomous members that new order will emerge. As a network matures, you sustain it by balancing its chaos and order. "The balance point"—explains Mitchell Waldrop in *Complexity*—"is where the components of a system never quite lock into place, and yet never quite dissolve into turbulence either." In a network, Waldrop's "balance point" exists somewhere in a continuum between having enough continuity to sustain the network and enough invention to evolve it, without having too much or too little of either.

Given the dynamics of the chaos–order tension, managing an ongoing generative network requires two things of network builders, whatever position they occupy in the network. First, you have to be obsessive about making and implementing decisions that enable the members. It's *their* network, whatever the governance structure that's been put into place, whatever the skills and intelligence of the coordinators doing much of the work. Second, you have to be adaptive, willing and able to constantly and often rapidly make and implement decisions that take into account the members' many different perspectives, a network's changing overall condition, and shifts in the context within which the network operates. When the Bridgespan Group studied more than 100 community-based collaboratives, it concluded that the successful ones "are by nature adaptive—adjusting their approaches based on new information, changes in conditions, and data on progress against goals." There's a lot to juggle and, in the process, you have to monitor the effect of the network's decisions and increase your understanding of what works and doesn't work when it comes to enabling network members.

Some of the network-management concerns that arise involve making adjustments to previous decisions about network design. For instance, as a network evolves, the topic of rightsizing its membership may come up again and again, and so may the question of how to grow the network. In this case, the basic guidance we offered in chapter 2 about start-up design still applies and so does what we explained in earlier chapters about various ways to expand network connections. Another reason for making adjustments can be shifts in members' value propositions—and this requires an understanding of the need to cultivate collective value propositions, and the sort of continuous monitoring of members' satisfaction (as we will describe in chapter 6). Governance is another potential adjustment point. The Learning Network of Greater Kalamazoo changed its governance model two times in its first few years. It started with seven founding members, an inner circle. "We put such care and thought into the people we gathered around the table in that group and so much importance in the access they had to other networks. But we had to recognize that there was a need to change in midstream," says Carrie Pickett-Erway, head of the Kalamazoo Community Foundation. "It had nothing to do with the people involved, but the world had moved on. We stepped back and looked at the larger network that was emerging. The structure we had designed so carefully, it was really difficult to let it go. We had created more emotional attachment to it than we realized, instead of treating it as version 1.0, then a 2.0, then a 3.0."

Some adjustments occur because things aren't working as well as you'd like. The Fire Learning Network has seen regional hubs come and go. "Where we didn't have the right kind of leaders, the hubs didn't materialize into a vibrant network," Decker says. And the network's management style had to change: "We focused on organizing and running the network from a top-down approach, and very quickly found that didn't work at all because people need you to work with them in a very different way. Running the network is similar to coaching—it's about relationships and finding out what makes people want to do the work."

Another driver of adaptation is success—finding something that works and doing more of it. In October 2013 the Partnership Fund for New York City, a 17-year-old network of individuals and companies in the city's private investment and corporate sectors, built on its experience in linking senior-level bankers with technology entrepreneurs to launch its fourth annual "FinTech" Innovation Lab. The lab starts with banks—14 of them in 2013—meeting together with 20 entrepreneurs who describe the financial services they are developing. The entrepreneurs make presentations, and then six or seven of them are selected for intensive mentorship. "Each bank picks one or two entrepreneurs it wants to spend time with," explains Maria Gotsch, the Fund's president and CEO, and then helps them test and fine-tune their services and business strategies. Five to 10 employees from a bank engage with the entrepreneur they select, joined by a mentor from a successful financial-technology company, as well as venture capitalists. The program lasts 12 weeks, but the relationships formed extend beyond that—"longer and stronger than any of us thought they would be," says Gotsch. For instance, some executives ended up investing in the companies, and some mentors joined companies' advisory boards. The matchmaking was so well received—alumni companies have raised

$47 million in venture financing—that the Fund initiated a similar model for 23 of the city's hospital systems and has considered expanding into other sectors.

Many adjustments that networks make respond to their specific contexts, but, in general, as generative social-impact networks evolve, their builders will face four management challenges that are peculiar to maturing networks:

1. *Member Engagement*: what to do about the variation in member engagement in the network
2. *Network Infrastructure*: which governance and staffing models to use as the network evolves and how much structure to build
3. *Provisional Planning*: how to be intentional about the future while open to emergence and surprise
4. *Periphery Relationships*: why, when, and how to engage with entities outside the network

In this chapter we discuss each of these challenges and the field-tested ways we've seen to think about and respond to them. But network management isn't about applying a standard formula for what to do; it's about understanding a situation and having a repertoire of possible decisions and actions from which to select. In chapter 6 we address another network-management topic of great interest to network builders and funders: how to measure, monitor, assess, and evaluate network health and impact.

Member Engagement

- Offer members a menu of varied activities in which to engage.
- Engage the unengaged.
- Bring new members onboard in ways that accelerate their engagement.
- Fix ineffective engagement processes.
- Enforce participation expectations.
- Raise participation standards.

Some members engage intensively in their network's activities, while others don't. Some step up to play roles in building and managing the network, others are satisfied just to participate in network activities. Some members start out engaging slowly and become much more active. Others engage quickly but fade away. Variation in member engagement is normal, but it can cause difficulties. For example, as the West Michigan Manufacturers Council matured, a case study noted, its members included "firms at very different stages of awareness and implementation of world class [manufacturing] processes" and that "as the early adopters move into new areas, it is easy to forget that many firms are at early stages of transformation." In networks with many members, variation in engagement can strain efforts for inclusion of members and reduce to a relatively low level a network's core of strongly connected members. In networks in which members depend on each other to achieve a shared goal, a less engaged member can slow down or damage the collective effort. When the Urban Sustainability Directors Network formed working groups of members to conduct monthly calls for peer-to-peer exchange, recalls USDN managing director Julia Parzen, "We were tracking who was on every call. If a member who had signed up was not on two calls in a row, we sent them an e-mail asking if they were still interested. This mattered because we wanted to build a sense of community within those groups." The potential negative effects of low member engagement can leave network builders wondering about which members to focus on, the engaged or unengaged, and what to do to boost engagement. We've seen several methods for managing membership engagement:

- *Offer members a menu of varied activities in which to engage.* If you think of the network as a "plug and play" system, then it's important to offer members different activities to plug into. Some activities require more commitment and time than others, but some don't require much of either. It's the difference between, for example, participating in a working group that meets monthly for an hour just to share members' insights about a topic or engaging in a six-month-long project that involves working closely with other members to produce something. Some networks offer members a "pyramid" of engagement opportunities—easy-to-participate-in activities that a broad base of members uses and harder-to-participate-in undertakings used by a narrower set of members. The pyramid's tiers can also serve as a ladder: members engage with base activities first and, as they become more comfortable and committed to participation in the network, they gradually progress up to more difficult activities. "It's important to have projects of many different sizes in the network," says June Holley in *Network Weaver Handbook*. She describes small projects as involving a handful of people for a few months and large projects as involving dozens of members and lasting a year or longer, with larger projects requiring higher levels of trust, coordination, and resources.

The Surfrider Foundation, a network-based nonprofit with more than 50,000 members in 18 nations, offers "a unique model of engagement" that allows members, strangers, volunteers, supporters, and leaders to participate in many different ways, report Beth Kanter and Allison Fine in *The Networked Nonprofit*. "Strangers and friends can buy T-shirts online and sign up for e-mail alerts. More involved supporters and members can download and listen to podcasts and organize local beach cleanups. Leaders can arrange to meet with elected officials to discuss legislation to protect the shorelines." In similar pyramid fashion, members of the Urban Sustainability Directors Network have many options for participation: join a learning group, present at a workshop, respond to other members' questions on the network's website, develop a regional network, serve on a USDN standing committee, and more.

- **Engage the unengaged.** Identify members who are only minimally engaged in network activities and engage them in a conversation about what they are getting and not getting out of the network, what sort of opportunities they are looking for. Then show them possible ways they could engage more to meet their value propositions. This is ultimately about connecting members to other members—that's what drives all network activities—and there are many ways to do it, as we described in chapter 3. But start by asking the unengaged what they are experiencing, what barriers they face, and what they want. In larger networks it's useful to systematize this sort of outreach, by asking core members to touch base regularly with unengaged members.

- *Bring new members onboard in ways that accelerate their engagement.* It takes time for most new members to get into the flow. They may not know many other members. They may not have worked in a highly collaborative environment before. They may not be sure which activities to try or how to initiate something they care about. There's a natural period for newcomers to acclimatize, make connections, feel things out. But this doesn't have to take forever! An orientation process can help. But don't just hand newbies some printed materials; have a network member engage with them. A buddy or mentor system can help—assign a network veteran to orient, check in, and stay in touch with an incoming member. A probationary period for new members can help—testing their engagement in and commitment to the network before fully accepting them as a member. Even a requirement for a certain minimum level of participation can help, because it signals the network's expectations. Whatever you try, at the end of six months ask new members for feedback about what worked and didn't work in the orientation process; they may have good ideas about how to improve the onboarding.

- *Fix ineffective engagement processes.* Most network activities require some facilitation. To enable a group of members to work together, one or more people (members or staff) support the process, setting the agenda, preparing materials, managing sessions, handling the logistics, and more. In most networks this gets done somehow. But that doesn't mean that it's being done in ways that engage the participants fully. Some network members and staff may not be especially skilled at this sort of facilitation, or the process may not have the resources or communications infrastructure it needs, or the focus of the group's work may not be as compelling as had been thought—any number of factors can inhibit engagement. Holley notes a simple standard that a network's every process should strive for: "Convert all your gatherings and activities from situations where participants are listening to one person speak to more engaging formats where participants can have discussions and interact with each other." It makes sense to set engagement standards for network activities, help prepare process facilitators, and get critical feedback from participants.

- *Enforce participation expectations.* There's no point in having standards for member participation if you're not going to enforce them. Of course the standards have to be known, clear, and objective—and in writing. For networks that support members' projects financially, this is especially important. For instance, the Shape Up Somerville community collaborative, an obesity-prevention effort in a Massachusetts city, used mechanisms like memorandums of understanding and contracts to spell out the commitments and accountability of all participating members. As long as participation standards are in place, not applying them diligently isn't just a cop-out; it's a disservice to the unengaged members and the rest of the membership. Some people or organizations just don't take to a network environment. Network builders should coach and coax them, but if they still haven't engaged after a while, they probably aren't going to. Tell them to leave.

- *Raise participation standards.* This may seem counterintuitive if you're concerned about members who aren't very engaged. Won't raising expectations squeeze them out of the network? It might, but it also might serve as a wake-up call that spurs them to up their participation. And, especially if there are others knocking on the door to get into the network, it signals to potential new members that the network's norm—its culture—is a higher, rather than lower, expectation of member engagement.

As a network becomes much more active and its actions become more ambitious, its members do more and have more at stake. To keep up, the network needs to adapt its basic infrastructure—the governance model for making collective decisions; the staffing model for supporting members; and the communications capabilities that enable member connectivity and action. Informal governance, minimal staffing, and just using e-mail probably won't be good enough anymore. In general, governance

Network Infrastructure

- Ensure that the governing group collects and studies information and activities throughout the network.
- Make room for new people to get into the governance process.
- Ensure the transparency of governance's decision-making processes and decisions.
- Develop a pipeline of members who may take responsibility for moving the network forward.
- Provide basic orientation to network-building practice.
- Only add staff to enable members in connecting, aligning, and producing—not to do the members' work.
- Build staffing to support the network's evolution, not just its immediate needs.
- Make sure new staffers are compatible with the network model for doing things.
- Reexamine the benefits of centralizing or decentralizing network staff.
- Make a serious and ongoing investment in the information technology that will meet your network's communication needs.

will need to become more inclusive, and staffing will need to grow and become more specialized. Along with these comes the matter of talent development—identifying and cultivating people who can step into governance roles in the network. You'll also need to make sure that the network's communications system keeps members informed without overwhelming them with information, and that it supports their project collaborations, not just their conversations.

Whether the network has an elected or self-appointed governing body, the first question about the governance model is whether it's working well for the membership. We've seen both models work effectively in mature networks with small and large numbers of members—their performance measured by how satisfied members were with the network. The RE-AMP network of advocates working on climate change has a Steering Committee with different seats determined in different ways. Some positions are filled by election of the voting members, while others are filled by working group chairs or elected by funders of the network. The arrangement results in a governing body with a wide range of perspectives from around the network and direct involvement in the network's key activities. A 2011 survey of the RE-AMP membership found strong satisfaction with the network. Since the membership felt enabled and satisfied, the network's evaluators said, there didn't seem to be anything about governance to fix. At each annual meeting of the Urban Sustainability Directors Network, members are asked if they want to change anything about the way the membership of their governing group, a self-appointed Planning Committee, is selected. Year after year the answer has been no.

We have a few basic suggestions for managing governance as the network develops:

- *Ensure that the governing group collects and studies information and activities throughout the network.* Members playing roles in governance must be aware of what's going on in the network, but this isn't easy in a busy network that's getting even busier. Two things are essential: Within the network there has to be a good, consistent flow of information about activities—meeting notes, progress reports on projects, and so on—that informs all members, including those in governance. And the governing body has to have a regular process with ample time set aside to review and discuss things before making decisions. Several networks we've worked with make sure that members in governance also are involved in the network's main projects. For instance, USDN's Planning Committee members are also co-chairs of some USDN working groups—an interlocking mechanism that helps assure the committee gets up-to-date, in-depth information about network activities and is in touch with lots of members.

- *Make room for new people to get into the governance process.* Fresh faces in governance bring new ideas and perspectives into play, and that's a good thing for an evolving network. Having an election for positions on a governance body doesn't guarantee turnover, so term limits might be a good way to force change in some seats. For a self-appointed governing committee, it's useful to require that a portion of the group be replaced regularly. The 10-member USDN Planning Committee replaces at least two members a year. "The members have confidence that their interests will be represented," notes Parzen.

- *Ensure the transparency of governance's decision-making processes and decisions.* As long as network members know, or can easily find out, what's being decided and how it's being decided, they're likely to be satisfied with governance, assuming they've had a hand in determining the governance model. This is a communications challenge: notice of governance meetings, agendas, background material, decisions taken—this and more (proposals sent to funders, for instance) should be made available to the network. At the same time, make clear whom in governance the members should contact if they have questions or suggestions.

- *Develop a pipeline of members who may take responsibility for moving the network forward.* Since the people who step up to take responsibility for network governance are likely to move on to other interests and work at some point, network builders have to pay attention to developing new talent to fill gaps. The network itself is the best "training ground" for members. Members who offer, for instance, to lead working groups and other processes may become good prospects for participating in governance. The same may be true of members who are natural hubs in the network and stay connected to many other members. Lawrence CommunityWorks provided developmental opportunities and stipends to members who performed certain functions in the network. "Members can only enroll in each of the . . . opportunities for one term—usually one year," notes Bill Traynor. "The idea is to have opportunities that members can cycle through and that can change with changing demand."

- *Provide basic orientation to network-building practice.* In addition to providing members with opportunities to contribute to the network's care, it's important to help members understand what building the network is all about. Not all members will be deeply interested in this topic, but some will be—and you can't predict which ones. Raising the members' literacy about network building helps to ensure that members who take governance roles will share a framework about how to conduct themselves. In 2011, the RE-AMP network used an in-depth, 20-page evaluation of the network as a "teachable moment" for the members—organizing a presentation to all and small-group discussions about each of the report's recommendations.

Although a network's development may not drive the need for big changes in its governance model, the same probably is not true for its staffing model. Typically the network will need to rethink the role of staff and also add more staff, and it may need to address the question of how centralized or decentralized staffing should be.

- *Only add staff to enable members in connecting, aligning, or producing—not to do the members' work.* As the network's needs change, it's important not to default simply to hiring more staff to do things. "If there are things members can do for themselves, staff should not be doing them," notes Rick Reed, who helped develop RE-AMP. A similar view has prevailed at USDN. "Be as lean as possible," advises Parzen. What's at stake is not just staffing positions, but the nature of the network. When a network's infrastructure starts to substitute staff work for member work, the network is likely beginning a shift toward becoming an association that provides a range of services to its members or a "backbone organization" that coordinates the activities of other organizations. This sort of transition may be precisely what's needed, but it should be intentional and strategic, and network builders must understand that it won't result in sustaining a member-driven generative social-impact network.

To minimize staff building, at least for a while, you can find partners who will work with the network and take on some of the new tasks. "We're not trying to do everything ourselves," says Parzen. Or you can use consultants to test work that the network wants to try. Using either partners or consultants, you can pilot new work until you know that it's work that should occur at scale and be under the network's direct control; then hire staff to enable members to do the work.

- **Build staffing to support the network's evolution, not just its immediate needs.** Yes, as the network expands its activities, you'll probably need more staff to provide increased coordination and communication. But as the network evolves, it may need staffing for entirely new types of tasks. At USDN, for instance, the members' desire to engage with periphery organizations, including the federal government, led to a decision to hire a staff person for national partnerships, someone to serve as the members' liaison to partners. A similar emphasis on connecting with the periphery occurred at Reboot, which allocated part of a staffer's time to be a national coordinator for community partners, a way of engaging traditional Jewish organizations in some Reboot projects.

  Other evolutionary trends can result in shifting needs for staffing. In the Opportunity Chicago collaboration of organizations, formed in 2006, the Chicago Jobs Council served as the backbone organization, but over the years its role changed. The Council served initially as a facilitator that convened the initiative's stakeholders. "As leaders and participants from partner organizations left to take on new roles, and new leaders and participants joined," reports a case study by FSG, "it helped maintain continuity and focus." Next, the Council started to "help other partners clarify roles and responsibilities and to create momentum for the initiative as a whole."

- **Make sure new staffers are compatible with the network model for doing things.** Whatever you do to hire for compatibility, it's likely that people you hire will hold organization-centric assumptions about how to do their jobs. You'll need to make clear to them what the network-centric approach is and what the network's culture is. This probably isn't just a quick talk; it likely involves ongoing coaching and feedback to staff about their performance—until they internalize the "network way."

- *Reexamine the benefits of centralizing or decentralizing network staff.* Some networks, especially those comprising organizations, build highly decentralized staff arrangements, usually as a way of ensuring broad membership buy-in and reducing the potential for a centralized staff to "hijack" the network. Both RE-AMP and the Learning Network of Greater Kalamazoo use this model. The Kalamazoo network hired staffers at five different organizations, all members of the network. This helped to defuse concerns in the community about who would lead the network, and it gave other organizations a meaningful stake in the network's success. Those benefits don't come without trade-offs. "A challenge is that there's no one organization that knows everything," notes Pickett-Erway. "Sometimes balls get dropped, people get surprised. The pace and intensity of people moving forward is hard to manage."

More typical is a centralized model for network staffing—with all staff under one command. But while this may ease the pressures of coordination and communication, it can always raise concerns about empire building and the membership losing control of the network. At different evolutionary points in a network's life, you may have to judge whether more or less centralization makes sense.

The communications challenges of an evolving network mostly involve ensuring that information flows well within the network so that members know what's going on and where the opportunities for collaboration are. Ineffective communications, as we noted in chapter 2, can hamstring efforts to build connections among members. With the increase in activities, the volume of information may get unmanageable for members. And as a network's membership and partners become more diverse, communication—access to information—may have to become more customized for particular members. "We have business, education, and nonprofits who all want to be a part of the work," says Pickett-Erway. "The information coming out of the network has to be customized for them. If I sit with education superintendents to talk about what is happening, they want very different information than business leaders want."

Communication is not just about the flow of information; it's also about the stock of information that a network may build. A directory of members, for instance, is a useful database for a network. Information about how to do things in the network is another example. Lawrence CommunityWorks posted material online about how to organize a neighborhood block party, something that many of its members might be interested in. It also provided digital space where members could document and share their experiences in the network.

For managers of maturing networks, our advice is simple:

- *Make a serious and ongoing investment in the information technology that will meet your network's communication needs.* The network's communications needs have become too important to be addressed on the cheap or ad hoc. And they may not be well served by purchasing off-the-shelf solutions. Instead, you may need to design a system that fits the way your network's members work. Whatever you decide to do, don't assume that it's a one-time expense. You'll likely have to make periodic updates in the communications capacity, and you'll also have to spend some effort on training members to use the system.

Provisional Planning

- Processes should provide every network member with opportunities to contribute ideas and identify priorities for the network.
- Processes should identify and reflect on what's been learned about operating the network effectively—and support continuous improvement.
- Notice surprises and don't dismiss or suppress them.

Networks live with a high degree of uncertainty about the future, a condition that John Kania and Mark Kramer astutely describe as "the paradox of combining *intentionality* (that comes with the development of a common agenda) and *emergence* (that unfolds through collective seeing, learning, and doing)." This edge-of-chaos tension requires a balancing act: too much planning can reduce the network's openness to emergence, while too little planning can reduce the network's capacity for cohesive, collective action. To manage this paradox, heed the insight of Dwight D. Eisenhower, the American general who planned D-Day in 1944, the largest amphibious invasion in world history: "In preparing for battle, I have always found that plans are useless, but planning is indispensable." In other words, it's the quality of a network's planning *process*, not of the plan itself, that matters most.

Networks do have plans, of course, but typically they are short term, a year or two at most; being provisional leaves room for testing, learning, and surprise. Referring to the West Michigan Manufacturers Council, a study found that "It is not possible to predict what the next 'generation' of the [network's] process will be, since much of it is 'made up as you go along.' . . . Real information comes from actual experience. Therefore, you don't really know what to do until you start doing it." Even if a network has developed a detailed plan, which is usually the case with networks of organizations such as community collaboratives that align the actions of many players, its members discover new possibilities as they implement the plan. Their intentions don't change, Kania and Kramer note, but the plans do, because as implementation occurs "solutions and resources are uncovered. . . . They are typically emergent, arising over time." In effect, some networks have "rolling" plans and nearly continuous planning processes. Traynor describes the provisional planning by Lawrence CommunityWorks in this way: "We try to keep all of our teams and committees loose and flexible. . . . This creates space for experimentation and allows things to grow and also allows for things to go away when they aren't useful anymore." USDN develops a new plan every year—a "zero-based budgeting" of sorts. Only a few network activities are assumed to carry forward; everything else must be reaffirmed by members or it dies. And it's not enough for members to say they want something to happen; they have to sign up to lead or work on it. In Canada, the community collaboratives in the Vibrant Communities poverty-reduction initiative revise

Main Elements of Network Work Plan

Eight regional networks of urban sustainability directors adopted a common work-plan format consisting of five sections:

1. Background about the network—purpose, member history, existing infrastructure (and more)
2. Goals/objectives for the next year or two—network condition/development and network external impacts
3. Partners working with the network to achieve goals/objectives
4. Activities to achieve the goals/objectives
5. Network infrastructure/management to achieve goals/objectives

For more detail, see Appendix C.

their goals and strategies continuously in response to ongoing analysis of key indicators of progress, changes in the broader environment, and the network's capacities. Their "openness to unanticipated changes," report Kania and Kramer, "enabled them to identify patterns as they emerged, pinpointing new sources of energy and opportunity that helped to generate quick wins and build greater momentum."

Many elements of a network plan resemble those of an organization: purpose, goals, and objectives, as well as the activities and competencies needed to achieve them. But in a network, these elements take a distinctly network-centric approach.

Managing the quality of a network's planning processes means paying attention to a number of factors:

- *Processes should provide every network member with opportunities to contribute ideas and identify priorities for the network.* At USDN, the Planning Committee develops an annual strategic plan—but only after spending several days with the members at the network's annual meeting, hearing their collective priorities, and seeing what members are willing to sign up to do and to lead. "The Planning Committee can allocate resources for the network, but it can't say what members are going to do," says Parzen.

- *Processes should identify and reflect on what's been learned about operating the network effectively—and support continuous improvement.* One thing network members know about is this: what is and isn't working for them in the network. You have to gather member feedback thoroughly and regularly, getting them to tell their network stories, and then figuring out what the implications are. It's smart to involve members in the process, not just as sources of information but as processors of the information. "Help people reflect on successes and failures and understand the underlying patterns of success," Holley urges network builders. And always show members how the feedback processes have and will lead to improvements; that is, show them that you're not wasting their time. But a network's internal learning/improvement processes are likely to falter if they are not considered to be crucial to the network's success. "Somebody has to really care about the learning and want to use it," says Reed. "If you have a core group having that learning conversation, then the information can become a change agent in the network."

- *Notice surprises and don't dismiss or suppress them.* Sometimes what emerges from network members can be problematic because network builders can't see how it fits in—or, worse, because it contradicts the network's current direction. We've seen several networks forced to deal with surprises that raised concerns about or directly challenged fundamental design decisions—the network's purpose, membership, or governance structure, for instance. Imagine that you've been building a network to increase the diversity and strength of leaders in a community, but after a while some members want the network to advocate for a public policy that you strongly disagree with. Or that you've been building a network with one type of member—environmental activists, say—but some members say it's important to bring a very different kind of member—community organizers, for instance—into the network. Or that some members challenge the network's strategy for achieving impact and suggest other approaches that could disrupt the network's focus.

What should you do? In an organization, potential shocks often stay below the surface, as part of a counterculture, out of fear that leaders will consider them to be insubordinate or irrelevant. If they do surface, they may be suppressed or finessed by leaders who disagree with the concerns or don't want the organization to be distracted. In a network, however, the members rule, and surprises should be acknowledged and considered. Instead of either embracing or rejecting fundamental new ideas for the network, you have to allow and help all members to work through the ideas, understand their implications, and then decide what to do. "You have to go where the network's energy is," notes Reed. "That's the network's job." This means creating space in the network for members interested in holding potentially disruptive conversations. It also means helping the conversations take a form that could eventually be incorporated into network strategies and activities, rather than continuing endlessly. Then have the members decide where, if anywhere, the surprise fits into the network's future. It could happen that the surprise doesn't fit and that what's really afoot is a split in the network, with some members leaving to pursue a collective value proposition that other members won't honor. If a conflict cannot be resolved, the departure of some members may be a healthy occurrence, as long as the network maintains a sufficient core to carry on.

Periphery Relationships

- Use branding to share credit throughout the network.
- Create ways for the periphery to engage with the network.
- Engage potential partners in ways that build trust; start with small steps.
- Look to funders as potential partners too.

A maturing network views the periphery of organizations and individuals around it as opportunities; they are potential sources from which to draw new energy and ideas and potential channels through which to impact the larger world. Engaging with the network's periphery involves two essential and interrelated tasks: branding—whether and how to project the network's image outwardly; and also partnering—why and how to join with organizations and individuals outside the network.

Branding makes a network visible to others. Many social-impact networks prefer initially to stay off the world's radar screen. Their focus is internal, on the members, not external. Especially in their early network-building years, they don't want to attract much outside attention. "USDN has been very private," notes Parzen. "Some people used to say we were like a secret society. We didn't have a presence like an organization. We had nothing to say collectively." Rebooters often heard from those outside the network that it seemed to be an exclusive club.

Some networks, after years of running dark, evolve to the point where developing a brand becomes useful. Typically, members have aligned around a common interest but cannot "move the needle" without engaging outsiders in the effort. "We're seeing a great desire among members to speak with a collective voice on particular needs they have," notes Parzen. Reboot wanted to engage with mainstream Jewish community organizations to help develop and distribute its innovative products for Jewish Americans, so it had to be able to explain what it was and how it could work with others.

But branding also comes with a requirement: when a network wants to "speak" to others, it should have something for which it can take credit. It has to project its potential value to others, not just its needs. It can show its capability to connect people and organizations, or align them, or engage them in collaborative production—but it must be able to make the case that as a collective it has something to offer.

In many ways branding a network is similar to branding an organization, but there's an important aspect of managing a network's brand that is a particular challenge.

- *Use branding to share credit throughout the network.* The social-change world is filled with stories about what happens when organizations fight over credit. For example, the Bridgespan Group notes that in the case of Boston's Operation Ceasefire, an effective collaborative that reduced youth violence in the 1990s, "one consequence of its success was that various stakeholders tried to claim credit for the achievement. Police, probation officers, social workers and the minister-led Ten Point Coalition all thought they stood to gain by being seen as responsible for the nationally acclaimed 'Boston Miracle,' even though it was really the sum of their efforts which made the difference. Credit claiming, in part, caused the collaborative to stumble." In one organization-based production network we know, some members became concerned about not getting enough credit for what the network was accomplishing—fearing that in the future their organization's case for funding of its own work would be weakened. This concern is typical among nonprofit organizations that must chase funders' dollars. As researcher Bonnie Shepard explains, "Part of the 'capital' of an NGO is its record of achievements, which is essential for publicity and fund-raising pitches." But in a network it is hard to claim credit for success, since "everyone" made it possible. "Even when an NGO has devoted considerable organizational resources to an achievement by a network of organizations, it cannot claim individual credit for it." This can concern organizations that are heavily dependent on donor funding. It may lead them not to join a network, preferring to go it alone. Or they may join a network but then act in ways that undercut the network in favor of promoting themselves. For example, Shepard reports that some members of an HIV/AIDS–prevention network in Chile organized a major public meeting without including other network members. "This exclusion set off severe internal tensions, with two major founding members leaving the network."

The bottom line when branding a network: be generous with the credit. "The more we can give people credit, the better off we are," says Pickett-Erway of the Learning Network of Greater Kalamazoo, which coordinates activities of more than 30 local organizations. Another community collaborative, Memphis Fast Forward, realized that celebrating successes and sharing credit were critical motivating factors to keep partners engaged and active. "Really make time to celebrate the progress of an activity," advises Blair Taylor, head of the effort's backbone

organization. "Do it loudly, and give people the credit they deserve." When the Fire Learning Network developed a logo for
the network, it made sure to include the seven federal agency
members and then put The Nature Conservancy's emblem at
the bottom. "Some people think TNC owns the network," explains Decker. "We're really careful to put all of the members'
logos on. All publications have seven logos on them and TNC's
is always last on the string. The federal partners know it's *their*
network."

Branding can be part of a network's broader effort to develop external
partnerships, since it attracts attention to the network. Partnering is not
the same as inviting in new members. It's about the network *as a whole* developing a relationship with external entities—organizations, individuals,
other networks, and even funders. A partner is engaged by the network,
but not included in it. Partnering always involves value creation that flows
both ways, to the network *and* to the partner.

There comes a time in a network's evolution when it makes sense to
engage the periphery to build partnerships. Sooner or later, for instance,
community collaboratives need "supporting policy and environmental
change" to thrive, says the Bridgespan Group. State and federal policies
may influence what happens at the local level, and allowing use of their
funding for collaborative staff and infrastructure "would make a significant difference in existing capacity." RE-AMP recognized that, in order to
build enough political strength to gain adoption of climate-friendly policies, it might need to work with new types of organizations—community organizers, social-justice advocates, and municipal governments. The
many organizations involved in the seven regional and national networks
of rural advocates developed in the Kellogg Foundation's Rural Places,
Rural Policies initiative started to align with other organizations that were
a part of the National Rural Assembly—in order to increase their influence on government policies. USDN developed a Memorandum of Understanding with the C40 Cities Climate Leadership Group— in order to
bring an international dimension to its learning and knowledge exchange.

It's important, though, to partner in ways that enhance the network
without changing its essence. The story of a rapidly expanding Internet-
based network is instructive. In 2006, two mothers founded MomsRising.

org, started blogging, asked people to sign up on their website as members, and provided them with e-mail updates and action alerts. After two years, MomsRising.org had 160,000 members. The network's purpose: to "take on the most critical issues facing women, mothers, and families by mobilizing massive grassroots actions." In 2009 the founders created a video, "Mother of the Year," which was viewed online 12 million times and led to the addition of 1 million members. "As remarkable as what MomsRising.org has done is what it has not done," observe Kanter and Fine in *The Networked Nonprofit*. The founders "knew it was important for them to stick to what they do best—outreach to and organizing of moms. They have formed partnerships with dozens of advocacy groups to extend their network without pulling themselves off task." In short, a network seeking partners must know what it's good at and should continue to do it—and know what it wants partners to do.

There's no magic formula for partnership development, but a network can take certain steps to manage the process:

- *Create ways for the periphery to engage with the network.* The network's branding helps outsiders to understand what it's about, but to build partnerships you have to let others see inside the network enough so they and you can measure each other up. "Create mechanisms for voices from the periphery to influence decision making," urges Holley. A low-risk way to start is for a network to create an advisory board of people with whom it might consider partnering. This involves regularly sharing information and thinking and talking together—about the network and its environment. RE-AMP established a leadership council of nonmembers, while the USDN Innovation Fund created an advisory committee stocked with funders and leading practitioners in urban sustainability.

- *Engage potential partners in ways that build trust; start with small steps.* A partnership is a relationship, and successful relationships depend on trust. If you've already got trust in a potential partner, that's a great start. If not, then take the time to build trust, just as you do when connecting members in the network. Some potential partners may not be used to working with a network, so it makes sense to help them understand how the network operates and makes decisions. Instead of jumping into a full-scale partnership, try a few experiments or pilots so everyone can get used to each other with relatively low stakes involved.

- *Look to funders as potential partners too.* This is not about getting funders to provide resources for the network's operations. It's about collaborating with funders on projects of mutual interest—value that the network can create that advances a funder's goals, too. Both RE-AMP and USDN created internal funds, managed by the networks but fueled by funders' money. Another way to engage funders as partners is to bring them into the network's internal learning and planning processes—as valued sources of information and dialogue, not as decision-makers. Not every funder will want to do this, and some may not be suited to it. But some funders might regard it as an opportunity. USDN's funders routinely attend its annual meetings and participate in discussions as equals. The Tamarack Institute in Canada, which guides the Vibrant Communities initiative, encourages funders to participate in initiative meetings and organizes a community of practice where funders can share knowledge and develop expertise. According to one report about the effort, "Tamarack has found that funder participation increases knowledge and trust, which in turn leads to greater commitment through challenges. It also opens the door for funders to recognize and offer relevant additional resources both financial and via connections to new groups of community people, including other funders, politicians, and community leaders."

Management Enabler

With all of the adaptive management challenges a network builder may face, it's probably hard to believe that networks settle into routines. But they do. They have one or two annual meetings of members, usually at predictable times of the year. Their working groups set up schedules of meetings and activities. Their governing bodies meet regularly and distribute meeting agendas and notes to the members. They routinely orient new members. They send out regular updates on network activities. They make pitches to potential funders on a cycle dictated by funders' calendars. They meet with partners. All of this offers a degree of order based on having the network's governance structure, engagement processes, and communications perform reliably to deliver what members need to connect, align, and produce together.

But there's something that's still not in place: a way to monitor and assess just how well the network is doing. Knowing what a network does and when it does it isn't the same as knowing its underlying condition, its healthiness as a network. It's not unusual for builders of a social-impact network to roll along without considering its fitness; there's so much else to worry about and work on. But network builders who don't seriously and regularly check on their network's robustness aren't likely to be able to continuously improve the network's performance or keep presenting funders with compelling evidence of the network's value.

CHAPTER SIX

Know Your Condition: Taking a Network's Pulse

Monitoring and assessing a social-impact network's condition and performance is the basis for improving its impact.

The starting point for improvement is to recognize the need.
— *Masaaki Imai*

In 2009, Adene Sacks and Julia Parzen were working with different social-impact networks, but on the same problem: how to assess the network's performance. They had different reasons for putting the networks under a microscope. Sacks, then a program officer for the Jim Joseph Foundation, had provided funding to build the capacity of the Reboot network. She wanted to evaluate the network's development and impact, to judge the effect of the foundation's $3-million grant. She wanted to understand what had happened, what other factors might have contributed to those results, and how Reboot could continue its evolution to increase impact. Parzen, managing director of the Urban Sustainability Directors Network, which was just starting up, wanted to monitor the network's condition as it evolved. Her eye was on continuously improving the network's performance. "The network is a living organism," she explains. "If you don't take its temperature, how do you know how it's doing?"

Both Sacks and Parzen needed information about the networks' performances, but before that they needed a framework to guide them: what to assess, how to assess it, and how to interpret and use what was learned.

They couldn't just grab a network-evaluation framework off the shelf, because there weren't any. As a rule, the Jim Joseph Foundation evaluated almost every grant it made, but it hadn't funded a network evaluation before. "When I talked to other funders," Sacks recalls, "no one knew what to do." She tried using traditional evaluators with Reboot, but it didn't work. "They weren't speaking the same language as Reboot. They would say, 'We want to see your business plan and metrics for success,' and Reboot would say things like, 'We're redefining Jewishness for a new generation.' And the evaluators would say, 'Can you put some numbers on that?' They wanted to tie organizational outcomes to the network. I was struggling to figure this out. We needed a framework that would help us understand what Reboot was trying to do."

Parzen also had to wrestle with the differences posed by a network. "I'm always asking, what really is happening here? Is this going to be something better, more valuable?" But it wasn't immediately clear what to ask about when building a network. "I wanted to have a set of principles that we'd use. Once we had them, they'd start to define the questions that you need to be asking."

Evaluation in the social-change world had focused almost exclusively on the effort of an individual organization, not on collaborations of individuals or organizations. In a network, performance is evaluated for the same reasons that an organization's performance is evaluated: to measure impact and ensure accountability for use of resources, to plan and improve network processes and development, to generate knowledge about what works and doesn't work. Network builders may feel the same anxieties about evaluation as organization leaders might. Lynn Decker hesitated at first to let evaluators into the Fire Learning Network that she managed and The Nature Conservancy had helped to start: "I was afraid of publications that might embarrass The Conservancy. But I think that's sort of natural." She realized that the potential benefits of assessment outweighed her concerns. "An outside evaluation would actually give me knowledge and perspective that I didn't really have. We had been monitoring our progress to make sure our strategy wasn't defective, but I found the prospect of outside evaluation really compelling."

Understanding a network isn't the same as understanding an organization. Unlike an organization, a network is a decentralized, member-driven platform of relationships that evolves its capabilities and underlying structure of connectivity. Its success depends crucially on the degree to which it organizes connections among its members to produce unique, flexible capacity and network effects. To assess a network, you have to examine closely its members' multiple value propositions and web of relationships, their highly diffused decision-making processes, and the stage of the network's evolution (connection, alignment, or production).

Due to these differences, when network builders come to the question of evaluation, whether for their own needs or those of a funder's staff or board of directors, they are likely to want to know about things that an organization-centric evaluation might not consider important. This was the case at USDN. "From day one," says Parzen, as the network's founders considered how to conduct continuous self-assessment, "we built a story about USDN around the idea of creating something based on the relationships."

Framework for Evaluating Networks

Our framework for network assessment contains three major topics: connectivity, health, and impact. These are the things you want to know about the network, and they matter whether, like Parzen, you want to self-assess a network for continuous improvement or, like Sacks, you want to externally evaluate a network to determine the return on an investment.

It shouldn't be a surprise that we emphasize *connectivity* among a network's members. After all, if members are not connecting with each other, then no value can be created by the network. As a 2012 report by the International Institute for Sustainable Development notes, whether you're building a network of organizations or individuals, you "need to understand how to build social capital among the various actors in the collaboration and how to measure whether social capital has been built and is sufficient for the collaboration to advance its work." And as we detailed in chapter 4, the connections made in a network result in connectivity structures that can be mapped, measured, and analyzed, with important implications for the network's evolution.

Network *health* is about the other essentials for developing a network—members' satisfaction and sense of shared purpose; the effectiveness of network infrastructure, including governance and communications; the network's resources; and additional subjects—and how well the network is evolving. In short, how is the network doing in creating the conditions crucial for its success and sustainability? The feedback you get from members could lead you to conclusions about what's working well and what isn't, and what to do next.

A network's *impact* has two dimensions: the impact that individual members of the network have on their separate worlds as a result of participating in the network and the impact network members have collectively. Either way, the basic question is the same: how much is the network changing the world? Of course, it's more complicated than that, since you have to sort out what part of any evident change can be attributed to the network, rather than to other factors.

With these three topics framed, there's also the challenge of figuring out how they interact. Network health depends to some extent on connectivity, and network impact depends to some extent on network health. And a network's impact can affect both its health and its connectivity.

An advantage of this framework is that it can work for both an insider's self-assessment and an outsider's third-party evaluation. In fact, the evaluation of Reboot that the Jim Joseph Foundation paid for was also used by Rebooters to help guide the network's development, and the continuous assessments that USDN conducts have been used by some of its funders to gauge the network's progress.

Framing the assessment inquiry and its key questions is just a first step. For each topic in the framework there are challenges in data collection and analysis, and some tools to help network builders along.

Assessing Connectivity

From the beginning of USDN's formation, the network developed maps and analyses of its members' connections with each other. Parzen got the idea from consultants who had worked with the Barr Foundation, which required the networks it was funding to do mapping to develop strategies and benchmark connections. "We decided that mapping was a way we could demonstrate the network's performance in the early years," she says. "We found that once we could show change in connectivity from year to year in those maps, it was very potent. It wasn't just an evaluation tool; it was a planning tool for the network." Before the network's first meeting, members answered a survey about their connections to other members, and every year since then they have done the same. By 2013, the network had amassed a large amount of longitudinal and recent data about member connections. Parzen reported in that year's "State of the Network" that highly efficient connectivity had been achieved—the average member either knew every member or knew someone who knew every member—and the quality of the connections among members was "getting deeper"—while the average member's number of stronger ties to other members had more than doubled in two years to 10.

When Sacks worked with Reboot's governing board members and staff to design their evaluation, they also decided to map the network's connectivity shape—but they had more than a decade of undocumented member connecting to catch up with. The Reboot maps revealed several patterns of interest to both funder and network members: Reboot had a "committed core of well-linked" members with "direct connections with large numbers of other Rebooters." Even though the network had added annual cohorts of about 30 new members since its start-up, there was a "substantial amount of connectivity across cohort years." And, while most Rebooters lived in one of three U.S. cities, there were differences in the patterns of connections among members within each city. For instance, "New York Rebooters form sub-clusters, often by neighborhood . . . while the LA network is the densest of the local networks, likely due to the shared professional interests of many LA Rebooters and effective network organizing."

Both of these mapping exercises delivered valuable information. The Reboot maps provided evidence of the network's strength, Sacks says. "It proved to me that the network was sustainable. It had key players—all these incredible individuals—and boundary spanners [between the major city clusters]. It had evolved cross-cohort connections. I felt hugely gratified seeing those network maps and understanding how much was happening in the network that had nothing to do with the founders or the organizational backbone [Reboot staff] for the network." USDN's maps reinforced the need to build additional opportunities for members to connect deeply. "The big story was that the strength of connections went up dramatically, because we've got so much more collaboration going on," Parzen says. "It's not surprising, but you have to keep thinking about what support the network needs to have even more of these collaborations."

Mapping reveals the structure of a network's connectivity, and a method called "social network analysis" can analyze the efficiency of the connectivity. As the Barr Foundation invested in increasing the connections among organizations that provided after-school programs for students, it also measured the degree to which their connectivity was changing. Consultant Stephanie Lowell reports that data were collected from some 1,000 organizations in sports and arts programming, including their links to each other. "Efficiency refers to the average number of steps it takes for any one node to reach another node in the network," she explains. "A rule of thumb in the network research field is to strive for efficiency at or near three." After Barr-supported weavers had been active connecting many of these organizations, the efficiency of connections among the sports organizations improved to 3.8 steps on average (from 4.6 steps) and that of the arts organizations improved to 3.2 average steps (from 6.0 steps).

None of this can be known without developing network maps.

Mapping Networks

As fascinating as network maps are, there's a lot to know about why and when to invest in creating them.

Network maps, which are created with special software, present complex information in a way that makes it easier to "see" connections and their patterns. Who is connected to whom? Who has more connectivity or reach than others in the network? Which nodes are strongly connected and which are weakly connected? Which are becoming more connected, which are losing connectivity? A network map of the Network of Korean American Leaders (NetKAL) early in that network's life revealed that two of 24 Korean American professionals who were members were much more connected to other members than the rest of the members were. But they were well connected in quite different ways. One was directly connected to about half of the members. The other connected directly to only a quarter of the members, but those people were well connected to other members. Working through just these two "hub" nodes, you could easily reach almost all 24 members of NetKAL. When we displayed to NetKAL members the map we'd made of their connectivity, many of them immediately began spotting patterns, such as which members were relatively unconnected to others. The exercise created some excitement among members because it made visible something—everyone's connections to each other—that was otherwise hard for anyone to see in its entirety.

You can map many aspects of a network's connections. In Boston, when a group of foundations mapped the funding sources for after-school programs, examining the financial links between funders and organizations, the maps revealed that many people's assumptions about the flow of money were incorrect. USDN maps its members' connectivity by the size of the member's city, the region the city is in, the member's tenure in the network, and other factors. In Michigan, a new network of community innovators started by mapping the combinations of "core competencies" that could be assembled from the organizations in the network. Both Reboot and USDN made maps that depicted connections among members participating in specific network activities.

Network mapping creates value for network builders in three ways:

- *Maps reveal opportunities to build connections that can maximize the power and potential of your network.* Who's not connected but should be? Where are the hubs and bottlenecks in the network? A network map of an eighth-grade class in Detroit, with 17 students who had been together for nearly three years, revealed that two of the students connected with every other student when it came to their learning activities (collaborating on projects or homework, for instance). At the other extreme of connectivity, three students connected to very few other students. The well-connected students were natural hubs in the classroom, and their teacher used them to build even more connectivity within the class by having them spend more of their time working with students who were relatively unconnected.

- *Maps show how a network's structure is evolving—and this can be used to assess the health of a network.* A map is a snapshot of a network's structure, and taking "before" and "after" pictures can reveal how a network is evolving. Has it moved, for instance, from the hub-and-spoke stage, as described by Holley and Krebs in chapter 4, to a more advanced structural stage? Has it expanded to include people who once were beyond the "horizon" of the network? Has it lost connections to some nodes? A map of nearly 500 Boston arts and culture organizations serving children found that they were not well connected with each other and that they relied on just a few people as connectors. On average, it was calculated that the organizations were six connections apart from each other—quite a "distance." However, the picture changed after a weaver spent a year connecting many of the organizations to each other. On average the organizations were then three steps away from each other, and the mapping also showed that a hub-and-spoke structure had emerged with the weaver at the center.

- *Network maps make members better networkers.* Every network member is also a potential network weaver. When network members see maps of their network, it can improve their "eye" for the network's connections and help them see what weaving they can do. In research on "structural holes" in networks, Ron Burt and Don Ronchi show that even minor training can improve people's ability to see and act on network opportunities. It turns out that most of us are not very good at recognizing bridging opportunities for closing "holes" in a network. But, the research shows, if you know what a network "bridge" is and looks like, you'll find and act on these opportunities more readily.

A simple network map with a small number of nodes can be drawn by hand. But the analysis and display of more complex network information are best achieved with special software that sorts, measures, and organizes data for easier interpretation. Although most of these software programs, having been developed for limited distribution by mathematicians, sociologists, or graph theorists, are difficult for the average user, the technical assistance and mapping tools themselves are increasingly being adapted to serve new lay markets. Examples of low- or no-cost tools include NodeXL, a free, relatively easy-to-use software application that works within Microsoft Excel; Gephi, a more recent entrant into the field of no-cost network visualization tools; and InFlow, which can be purchased through orgnet.com and comes with coaching and support from its creator, Valdis Krebs. (One source for more information about mapping software is Patti Anklam's website, listed in the Resources section.)

The basic steps for mapping a network are as follows:

- *Identify the network you want to map.* What is the set of members (people, organizations) that you want to include? For instance, will you monitor core members only or anyone active in the network? What type of connections do you want to track? A relationship between individuals or organizations may be defined in many ways, from simple contact (who talks to whom?) to more-complicated exchanges (who supports whom? who learns from whom?).

- *Gather network data.* Software programs do the calculating and display results, but relational information has to be collected and entered into the database. Information about network relationships can be gathered through various methods, including observation, interviews, documents, and electronic records, as well as from surveys (either direct or online). For the Reboot evaluation, consultants first met with three separate focus groups of members, one in each of the network's major cities, and used those 90-minute conversations to develop a survey questionnaire that was sent to every network member. In USDN, a participation requirement is that members respond to two surveys a year. One of the surveys focuses on members' connections and satisfaction with the network.

  Network questions typically establish the existence of a link, the kinds of relationships or flows between nodes, and the frequency of contact and strength of the connection. Mapping software sorts and displays nodes with different attributes (such as people working in the same region or serving particular constituencies), but only if these data are also gathered and entered into the network database. A map of a network can depict many aspects of the relationships between nodes. Most simply, it can show who is connected to whom. But it can also show qualitative aspects of the relationships, such as the strength or weakness of ties between nodes, or which nodes share a value proposition, or which nodes connect to people outside of the network that others in the network want to connect with.

- **Generate and interpret maps.** A simple display of "who's connected to whom" can be a powerful tool for detecting network patterns and designing network strategies. Typically, you will be able to "interrogate" the data along these lines: Where are the strong connections in the network? Where are the weak ones? Where are the gaps in connectivity? What structure(s) is the network taking on? It's important to remember, however, that no particular pattern of links is desirable in itself. A small, closely knit network may be ideal for exchanging complex information, but not for finding new ideas. A spoke-and-hub structure may be effective for starting up a network, but can become a barrier to network evolution. Judgments about what the mapping means have to take into account the network's context.

Assessing Network Health

When some members of Lawrence CommunityWorks met to discuss how they would know whether or not their network was "healthy," they identified several measurable conditions they felt were essential for the network to achieve its long-term goals: growth of membership; increase in the proportion of members actively involved in the network; engagement of members in multiple kinds of activities provided by the network; increasing levels of member participation in the stewardship and management of the network; increasing diversity of network membership; members coming together in different combinations in the network (for example, youth and adults, members with different social and ethnic affiliations, new members and more experienced members, leaders and others); and members making and taking advantage of both strong and weak ties in the network.

Any network can come up with a similar set of indicators by which to gauge its vital characteristics. In general, you can start with the design elements of networks detailed in chapter 2: purpose; membership; value propositions; coordination, facilitation, and communication; resources; governance; and operating principles/culture. Some of what you want to measure will vary due to the network's purpose. For instance, LCW is a community-based network of individuals, so it focused especially on membership growth and diversity. In Boston, the Barr Foundation evaluated its efforts to boost capacity of after-school programs by using network-building metrics that included the strengthening of intermediary organizations in the network, improvement of information flows, the spread of "best practices," getting an increased number of voices to the table for discussion of after-school issues, and the emergence of new network weavers and hubs. Other networks have identified various indicators of health: distributed control of the network, sufficient financial resources, attractive value propositions and the right balance of individual and collective value propositions, and adaptive management culture. When we developed a Network Health Scorecard for general use, it focused on a network's shared purpose, goals, and plans; collaboration among members; communication among members and with external stakeholders; funding; decision-making processes; accountability of members; and the network's collective capacities. (See Appendix D for full Scorecard.)

Whatever factors you want to emphasize, make sure you check in on the members' value propositions, a most crucial indicator of network health. In USDN's 2013 survey of members, 90 percent of respondents said the network was delivering "access to trusted information"—one of the membership's top-three value propositions. The survey also found that satisfaction with all three had increased over the previous year and that several other value propositions were growing in importance to members. Weighing this information, the network determined that one of its priorities in the coming year was to maintain, rather than change, most of its activities.

An important factor in health assessment is the stage of a network's evolution. For instance, is the network in an early stage during which establishing connectivity matters much more than anything else? Or is it in a more evolved stage in which a large amount of collaboration among members should be expected? In 2013, we examined the condition of eight regional networks of sustainability directors in the United States, their connectivity and some elements of their health (leadership, type of

activity, level of communication, coordination, and member satisfaction).
Seven of the networks were one to three years old; the eighth was six
years old. Three were recent start-ups with committed founders, but they
had only met once or twice so far. They had few strong connections between members, relatively little communication between meetings, and
ad hoc coordination. Not surprisingly, most of their members reported
that they could see the potential value of the network, but that the network was not yet delivering the value. The oldest network had reached
maturity, with a relatively large core of strongly connected members, a
second generation of network builders in place, consistent and effective
coordination, and a strong communications infrastructure often used by
members. Its members reported a high level of satisfaction. The development of the four other networks fell in between the start-up and more-
mature stages. They had partly left behind the start-up stage but hadn't
yet reached full maturity. These fine-grained differences in the networks'
evolution affected the advice we offered about each network's next steps.

There are three main ways to gather data about a network's health:
survey and interview the members, document members' participation in
network activities, and observe network members as they engage.

- *Conduct regular surveys, focus groups, and interviews of members.*
  It's not unusual for networks to get feedback from members, but
  most don't do it comprehensively—probing the many elements
  we mentioned above—or regularly. That means they're not seeing the whole picture or how the picture is changing over time,
  which stymies the use of the data to make beneficial changes.

  The Southwest Rural Policy Network surveyed its members
  on a quarterly basis over a period of three years using the Network Health Scorecard. Results were used to identify and address challenges such as uneven member participation, and to
  reinforce effective network practices such as quarterly face-to-
  face meetings and the engagement of a high-performing coordinator. Graphing survey results over time also helped members
  see the value of investing in their network over the long term.
  Despite several "dips" in Scorecard tallies along the way, members had evidence that during the three years their network's
  health had improved.

When we conducted an evaluation of a homelessness initiative of the Massachusetts Interagency Council on Housing and Homelessness (ICHH), which used 10 regional networks of provider organizations to test innovative services, we used a modified version of the Scorecard to survey members. The results led to mid-course corrections in the operating procedures of several networks in order to ensure that all of their members were well informed and involved in key decision-making processes.

- *Document members' activities.* If you don't know who is doing what, it's hard to assess the engagement of members, a critical indicator of health. Yes, it takes time and energy to track activities, and, yes, monitoring members closely may make them feel "watched." But the point is to gather data that will allow the network to figure out how to improve its performance. For instance, the 2013 "State of the Network" presentation to USDN members reported on the percentage of members meeting participation requirements, participating in at least one working group or committee, applying for project grants, and engaged in a regional network. These data—and much more—had been collected routinely during the year and were a basis for recommending network priorities for the coming year. Reboot also documented the participation of its members in a wide range of the network's activities, and these data were subsequently incorporated into the network maps to help identify the most-active and well-connected members.

- *Observe member engagement.* It's also useful to watch the network at work, looking for how members participate and interact, how much sharing is going on, and how collective decisions are made. Surveys can tell you a great deal, but observation can enhance these data. When we evaluate networks, we find that both observing network activities and engaging with network members to discuss evaluation findings can provide additional insight into the network's health.

  RE-AMP invited us to present evaluation findings at its annual meeting of members, and then had members break up into small groups to fully discuss each of the findings and its implications, after which each group reported out to the whole membership. This kind of attention to a report about the network's health has the benefit of increasing members' awareness of the challenges of network building. It can also enhance an evaluator's perspective about the network.

Assessing a Network's Impacts

Networks have the same difficulties as organizations when it comes to providing evidence of the impact of their activities and outputs. It's not always easy to establish a cause-and-effect relationship between what a network or organization has been doing and the impact it has. Significant change processes take time, and the contribution of the network or organization to these processes is often difficult to measure, especially in the short to medium term. This is especially true when a big, generative social problem—climate change, homelessness, or cultural identity, for instance—is being tackled.

In networks, however, the usual problems of impact assessment are compounded by the way that decentralization creates a "chain of impacts." First in the sequence, the network affects its members—providing each of them with something new that they value and can use. In Reboot, for example, participating in the network might impact members' sense or understanding of their Jewish identity. The evaluation survey asked many questions about this, and, in response, 86 percent reported that being in the network had an impact on how they feel or think about themselves as Jews, and 79 percent said that for them Reboot was a "bridge back to Jewish experience I can relate to." At USDN, most members reported in 2013 that the network made it possible for them to "get to know many colleagues" and "keep abreast of others' accomplishments." There's a similar dynamic at work in community collaboratives of organizations when they align around a shared goal. The organization-members are acknowledging that being in a network relationship with each other enables them to seek an outcome they could not achieve on their own.

In the sequence's second step, individual members of a network start to use in their own situations the value they get from the network. In the case of USDN's local sustainability directors, the members engaged in their cities' setting and began to influence the thinking and actions of others in local government. In a 2011 evaluation of the RE-AMP network, 65 percent of member-organizations said that as a result of participating in RE-AMP they were using better strategies, and 63 percent reported that foundations and advocacy organizations in the network had become better aligned with each other. Nearly all of the foundation members agreed that participation was helping them make better funding decisions. And in Reboot's case, the members' local environments included their personal (family and friends) and professional networks, as well as the local Jewish community and its infrastructure of organizations. In this way, a network has an outward rippling effect on nonmembers.

The third step in the sequence has two dimensions: individual and collective impacts. What the individual members do directly or through others "back home" results in actual changes locally. In USDN, this might involve the introduction of a new practice that the member learned about through the network, with the impact of saving money or reducing carbon emissions. In 2013, according to the USDN annual report, about two-thirds of members reported that as a result of being in the network they had been able to "find a solution to a key challenge," and more than half said they had "made a change in policy, program, or process." In Reboot's case, many individual members started to produce new "Jewish products" for their family and friends or for others in the local Jewish community. "Rebooters are leading or supporting the development of engaging local religious and cultural entities," the Reboot evaluation reported. "A number of Rebooters now consult or work for mainstream Jewish organizations, often to provide expertise about connecting with young Jews."

Even as the network produces individual member impacts, members who are working together, in small clusters or as a whole network, may start to have a collective impact. In some cases, the impact is evident on many local environments at once; in other cases it's on the larger environment within which network members operate, such as when USDN members from cities seek to influence U.S. federal government agencies. As we reported in chapter 1, some Rebooters worked together to create books, movies, events, and music CDs that reached mass audiences. Their impact on these people, while not part of the scope of the 2012 Reboot evaluation, can be measured. In USDN, teams of members have collaborated on more than a score of innovative projects that impacted multiple cities, and the network as a whole has explored how to use its "collective voice" to impact the development of the urban sustainability field. A September 2013 USDN report identified multiple ways in which USDN could achieve collective impact, including pooling financial resources to invest in innovations, building long-term research partnerships with universities and businesses, and aggregating city purchasing power to influence the design and adoption of green-friendly products.

As networks evolve, they become more capable of enacting this impact sequence effectively, but it takes time and it's not necessarily a linear, orderly process. This is why some funders may be more comfortable with creating a set of milestones—intermediate indicators of progress—for impact.

Whatever the impacts a network is supposed to have, a formal evaluation will usually ask whether or not using a network approach to produce the outcomes has been worth it. Would a different approach—relying, for instance, on a single organization—have been more effective or less costly? For some network builders this is an unnecessary question; they've already concluded that a network approach will be more powerful than what a single organization can accomplish. But because networks are considered to be a new, untested approach to social change, they may be required to prove themselves against alternative models for getting things done.

The evaluation of 10 regional homelessness networks in Massachusetts provides one of the few examples we've seen of an effort to assess the connection between use of a network model and the impacts achieved. The pilot project was designed to test the hypothesis that network-based approaches to implementing housing-focused interventions would more effectively address the needs of Massachusetts residents who are homeless or at risk of homelessness. Each region had a different starting point, put together its network of government and nonprofit service providers a bit differently, and pursued a variety of innovations, with the regional state agency acting as the convener. And in different parts of the state, factors such as the local economy affected homelessness differently. During the 18-month pilot period, the networks submitted quarterly reports on their activities and also used the Network Health Scorecard, providing data that, evaluators said, "enabled the ICHH to correlate Network efforts with effects on the shelter system on an ongoing basis." The evaluation results showed that new regional cross-sector collaborations measurably increased the likelihood that vulnerable families and individuals would be diverted from shelters or rapidly rehoused. "Regional coordination of services minimized duplication and increased the efficiency and effectiveness of service delivery," according to the report, which concluded that "reducing the need for shelter among chronically homeless adults, including long-term shelter stayers, can be achieved through Network-based collaborative efforts to identify and serve clients using housing first approaches." The evaluation also found that one of the state's highest leverage investments was in network coordination. This informed the state's decision to continue to support regional network-based efforts and encouraged the state and other funders to pay for regional network coordinators.

Four Lessons about Assessing Networks

1. Don't underestimate the need to educate funders—staff and board members—and network members about network basics.
2. Anticipate and build the assessment system your network will need as it evolves.
3. Don't be funder-centric in thinking about evaluation.
4. Assess multiple dimensions of the network: the results it is producing, how it produces them (as a network), and the development of the network itself.

1. *Don't underestimate the need to educate funders—staff and board members—and network members about network basics.* Sacks worked hard to help her foundation's board understand what the evaluation could tell them about the Reboot network. "I wanted the board to understand network evaluation and network-building process metrics, in order to appreciate how networks build value and why greater connectivity was good." She used the presentation of evaluation findings as an opportunity for the board to consider the connection between

network strength and impact. "The board used Reboot to teach themselves about networks." USDN had the good fortune to attract funders early on who recognized that it would take time to build the network's capacity—and some of them used the network's connectivity and health assessments to inform their efforts in supporting other networks.

2. *Anticipate and build the assessment system your network will need as it evolves.* Sooner or later a network's builders, members, and funders will want to know how well the network is performing. It's smarter to tackle the topic sooner, since a good assessment requires data that are easier to collect at the time things are happening rather than much later. It's also better to build the feedback and learning process in early, so that it is clear to the network that assessment is essential to managing the network, not just an add-on chore.

The Southwest Rural Policy Network began using the Network Health Scorecard at a pivotal moment in its history, when it was transitioning from connectivity and alignment to production by developing projects for member collaboration. Members understood that their network's health was critical to network performance and so began systematically monitoring network conditions. When the Scorecard's cumulative results were shared with outsiders, it helped to make the case that the network had managed its evolution in a deliberate way to build capacity and improve performance.

3. *Don't be funder-centric in thinking about evaluation.* Network organizers who worry mainly about their funder's demand for an evaluation should more closely consider the "emergent demand" from their own network members for more self-assessment and accountability. When a funder requires evaluation, align that process so that it can also meet the feedback needs of network organizers and members. Note the Reboot case, in which the funder and the network jointly designed the evaluation to meet both of their needs.

4. *Assess multiple dimensions of the network: the results it is pro-ducing, how it produces them (as a network), and the development of the network itself.* To have a well-rounded assessment that in-forms organizers, members, and stakeholders such as funders, you need to know all of these things—and much of the data that you need can be gathered all at the same time.

Tracking a network's performance and reflecting on what it means—"noticing the network," June Holley calls it—is essential to the network-building process. With the information, network builders can make sure the network stays adaptive. And assessment provides a feedback loop that is important in other ways. "Seeing the maps of connections get denser was a real pleasure," Parzen says. "And funders found it impressive too." With careful, thorough assessment, a network takes a step on the path of continuous improvement.

Sometimes, though, what a network needs isn't continuity. Instead, it needs to step back and consider its options, because it's stuck or fading away.

CHAPTER SEVEN

Back to Basics: Resetting a Network's Design

Making an existing network more generative, with more engaged members and impact, requires resetting of key design decisions to boost members' connectivity.

We cannot solve our problems with the same level of thinking that created them.

— *Albert Einstein*

"*There's not a lot of follow through by members after meetings.*"

"*Our investors are outcome focused and don't think about what it takes to invest in network building.*"

"*We had a collaboration/chat room on our website, but no one played.*"

"*There's confusion about what types of results the network needs to see right away.*"

"*We don't get the right people on the calls—sometimes it's the members, sometimes it's their staff.*"

"*We're not enforcing membership eligibility guidelines and participation requirements.*"

"*The network is being managed like it is some sort of club.*"

"*We don't have members who are willing to lead the network.*"

That's some of what concerned network builders have said when they sought our assistance. Their efforts to build social-impact networks haven't resulted in the sort of network effects and generative capacity we've described in earlier chapters. Their members meet and talk, but not much collaborative activity happens. The members' engagement in network activities diminishes. Funders lose confidence in the network's ability to have impact. No one is sure what to do next, but staying the course isn't an option.

In other cases, network builders worried about how to evolve the network further to get more member engagement and impact; the network seemed stalled. That concern was on Leslie Ethen's mind in October 2013. The director of conservation and development for the city of Tucson, Arizona, she had helped for three years to build a 12-city network, the Western Adaptation Alliance (WAA). It had undertaken several projects and expanded its membership, but Ethen and other builders were concerned about its future. "We're almost at a turning point," Ethen says. "We need to be intentional and thoughtful about where we go from here, because if we don't I'm afraid next year will be our last year. There's nothing bad or wrong happening, but there's enough investment and desire to take the network to another level that if this doesn't happen, it will fragment and go away."

What's a network builder to do?

The answer is: go back to basics. We're not talking here about the sort of management challenges detailed in chapter 5, which present themselves in networks that are maturing nicely in their capabilities and connectivity structure. We're talking about networks that have not yet developed the conditions that spur healthy evolution—and whose very existence may be at stake. In response to this peril, you have to closely examine the decisions the network has made explicitly, or implicitly, since its origin, with regard to five key design issues: its purpose, membership, value propositions, governance, and operating principles. What may be needed is a total reset of the network. (Your network may also be having difficulty with the other design issues—coordination, resources, and assessment—but these often arise from problems with the five we're focusing on, or they can be fixed without hitting the reset button.)

It's not unusual to find that when a network started up it wasn't ready to undertake deliberate design work. So now is the time. "When we first started I don't think we could have done this," Ethen says of the WAA.

"But we've grown since then. Even if we haven't developed our connections to each other as intentionally and strategically as we could have, we've reached a point where we're mature enough to look at this from a structured and very intentional perspective."

Unleashing the power of a network depends on establishing a set of social relationships—connections and shared identity—that are both highly decentralized and strongly collective. There's no single right way to do this and, like Ethen, a network's builders may find after a few years that they are better able to address design issues that they may not have even recognized earlier. At that point, it's important not just to treat the symptoms but to focus on the fundamentals. That's where the path forward begins, whatever the network's unrealized potential.

Purpose

Some social-impact networks are networks in name only. If a network is being driven by staff or by an outsider's purpose, then it's not likely to become a generative network. It may be an organization or an association that provides members with services. It may be a funder's initiative involving multiple grantees. There's nothing wrong with these approaches; they are viable means of achieving social impact. But they shouldn't be expected to become generative networks with highly engaged members and impressive network effects; that development is simply not in the cards.

We've seen "networks" that involved occasional conference calls with "members" to listen to experts talk about a topic of interest. The members didn't connect much with each other and didn't align around ideas or goals. But they were satisfied, because learning about a topic from an expert was what they wanted. It's possible that some participants in this activity might develop work to do together, but this is not a model for stimulating a lot of collaboration. If a member-services organization, association, or coalition wants to generate more member energy and sustained collaboration, it will have to use methods that help members connect, align, and produce together. But first, it should find out if there are members who want that sort of peer-to-peer opportunity. Assuming that there are, then instead of trying to transform existing practices of the network, which may prove difficult due to habit and inertia, pilot a few new efforts—experiments—with a focus on building connectivity. The pilots can attract the members interested in collaboration without disturbing other members. With pilots under way, the organization or association could shift into a hybrid model in which one of the services it provides members is the opportunity to participate in an effective generative network.

We've also seen "networks" that started when a funder convened grantees to be its "members" and then assigned them a collective purpose. The members enjoyed their time together and responded well to the funder's pledge of ongoing financial support for the network, but they didn't feel that the network was theirs or that creating value for each other, rather than for the funder, was the purpose. Without that feeling, they weren't going to invest serious time, energy, and hope in building a network. If a funder or other network engineer—even an "inside" founder—has a deeply held vision for the network and dominates the design decisions to ensure that the vision will be achieved, then there's little prospect of building a generative network. But if a dominant node recognizes that it must genuinely share power with network members, then it may be possible to transform the relational dynamics in the network. Some of the guidance we provided in "Bonus Track—Advice to Funders and Other Network Engineers," starting on page 75, may help engineers to let go. But the funder/engineer should not just abandon the network; instead of walking away, taking responsibility for what has happened in the network's development and playing a constructive role in its transformation is much more likely to give the network a fighting chance to develop.

Finally, we've seen networks that were confused about what they wanted the network to be able to do: was it to help members connect, or align, or produce together, or all of these? In early chapters we pointed out that you can create social-impact networks with any of these three basic capabilities, but that each function brings with it different requirements for network design and operations. Some network builders hadn't reckoned with these differences, so the network's infrastructure was not set up to enable the capability that was desired. Others start out to build a connectivity network, then decide they want members to align and produce, but they don't change the design or operations to accomplish that. We also noted earlier out that if co-production by members is your goal, then you have to develop that capability by connecting and then aligning the members. But some impatient network builders and engineers short-change the necessary investment in making connections among members. The first step in responding to these situations is to clarify the type of network that you want to build and to recognize what it takes to develop and enable such a network.

Membership

We've worked with networks whose members weren't even sure why they were participating. They represented member-organizations but they didn't know how they or their organization might benefit. One way this disconnection occurred was when the organization's top leadership—the executive director or board chair, for example—embraced the idea of creating a network and then assigned a lower-level staffer to participate. The representative didn't share the leader's enthusiasm and/or had no idea why a network might be useful. When the designated players got together, it was hard for them to connect with each other usefully because they didn't really know why they were there or what to do. The designated members didn't feel ownership of the network's birth and didn't hold a vision for the network's value that could help to pull them together and forward. A remedy is to let the designated members come together and design a network from scratch to meet *their* needs. What they come up with may affirm their leaders' sense of purpose, but if it differs from that, then it's up to them to try to sell their shared view to their organizations' leaders.

We've also observed networks in which the highly committed members were nearly outnumbered by much less committed and active members or even by nonmembers. Having associate members and other categories of membership—observers, learners—helps to grow a network without expanding its core membership, as we described in chapter 2. But the balance of non-core to core members matters. When a network has too many members who take from but don't give much to the network, then network activities have to shoulder that extra burden, and the "gift economy" culture of the network can become stunted. For deeply committed core members, spending time with a great many far less committed members will feel like a waste of energy, a reduction of the network's ability to deliver efficiently on prized value propositions. Responses to this imbalance include reducing and limiting the number of non-core members in the network so that they are only a small fraction of the overall membership, and raising participation standards for non-core members, so that they're focused on actively contributing value to the network, not just drawing from it.

Sometimes many of a network's members aren't especially open to connecting and collaborating with others. The constraint may be institutional: their organizations value taking credit rather than sharing it. Or it may be professional: the members' training and professional identity honors individual expertise and effort, the "lone wolf's" accomplishments. (Of course, one's reticence to engage with others may be personality-based, but it's unlikely that the network is an assembly entirely of introverted people.) These sorts of limitations make it extremely difficult for a strong group dynamic to emerge. One response could be to provide members with training in how to be more collaborative. This may be especially helpful if the organizations have been competitors and are nervous about confiding in one another. Another reaction could be to find those members who are comfortable collaborating and get them busy modeling the behavior and engaging other members. A third response could be to reexamine the network's purpose and perhaps conclude that more compelling incentives to collaborate are needed to help members break with past attitudes and behaviors.

In some networks the membership can be so diverse that members have trouble finding affinities around which to connect with each other. This isn't meant to be an indictment of diversity; a diverse membership can be a powerful asset for a network that seeks innovation. But to realize the benefits of diversity, a network has to grapple and come to grips with its members' differences—a process that can work, but is sure to take a lot of time and generate some confusion and frustration. Maybe the network's membership has been constituted too broadly; maybe there's more than one network within the network.

Value Propositions

Start with this question: whose value proposition is driving the network? If it's a funder's or an engineer's, then have the network members fully embraced it, too? If they're just going along for the ride, then they simply won't make the commitments to the network that create evolutionary momentum; instead, connectivity and development of a core of strong relationships will be short circuited. In such a case, it's up to the dominant decision maker to change the dynamics.

Sometimes the problem comes from within the network: members have not gelled beyond their individual value propositions. Each may know "what *I* want to get out of participating in the network," but not what *we* want to get out of it. In other words, there's no collective value proposition to motivate collaboration. This can arise especially if members formed the network in order to obtain funding for their efforts. They may have expressed a shared goal, but each had eyes mainly for their individual slice of the pie.

Another difficulty may occur when the network's collective value proposition is shifting, but members don't have a way to satisfy whatever's emerging. Although the members of the Urban Sustainability Directors Network embraced three priority value propositions for the network's first five years, the 2013 member survey indicated that two quite different value propositions were gaining in importance to members. Being aware of this kind of change helps a network to develop or strengthen efforts aimed at meeting members' potential future interests. Imagine not knowing that such changes were afoot—and your members being left hanging.

A collective value proposition that network members find compelling provides the glue for members' sustained connectivity and the fuel for members' shared action. If the network hasn't established a collective value proposition, or if the ones it has established are wearing thin, then you have a fundamental problem, not something that can be fixed with better communication or by securing more resources. We've seen two ways of handling this. One is to stop everything and get network members to focus on, discuss, and answer this question: What in our experience together do we know about each of our individual value propositions and what opportunities are there for developing a collective value proposition? In other words, is there really some collective value around which the network might organize? If members do identify something, the next step is to find out what commitments each is prepared to make to work with other members in order to create the value. Driving a network through a process like this can be difficult, especially if members have started to lose interest, but it can be helped with an outside facilitator. A second way is to change the network's membership—typically by adding members—so that new ideas and voices join the conversation about value and, hopefully, help it to reach a useful conclusion.

Governance

Three types of governance problems may plague networks: domination, exclusion, and lack of succession. In the first, a dominant node controls or excessively influences the network. The hub might be a funder or a founder, and has choked off decision making by the membership. In the second, governance of the network has stayed in the same hands for too long, leaving members with a feeling that others' ideas are not valued; an exclusive cluster is running the show. As Beth Kanter and Allison Fine note in *The Networked Nonprofit*, "Networks made up entirely of strong ties don't expand; they are tight-knit cliques."

In both cases the answer is to change the governance model by opening it up to other members, difficult as that may appear to be. As we discussed in the section about purpose, if the dominant node or core group recognizes that the network faces an existential crisis unless governance improves, it may decide to release its grip. If not, then little else will solve the difficulty.

In the third governance problem, the network has guiding members, but they have started to burn out after a few years, and no new members are volunteering to share the chores or take them over. It's up to members in governance to prepare successors; it won't happen magically. Holley explains that "a network can become stuck . . . and never expand, if the organizing group does not also engage others in the larger network in the developmental process." Of course, if members don't know any better, they might think that the network just happens somehow. They don't realize that there are things to tend to. They're happy just to be participating as members, not trying to be stewards of the network. This is one reason to make network-building activities and the health of the network visible to its members; it's educational, and some members may become interested in learning more.

Operating Principles

Did the network's culture get off on the wrong foot? Have network members defaulted to organization-centric approaches: Hiring staff rather than doing the work themselves? Acting solo rather than together? Maintaining activities that have little participation, rather than letting member interest drive decisions? Planning every detail for the foreseeable future rather than leaving room for surprise and adaptation?

It's not easy to stop doing behaviors that are routine in organizations but not appropriate in networks. It's not even easy to be aware that there's a difference. But there is—and it matters enormously. As we detailed in chapter 2, a network's culture—"the way we do things around here"—looks very little like an organization's culture. This means that members have to adjust the ways in which they behave. If the network hasn't been explicit about which net-centric behaviors are suitable, then it should do so. If the network has been clear about a code of behavior but hasn't been enforcing it, then it should start. This isn't just a matter of talking about the network's culture. Most essentially, some network members must start to consistently model—that is, promote, support, and insist on—the behaviors and attitudes that build a network's gift economy.

Network builders must have the nerve to call the network's attention to fundamental weaknesses in its design. And they have to guide the network through the process of resetting its design. Resetting a network, like continuously monitoring, assessing, and improving the management of a network, comes with the territory. It's a natural part of a network builder's practice—another test of the skills and knowledge it takes to generate collective capacity. But it's a test of something more than know-how. It's a test of what in an organization setting would be called "leadership." In a network setting, though, that intangible quality is somehow different from what we are familiar with, and it follows its own set of rules.

CHAPTER EIGHT

Three Rules to Build By

In addition to skills and knowledge, network builders hold a distinct net-centric point of view with its own rules.

If you want to lead the people, you must learn to follow them.
— *Lao Tzu*, Tao Te Ching

Michael Armstrong wasn't looking to be a network builder. In mid-2009, he received an invitation to a meeting in Chicago. The agenda and workshop topics looked just right for the senior sustainability manager for Portland, Oregon, even though he didn't know the organization behind the event. For two days he soaked in "rich content" and connected with other city officials. But one session left him wondering. "We had a session about the state of the network. I thought, why are we talking about this? It was more information than I cared to know about the inner workings of what, on the surface, seemed to be an organization doing good things."

Armstrong wasn't at a conference; he was at a network-building event. The meeting's convener wasn't an organization; it was a brand-new network—the Urban Sustainability Directors Network—looking for members. "At the time I didn't realize what I was hearing." But, he adds, "it planted a seed—that you need to understand about the network because this network is you; it's not generated and delivered by an external thing. When you first show up you want to sit in the back of the room and absorb all the information. But you gradually realize that you can't just sit in the back, because otherwise there's no one to give the information."

A year later, Armstrong attended USDN's second annual meeting in Boston. Again he participated in valuable discussions about the content of urban sustainability and met dozens of people in jobs like his. But this time, he says, "I noticed how this beast worked." An informal planning committee had set a meeting agenda based on conversations with network members about what interested them. A network coordinator, Julia Parzen, provided "nearly invisible support and guidance." And then there were all the members sharing information and ideas with each other. Armstrong, without being invited, sat in on the planning committee's after-meeting session. "They were getting their heads around what had happened and who wanted to continue to be on the committee. The structure of the committee, how people joined it, how many there would be—it was fairly loosely defined. I realized that this wasn't the usual leadership thing where someone's in charge and you passively follow their lead. I was interested in the way the network got its direction, surfaced opportunities, and made decisions." He joined the planning committee.

By November 2013, Armstrong, still working in Portland city government, was serving on the USDN team searching for a successor to Parzen. He was chair of the Cascadia Network of local-government sustainability directors in the Pacific Northwest. He was cochair of a USDN working group to develop a USDN partnership with the U.S. federal government. He was talking the network talk that back in 2009 mystified him. "The health of the network is strong, but it's also delicate. It needs maintenance and that doesn't happen automatically. I've been interested in understanding all of that. USDN is going into a new phase of evolution that will really challenge the identity of the network and the mechanics of how we all work together. We will have to be really disciplined." And Armstrong was still on the planning committee. "I love being on the committee. It's such a great group of people and such an interesting set of topics to work on. But I'm willing to leave the committee, because there's such value in letting other members have the same experience."

Armstrong's journey from would-be conference-goer to tireless network builder contains steps that will be familiar to other network builders: You learn what a network is, how it's different, and how it works. You participate in the network's gift economy and benefit from its easy reciprocity. You volunteer to help with network tasks and take on "leading edge" activities. You anticipate the network's future evolution, assess the network's leadership needs, and help others to step into important network roles. (You might even start another network on the side.) This is a path to network leadership—but not the sort of leadership we usually think of. "It's leading from behind," Armstrong reflects, "but it's not a passive role. It's a highly responsive role."

Serving the Network

In organizations, a leader is a take-charge person, someone who commands and directs others. As Peter Senge explains in *The Fifth Discipline*, "Our traditional views of leaders—as special people who set the direction, make the key decisions, and energize the troops—are deeply rooted in an individualistic and non-systemic worldview. Especially in the West, leaders are *heroes*—great men (and occasionally women) who 'rise to the fore' in times of crisis." This is leadership in a top-down, centralized model, not a bottom-up, decentralized model. "At its heart," Senge continues, "the traditional view of leadership is based on assumptions of people's powerlessness, their lack of personal vision and inability to master the forces of change, deficits which can be remedied only by a few great leaders." These assumptions don't hold for a generative social-impact network. The members, whether they are individuals or organizations, have the power and provide the network's vision and purpose. The network is a way for members to collectively adapt to change, not fall victim to it.

A network's essential decentralized collectivity should be reflected in the very language used to discuss it. To avoid falling into the trap of traditional views of leadership when discussing network builders, we usually avoid using the word *leader*. But it's not easy to find an alternative. A thesaurus offers many options: *head, manager, organizer, principal, chief, boss, director, guide, mentor, guru, superior, frontrunner, trailblazer, supervisor, kingpin, person in charge,* and *top dog.* But all are unsatisfactory. Sometimes we use *steward*—someone who carefully and responsibly manages something that has been entrusted to his or her care. To some, though, that sounds too passive, too much like a caretaker. We've heard some network builders describe the role as "servant leadership," a phrase coined by Robert Greenleaf in 1970. He wrote that "the servant-leader" takes care "to make sure that other people's highest priority needs are being served."

A network servant leader or steward looks after the network's collective interest, whatever his or her self-interest may be. This isn't always easy for organization leaders to do; as Beth Kanter and Allison Fine note: "The first and perhaps hardest step is for organizational leaders to overcome their fear of losing control." Carrie Pickett-Erway, president of the Kalamazoo Community Foundation, experienced that challenge while helping to build the Kalamazoo learning network. "You have leaders in the community who have lived their whole lives in hierarchical organizational roles who have trouble seeing that this is different." She puts herself in that category: "I've become more aware of how my reactions—disappointments and frustrations—might be coming from an old organization-centric mental model. In the community foundation, I have control. In the network, I have to depend on others to engage in the work. I've been getting better at setting more realistic expectations." (See Appendix E for one astute list of network leadership attributes.)

How much about being successful as a network builder depends on one's personality, not just skills, knowledge, and experience? When USDN searched in October 2013 for a new managing director to replace Julia Parzen, a committee of five members deliberated on the skills and experiences they wanted in an ideal network coordinator. But they also considered what the ideal personality of a network builder might be, and turned to Spencer Stang, an industrial psychologist, for assistance in screening that aspect of candidates for the job. Stang provided a set of five general personality traits—Extroversion, Agreeableness, Conscientiousness, Neuroticism, and Openness to Experience—with 29 facets or sub-traits, which can be used as predictors of a candidate's job performance. (See Appendix F for a full list and description of these facets.) The committee set up a scoring range for what it was looking for in each facet. (Candidates were assessed using their answers to more than 100 multiple-choice questions.)

When Stang compared the committee's scoring of traits for a network coordinator with those of organizations searching for high-level business positions, he noted two big contrasts with what the USDN network builders were looking for. "The most extreme difference was in the modesty score," Stang reports. Modesty is a facet of Agreeableness, defined this way: people with high scores on this scale do not like to claim that they are better than other people. "Searches for business managers weren't concerned about modesty at all, it's a nonfactor," Stang continues. "There are pros and cons to modesty. If someone is overly modest, they could come across as not competent. It's not necessarily better at the other end of the scale, if they are always trying to take credit. But for a network coordinator, modesty is seen as essential. This person has to be comfortable being behind the scenes; they're not out on the podium directing everyone. They're connecting the dots, and they don't always get credit for that."

The second big difference in an ideal personality was in the general trait of Openness to Experience, whose facets include Emotionality and Adventurousness. Typically, Stang says, this trait is not a strong predictor of job performance. "But a network coordinator has to be open to all different kinds of ideas. They're not running a Subway franchise where it's very clear how to be successful. They have to work with all these different personalities and be open to many paths to success, and those paths can change. They don't have a map in front of them."

For the USDN members searching specifically for a new network coordinator, Modesty and Openness to Experience were must-have aspects of the temperament they wanted in someone serving the network.

Three Rules to Live By

---

1. Trust the network.
2. Serve the network, but don't wait for it.
3. Embrace vertigo.

A network builder must be a jack-of-all-trades: founder, designer, weaver, coordinator, planner, maybe a funder, and more. Pulling all of this off requires the skills and knowledge about network building that we've covered in preceding chapters, as well as certain personality characteristics. But there's something else that matters: a way of being that's a combination of personality, understanding, and skill—a network-centric point of view that network builders hold personally and apply consistently. It's their default position, where they turn when knowledge and skill are insufficient. From our many discussions with network builders and observations of networks, we've pinpointed three rules for network builders.

1. *Trust the network.* As a network builder, says Armstrong, "You have to be willing to accept the network's direction, although it may not always seem wise." This is why modesty is a defining personality trait for network builders: they put the needs of others ahead of their own needs. Unlike leaders in most organizations, your role as a network builder is not to get everyone to do what *you* think is right. It's to help them to connect, align, and produce—to do what *they* think is right.

   Even a network builder with more than modest ego needs can be effective in a network, says Parzen—"as long as they trust the network." Trusting a network starts with understanding what a network is and why and how it works. For most network builders that's a learning process. For instance, the Fire Learning Network's Lynn Decker recalls her earliest conversations with outside network evaluators who studied the network: "I learned an incredible amount. . . . It gave me access to their insights on network theory and collaboration science, and I'd take those insights and immediately make small adjustments to improve the network's functions and outcomes." But trusting a network also requires unwavering belief in the network way of working. As Armstrong puts it, you have to believe that "the durable value of the collective process over an individual outcome is paramount."

   When you trust the network and show it by enabling members without determining their direction, the network will trust you too. And that reciprocity between builder and network sets up the second rule of network building.

2. *Serve the network, but don't wait for it.* The work of network building, says Bill Traynor, is "to 'stay close to the demand' and 'resource the opportunity.'" You listen to and see what's happening in the network, and respond in ways that enable members. But the network servant also has a little more to do: anticipate and suggest. "You have two roles," says Parzen, "facilitating network processes and also bringing new ideas into it. If you're only bringing new ideas, you won't be able to empower others. But if you're not bringing any new ideas in, then you could end

up going a little slow."

One source of network builders' new ideas is their understanding of how the network has been evolving and what its management challenges and potential are. "Somebody has to have a big-picture view, while most people are too busy and grounded in what they want to accomplish immediately," Parzen notes. The network members' willingness to consider your ideas depends on their trust that you're trying to enable them, not steer them. The way to maintain that trust is to be ready to let your ideas fail. "You are feeding in ideas that people haven't had yet," Parzen says, "but you also have to be willing to have them drop."

Even when a builder's idea is embraced by the network, it's important to test its value with experiments, not just leap to large-scale implementation. That way, Traynor notes, you "learn by doing" just how much members care about the experiment and what effects it might have. You just might learn that it's not a very good idea and that whatever member support existed has evaporated. A network, Traynor explains, is an environment that can "starve bad ideas and things that don't have genuine value."

3. *Embrace vertigo.* Network builders search constantly for a network's balance points, as we detailed in chapter 5. Their mantra could be "not too much order or chaos, not too much continuity or change." But endlessly rebalancing means being off-balance some of the time. "Our job is to know when to change," says Pickett-Erway, reflecting on the experience of changing the Kalamazoo Learning Network's governance twice in just a few years. It can be dizzying work, made even more so by its unfamiliarity. "Moving from a traditional environment to a network or connected environment can cause a kind of vertigo because the environment is so radically different," says Traynor. "It operates by different rules and responds to different stimuli."

You have to be comfortable with uncertainty, offers June Holley. You have to be comfortable letting go. You have to remember what you've learned about being in a network. You have to deal with criticism that you're taking too much control or that

you're not taking enough control. It's a deeply personal challenge. Traynor says that he makes mistakes as a network builder
when he lacks "the emotional energy to be truly engaged," or
forgets what he's learned, or fears "the imperative" of letting go.
"In those moments I pull in, try to prod, feel like a victim, and
let my ego rule the day."

It's personal, but you can't depend on just yourself to keep
your balance. Sometimes you need others to help. "I am lucky
in those moments that I am a part of a team of people here and
with colleagues around the country," Traynor says. "Increasingly we are struggling together and intentional about supporting each other—through both forgiveness and truth telling—so
that we can continue to build 'connected environments' that
feed the world by feeding the best of what it is to be human."
To cope with the vertigo, network builders need their own networks of support.

Walking the Talk

We said at the beginning of this book that building social-impact networks
is a practice, that there is much more to it than just connecting with others. And we said that the practice can be mastered by learning what makes
networks tick and noticing what has worked in other networks—their
design options, developmental paths, and management approaches.

It can be a somewhat lonesome practice. Most network builders don't
get to be recognized as stars. Their success depends on what others do.
They work behind the scenes and in a crowd, focused on enabling the
members. Out of sight, they anticipate what it will take to keep the network going. In response to changing conditions, they help the network
to make adjustments in order to keep its balance and momentum. Doing
this well requires knowledge and skills and, as noted earlier, even certain personality traits. It also takes a strong dose of curiosity, like Michael
Armstrong had.

All of this also requires a great deal of self-discipline and grit. Network
builders don't succeed overnight, so they have to be persistent. They don't
get to follow a wide, smooth path; it's more like walking a moving tight-
rope and trying to maintain balance.

One of the most mind-blowing balancing acts ever performed occurred in 1974 when a 24-year-old Frenchman, Philippe Petit, walked on a 200-foot long, ¾-inch wide steel cable stretched between the twin towers of the World Trade Center, a quarter-mile above the streets of Manhattan. Holding a 26-foot-long, 55-pound homemade balancing pole, he crossed the gap eight times and sat on the wire. One of the police officers sent to stop him described Petit's reaction to their arrival: "He started to smile and laugh and he started going into a dancing routine on the high wire. . . . He was bouncing up and down. His feet were actually leaving the wire and then he would resettle back on the wire again."

It was an unbelievable act of daring, but it was also a performance built on a disciplined practice of skill and knowledge. Petit had walked on wires since the age of 16 and had walked between the towers of Notre-Dame Cathedral in Paris and between pylons of the Sydney Harbour Bridge in Australia. He had planned the World Trade Center crossing for six years, studying the buildings, especially to gauge the swaying of the towers, and sneaking into the site several times. He interviewed workers on the roof and made a scale model of the towers.

It looked like a solo act, but it wasn't at all. Petit had a team of supporters and funders.

It was an act of physical courage, but it was also the result of a deeply personal point of view. Petit told a reporter that when he'd been training himself in magic, juggling, and tricks on the wire, "I thought, 'What is the big deal here? It looks almost ugly.' So I started to discard those tricks and to reinvent my art." Instead of working in circuses, he wanted to achieve artistic coups. Asked later why he'd done the Twin Towers stunt, Petit said, "When I see three oranges, I juggle; when I see two towers, I walk."

Something similar goes on with the network builders we know. When they see a complex social problem to solve, they build a generative social-impact network. Theirs is a constant balancing act on a slender, springy wire amidst swirling winds. They run, turn, bounce, resettle; they laugh, they cry. Their daring and mastery may not be as visible and celebrated as Petit's, but it too is a disciplined practice. Clutching a balancing pole of what they know, know how to do, and believe deeply, they step out onto the wire . . . and walk.

Afterword

Educating a person is collaborating with the forces of creation, and he who instructs another undertakes anew the creation of the world.

— Gabi Gleichmann

While we wrote this book we kept learning new things from network builders, and tried to update the manuscript as best we could. Talk about continuously improving! But ultimately a book is a time-limited snapshot; at some point you have to stop writing.

We hope you've enjoyed this guided tour of the practice of building generative networks to achieve social impact at scale, as we have learned it from diverse experiences in the field, extensive reflection, and the work and writing of others. We've tried to carefully differentiate this practice from other valuable ways to work on social good. We wanted to avoid turning the practice into an ideology or a brand that might overshadow or negate those other approaches. It is well suited to address complex, changing challenges, but it's not a panacea for every social problem. If it's the right tool for you, then perhaps our insights and advice will help you to increase your effectiveness.

We see network building as fundamentally a matter of design and management that should be informed by an understanding of the unique nature of networks. To illustrate this in depth, we've drawn on cases of network building, nearly all of them ongoing and, therefore, incomplete. These networks are in motion; they may be evolving nicely and may have achieved impressive trajectories, but their next years are filled with both the potential that attracts and the uncertainties that afflict network builders.

Hopefully, you will have found that our framework for understanding networks is something you can build on, amplify, and deepen. We can imagine that practitioners of generative social-impact network building have much to share with each other about their practice in the social-impact network field: their definitions of the field's boundaries and variations; their frameworks for organizing practical knowledge, portfolios of well-defined, tested practices that form the "state of the art," and growing inventories of cases examined in depth; their agendas for developing and spreading practice innovations.

We hope this book contributes to the development of this promising, emerging field.

Acknowledgments

I n a network's gift economy, gratitude is currency—and we have plenty of it to offer to the many friends, colleagues, and clients who helped in the creation of this book. Your work, thoughtfulness, responsiveness, and attention shaped the stories, ideas, and even the language we've used. Your enthusiasm for the project helped to propel it. For these gifts we are grateful.

We have learned from many networks, network-building organizations, and funders, and it's only right to name them here: Appalachian Center for Economic Networks, Advanced Energy Economy, Barr Foundation, Boston Green Ribbon Commission, Boston University–School of Public Health, C40 Global Cities, Cascadia Network, Central Appalachia Regional Network, Continuous Quality Innovation Network, Family Independence Initiative, Fire Learning Network, Greater Detroit Network of Social Innovators, Great Plains Rural Policy Network, Green Cities California, Green Justice Coalition, Heartland Local Government Sustainability Network, Instituto de Cidadania Empresaria (Brazil), Jim Joseph Foundation, W. K. Kellogg Foundation–Rural People, Rural Policy Initiative, Lawrence CommunityWorks, Learning Network of Greater Kalamazoo, Maine Community Heritage Network, Maine Philanthropy Network, Massachusetts Interagency Council on Housing and Homelessness, Massachusetts Smart Growth Alliance, Michigan Green Communities, Michigan Rural Network, Mid-South Network, National Alliance for Rural Policy, Network of Korean American Leaders, Networks United for Rural Voice, New England Municipal Sustainability Network, Northern Forest Center, O-K-I Network, Partnership Fund for New York, Physicians for Human Rights, RE-AMP, Reboot, Southeast Sustainability

Directors Network, Southwest Rural Policy Network, Summit Foundation, The Funders' Network for Smart Growth and Livable Communities, Tulsa CAP, Urban Sustainability Directors Network, Western Adaptation Alliance, West Michigan Manufacturers Council, West Michigan WIRED Innovators Network, West Virginia Community Development Hub.

We thank Patti Anklam for producing the network connectivity shapes used in chapter 4. We also thank the readers of various sections of early manuscript drafts whose critiques reshaped parts of the book to the benefit of future readers: Laura Bartsch, Jennie Curtis, Richard McCarthy, Julia Parzen, Suprotik Stotz-Ghosh, and Susan Wintroub. David Plastrik provided close editing of the manuscript that revealed subtle problems and boosted confidence in the narrative's quality. Deb Plastrik, proofreader extraordinaire, provided a last cleansing read. At Island Press, Chuck Savitt and David Miller made this book possible; they wanted and believed in the product. Miller, as editor, provided important, high-touch guidance, and the Island Press team polished the product and took it to market.

Thank you, thank you, thank you.

Notes

All quotations that are not attributed in the text or in these endnotes are from interviews with the authors or from presentations attended by the authors.

Epigraph

1. Stephen Colbert quotation: Stephen Colbert for President 2008, accessed December 1, 2013, http://stephen-colbert-2008.blogspot.com/2007/10/101-greatest-stephen -colbert-quotes.html.
2. Kevin Kelly quotation: Kevin Kelly, *New Rules for the New Economy: 10 Radical Strategies for a Connected World* (New York: Viking Penguin, 1998), 9.

Introduction

1. Barabasi quotation: Albert-László Barabasi, *Linked: The New Science of Networks* (Cambridge, MA: Perseus Publishing, 2002), 7.
2. "By 2008 the U.S. alone . . . nonprofits": Beth Kanter and Allison H. Fine, *The Networked Nonprofit: Connecting with Social Media to Drive Change* (San Francisco: Jossey-Bass, 2010), 11. Between 1978 and 2008, the number of private foundations grew more than 60 percent to 115,000.
3. "In 1997 *Fast Company*'s cover story . . .": Daniel H. Pink, "Free Agent Nation," *Fast Company*, December 1997/January 1998, www.fastcompany.com/33851/free-agent -nation.
4. Lipnack and Stamps quotation: Jessica Lipnack and Jeffrey Stamps, *The Age of the Network: Organizing Principles for the 21st Century* (New York: Wiley & Sons, 1994), xvii.
5. Kelly quotation: Kevin Kelly, *New Rules for the New Economy: 10 Radical Strategies for a Connected World* (New York: Viking, 1998), 9.
6. Dean campaign, see: Gary Wolf, "How the Internet Invented Howard Dean," *Wired*, January 2004, www.wired.com/wired/archive/12.01/dean.html.
7. Trippi blog: Cited in Morley Winograd and Michael D. Hais, *Millennial Makeover: MySpace, YouTube, and the Future of American Politics* (New Brunswick, NJ: Rutgers University Press, 2008), 157.
8. Friedman quotation: Thomas L. Friedman, *The World Is Flat: A Brief History of the Twenty-First Century* (New York: Farrar, Straus and Giroux, 2005), 8.
9. Watts quotation: Duncan Watts, *Six Degrees: The Science of a Connected Age* (New York: W. W. Norton & Company, 2003), 13.
10. Winograd and Hais quotation: Winograd and Hais, *Millennial Makeover*, 83.

11. Kanter and Fine quotation: Kanter and Fine, *The Networked Nonprofit*, 15.

12. Kasper and Scearce quotation: Gabriel Kasper and Diana Scearce, "Working Wikily: How Networks Are Changing Social Change" (Monitor Institute and the David and Lucille Packard Foundation, 2013), www.workingwikily.net/Working_Wikily.pdf.

13. Friedman quotation: Thomas L. Friedman, "It's a 401(k) World," NYTimes.com, April 30, 2013, www.nytimes.com/2013/05/01/opinion/friedman-its-a-401k-world .html?_r=0.

14. Benckler quotation: Yochai Benkler, *The Wealth of Networks: How Social Production Transforms Markets and Freedom* (New Haven, CT: Yale University Press, 2006), 5.

15. Noveck quotation: Beth Noveck, "Demand a More Open-Source Government," TED talk, posted September 2012 (TEDGlobal, 2012), www.ted.com/talks/beth_noveck _demand_a_more_open_source_government.html?quote=1870.

16. "When we first wrote about networks . . .": Peter Plastrik and Madeleine Taylor, "Network Power for Philanthropy and Nonprofits," Barr Foundation, April 2004, www.barr foundation.org.

17. Kania and Kramer quotation: John Kania and Mark Kramer, "Collective Impact," *Stanford Social Innovation Review* (Winter 2011): 38–39, www.ssireview.org/articles/entry/ collective_impact/.

18. Bornstein quotation: David Bornstein, *How to Change the World: Social Entrepreneurs and the Power of New Ideas* (New York: Oxford University Press, 2004), 7.

19. *Civic Revolutionaries* quotation: Douglas Henton, John Melville, and Kim Walesh, *Civic Revolutionaries: Igniting the Passion for Change in America's Communities* (San Francisco: Wiley & Sons, 2004), 55–56, 57.

20. Gladwell quotation: Malcolm Gladwell, *The Tipping Point: How Little Things Can Make a Big Difference* (Boston: Little, Brown and Company, 2000), 38.

Chapter 1

1. Wei-Skillern, Silver, and Heitz quotation: Jane Wei-Skillern, Nora Silver, and Eric Heitz, "Cracking the Network Code: Four Principles for Grantmakers" (Grantmakers for Effective Organizations, 2013), 24, www.geofunders.org.

2. "Membership grew to 19 local manufacturing . . . needed for world-class manufacturing": John Cleveland, "West Michigan Manufacturers Council: A Case Study of Inter-Firm Collaboration" (Regional Technology Services, 1995). Cleveland is a coauthor of this book.

3. Manufacturing Council quotation: "remains committed . . . collaboration": Right Place, www.rightplace.org/For-Local-Business/Industry-Councils/Manufacturers-Council.aspx, accessed January 11, 2014.

4. "Keller's company . . . Europe": "History of Cascade Engineering," Cascade Engineering, www.cascadeng.com/history, accessed December 1, 2013.

5. "The number of large wildfires . . . decade": Bruce Evan Goldstein and William Hale Butler, "The Network Imaginary: Coherence and Creativity within a Multiscalar Collaborative Effort to Reform US Fire Management," *Journal of Environmental Planning and Management* 52, no. 8, December 2009, 1013–33.

6. Butler and Goldstein quotation: William Hale Butler and Bruce Evan Goldstein, "The US Fire Learning Network: Springing the Rigidity Trap through Multiscalar Collaborative Networks," *Ecology and Society* 15 (3), no. 21 (2010), www.ecologyandsociety .org/vol15/iss3/art21.

7. "Facilitated by a consultant": Coauthor Plastrik served as the consultant and helped to develop the proposal to the W. K. Kellogg Foundation.

8. Garfield Foundation investment in RE-AMP: E-mail from Jennie Curtis, December 7, 2013.

9. "A set of seven . . . RE-AMP member projects": E-mail from Rick Reed, January 10, 2014.

10. "The Nature Conservancy and its . . . policies": Butler and Goldstein, "The US Fire Learning Network."

11. Quotations from 2010 assessment of U.S. Fire Learning Network: Ibid.

12. "50 million humans . . .": "World Population Growth History," Vaughn Aubuchon, www.vaughns-1-pagers.com/history/world-population-growth.htm#population -growth-chart, accessed December 1, 2013.

13. Aristotle quotation: Goodreads, "Aristotle Quotes," www.goodreads.com/ quotes/183896-man-is-by-nature-a-social-animal-an-individual-who, accessed December 1, 2013.

14. "Raising a child . . . a complex problem": Frances Westley, Brenda Zimmerman, and Michael Quinn Patton, *Getting to Maybe: How the World Is Changed* (Toronto: Vintage Canada, 2006), 9.

15. "Complex social problems . . . understanding the problem": "Wicked Problem," www. wikipedia.org/wiki/Wicked_problem, accessed January 10, 2014.

16. "As Adam Kahane . . . unfamiliar ways": Adam Kahane, *Solving Tough Problems: An Open Way of Talking, Listening, and Creating New Realities* (San Francisco: Berrett-Koehler, 2004), 1–2. Other authors have contributed to our understanding of generative social problems. The problems defy predetermined solutions because, as John Kania and Mark Kramer, leaders of FSG, a nonprofit consulting firm, describe in a 2013 article in the *Stanford Social Innovation Review*, they present "conditions of complexity—conditions that apply in most major social problems—when the unpredictable interactions of multiple players determine the outcomes." In an earlier article, "Leading Boldly," *Stanford Social Innovation Review* (Winter 2004), coauthored with Ronald Heifitz (www. ssireview.org/articles/entry/leading_boldly), they defined as "adaptive problems" what we are calling *generative problems*: "Adaptive problems are entirely different. They are not so well defined, the answers are not known in advance, and many different stakeholders are involved, each with their own perspectives. Adaptive problems require innovation and learning among the interested parties and, even when a solution is discovered, no single entity has the authority to impose it on the others." And Stephen Goldsmith, a leading government innovator, notes (in: Stephen Goldsmith with Gigi Georges and Tim Glynn Burke, *The Power of Social Innovation: How Civic Entrepreneurs Ignite Community Networks for Good* [San Francisco: Wiley & Sons, 2010], 8) that the complexity of generative problems can't be addressed successfully by dictates from on high. "We cannot solve complex horizontal problems [across sectors and institutions] with vertical command-and-control solutions."

17. "Some are well defined . . .": John Kania and Mark Kramer, "Collective Impact," *Stanford Social Innovation Review* (Stanford University, Winter 2011), 39, www.ssireview.org /articles/entry/collective_impact/.

18. "Other problems may require . . .": In addition to the examples shown here, it should be clear that you don't need a generative network to do tasks that absolutely require someone to be in charge and enforce the rules and procedures. "You use command-and-control to keep order in your organization, to make it efficient, and to function from day to day," note Ori Brafman and Rod Beckstrom, authors of *The Starfish and the Spider*, a best-selling shout-out to decentralized organizing. "When you get on an airplane, you had better hope it's a coercive system. You certainly don't want Johnson

from seat 28J to decide that right about now is a good time to land." (Ori Brafman and Rod A. Beckstrom, *The Starfish and the Spider: The Unstoppable Power of Leaderless Organizations* [New York: Penguin Group, 2006], 19).

19. Zuckerberg quotation: Randi Zuckerberg, foreword to *The Networked Nonprofit: Connecting with Social Media to Drive Change* by Beth Kanter and Allison H. Fine (San Francisco: Jossey-Bass, 2010), viii.

20. "In November 2013, comedian . . .": Stephen Colbert, www.colbertnation.com/the-colbert-report-videos/430605/november-18-2013/philippines-relief-from-the-colbert-nation, accessed December 1, 2013.

21. Holley quotation: June Holley, *Network Weaver Handbook: A Guide to Transformational Networks* (Athens, OH: Network Weaver Publishing, 2012), 53.

22. "They cite . . . and schools": Kania and Kramer, "Collective Impact."

23. Coauthor Plastrik has written previously about the New York City Investment Fund network. See case studies in Resources section.

24. Brafman and Beckstrom quotation: Brafman and Beckstrom, *The Starfish and the Spider*, 202.

25. Fire Learning Network evaluators' quotation: Butler and Goldstein, "The US Fire Learning Network."

26. Kanter and Fine quotation: Kanter and Fine, *The Networked Nonprofit*, 107.

27. NetKAL quotation ("to create . . ."): University of Southern California, Center for Asian Pacific Leadership, "About NetKAL," one-page description, 2011.

28. Garfield Foundation Letters of Inquiry quotation: Letters of Inquiry solicitation obtained by the authors.

29. 2011 evaluation of Massachusetts homelessness program quotation: Massachusetts Interagency Council on Housing and Homelessness, "Regional Networks to End Homelessness—Pilot Project: Final Evaluation Report," February 15, 2011, 8, http://www.ppffound.org/documents/ichh_final_report.pdf.

30. Kelly quotation: Kevin Kelly, *New Rules for the New Economy: 10 Radical Strategies for a Connected World* (New York: Viking, 1998), 60.

Chapter 2

1. *I-Ching* quotation: Interpreted by Wu Wei, *The I-Ching: The Book of Answers* (Los Angeles: Power Press, 2005), 87.

2. "This called for building . . . robust growth": We wrote about the early days of Lawrence CommunityWorks in: Peter Plastrik and Madeleine Taylor, "Lawrence CommunityWorks: Using the Power of Networks to Restore a City" (Barr Foundation, 2004), www.barrfoundation.org.

3. Lawrence CommunityWorks quotation: Lawrence CommunityWorks, www.lawrencecommunityworks.org/about, accessed January 19, 2014.

4. USDN mission statement: Urban Sustainability Directors Network, "Welcome Package & Overview of USDN" (undated), 3, obtained from Julia Parzen.

5. "RE-AMP declares that . . .": RE-AMP, www.reamp.org/, accessed December 1, 2013.

6. "For instance, the many organizations in the Cincinnati, Ohio . . .": John Kania and Mark Kramer, "Collective Impact," *Stanford Social Innovation Review* (Winter 2011): 38–39, www.ssireview.org/articles/entry/collective_impact/.

7. Kania and Kramer quotation: Ibid., 40.

8. "Heather Creech . . . good network citizen": Heather Creech, "Form Follows Function: Management and Governance of Knowledge Networks," International Institute for Sustainable Development (2006), 4–6.

9. Creech quotation: Ibid., 7.

10. "When researcher Bonnie Shepard . . .": Bonnie L. Shepard, "NGO Advocacy Networks in Latin America: Lessons from Experience in Promoting Women's and Reproductive Rights," North-South Agenda Paper No. 61, Dante B. Fascell North-South Center at the University of Miami, 2003, 14–15.

11. Creech quotation: Creech, "Form Follows Function," 14.

12. "The Fire Learning Network . . . set of practices": Bruce Evan Goldstein and William Hale Butler, "Collaborating for Transformative Resilience: Shared Identity in the U.S. Fire Learning Network," in *Collaborative Resilience: Moving Through Crisis to Opportunity*, ed. Bruce Evan Goldstein (Boston: MIT Press, 2011), 340, http://conservation-learningnetworks.weebly.com/uploads/3/2/1/8/3218918/collaborating_for_transformative_resilience.pdf.

13. Patrick Chung quotations: University of Southern California School of Social Work, "USC NetKAL: Network of Korean American Leaders," undated brochure obtained by authors.

14. "RE-AMP, for instance, described . . .": RE-AMP, "Position Announcement: Re-Amp Network Chief Executive Officer, Search Launched January 30, 2013," RE-AMP document obtained by the authors.

15. Creech quotation: Creech, "Form Follows Function," 17.

16. Kearns quotation: Marty Kearns, "Network-Centric Advocacy," Green Media Toolshed, www.greenmediatoolshed.org, accessed December 1, 2013.

17. Taschereau and Bolger quotation: Suzanne Taschereau and Joe Bolger, "Networks and Capacity: A Theme Paper Prepared for the Study 'Capacity, Change and Performance,'" European Centre for Development Policy Management, September 2006, 14, http://lencd.com/data/docs/119-Networks%20and%20capacity.pdf.

18. Bridgespan quotation: Michele Jolin, Paul Schmitz, and Willa Seldon, "Needle-Moving Community Collaboratives: A Promising Approach to Addressing America's Biggest Challenges," Bridgespan Group, 2012, 11, www.bridgespan.org/Publications-and-Tools/Revitalizing-Communities/Community-Collaboratives/Needle-Moving-Community-Collaborative-s-A-Promisin.aspx#.Urbzbs-A02E.

19. Creech quotation: Creech, "Form Follows Function," 23.

20. Massachusetts Smart Growth Alliance: The seven organizations in the alliance initially were: the Boston Society of Architects, Citizens' Housing and Planning Association, the Conservation Law Foundation, the Environmental League of Massachusetts, the Fair Housing Center of Greater Boston, Massachusetts Association of Community Development Corporations, and the Metropolitan Area Planning Council.

21. "The Alliance found . . . a self-assessment by the network": Mary Wissemann and Kristina Egan, "Building a Multi-Interest Movement for Smart Growth: The Massachusetts Smart Growth Alliance Story of What Works and How We're Facing Our Challenges," report, May 2006, 5.

22. "A Bridgespan Group study . . . governance structure": Jolin, Schmitz, and Seldon, "Needle-Moving Community Collaboratives," 8.

23. "The Massachusetts Smart Growth Alliance decided . . . begin to erode": Wissemann and Egan, "Building a Multi-Interest Movement," 11.

24. Holley quotation ("Make your motto . . ."): June Holley, *Network Weaver Handbook: A Guide to Transformational Networks* (Athens, OH: Network Weaver Publishing, 2012), 34.

25. Holley quotation ("When we share . . ."): Ibid., 123.

26. Traynor and Andors quotation: William J. Traynor and Jessica Andors, "Network

Organizing," *ShelterForce*, March/April 2005, 11,www.nhi.org/online/issues/140/LCW.html.

27. Kelly quotation: Kelly, *New Rules for the New Economy*, 18.

28. Brafman and Beckstrom quotation: Ori Brafman and Rod A. Beckstrom, *The Starfish and the Spider: The Unstoppable Power of Leaderless Organizations* (New York: Penguin Group, 2006), 189.

Bonus Track

1. "Funders succeed . . . operations for themselves": Jane Wei-Skillern, Nora Silver, and Eric Heitz, "Cracking the Network Code: Four Principles for Grantmakers" (Grantmakers for Effective Organizations, 2013), 16, www.geofunders.org.

2. "Funder-driven relationships . . . for funding": Ibid., 13.

3. Lois Savage quotation: Grantmakers for Effective Organizations, "Working Better Together: Building Nonprofit Collaborative Capacity," 19, http://geofunders.org/geo-publications/704-working-better-together.

4. Creech quotation: Heather Creech, "Form Follows Function: Management and Governance of Knowledge Networks," International Institute for Sustainable Development (2006), 6.

Chapter 3

1. Gladwell quotation: Malcolm Gladwell, *The Tipping Point: How Little Things Can Make a Big Difference* (Boston: Little, Brown and Company, 2000), 54.

2. Holley quotation: June Holley, *Network Weaver Handbook: A Guide to Transformational Networks* (Athens, OH: Network Weaver Publishing, 2012), 21.

3. "During the next five years . . . every other member": Julia Parzen, "2013 State of the Network," presentation to the Urban Sustainability Directors Network, September 16, 2013.

4. Holley quotation ("Does the core . . ."): Holley, *Network Weaver Handbook*, 81.

5. Holley quotation ("skilled at discovering . . ."): Ibid., 100.

6. Traynor quotation: Bill Traynor, "Vertigo and the Intentional Inhabitant: Leadership in a Connected World," *Nonprofit Quarterly*, August 5, 2009, www.nonprofitquarterly.org/management/1454-vertigo-and-the-intentional-inhabitant-leadership-in-a-connected-world.html.

7. Shepard quotation: Bonnie Shepard, *Running the Obstacle Course to Sexual and Reproductive Health: Lessons from Latin America* (Westport, CT: Praeger, 2006), 60.

8. Stevenson quotation: Karen Stephenson, "Towards a Theory of Government," in *Network Logic*, ed. Helen McCarthy, Paul Miller, and Paul Skidmore (London: Demos, 2004), 40.

9. Kanter and Fine quotation: Beth Kanter and Allison H. Fine, *The Networked Nonprofit: Connecting with Social Media to Drive Change* (San Francisco: Jossey-Bass, 2010), 35.

10. Holley quotation ("Asking someone to help . . ."): Holley, *Network Weaver Handbook*, 101.

11. Holley quotation ("When people are . . ."): Ibid., 31.

12. Holley quotation ("Sometimes people just need . . ."): Ibid., 31.

13. Holley quotation ("Make sure every meeting . . ."): Ibid., 37.

Chapter 4

1. Covey quotation: Steven R. Covey, "The Community," www.stephencovey.com/7habits/7habits-habit2.php, accessed December 1, 2013.

2. "It had nine categories . . .": John Cleveland, "West Michigan Manufacturers Council: A Case Study of Inter-Firm Collaboration" (Regional Technology Services, 1995), 10.

3. Bridgespan Group quotation: Michele Jolin, Paul Schmitz, and Willa Seldon, "Needle-Moving Community Collaboratives: A Promising Approach to Addressing America's Biggest Challenges," Bridgespan Group, 2012, 11, www.bridgespan.org/Publications-and-Tools/Revitalizing-Communities/Community-Collaboratives/Needle-Moving -Community-Collaborative-s-A-Promisin.aspx#.Urbzbs-A02E.

4. USDN Innovation Fund: Authors John Cleveland and Peter Plastrik have served as managers of the USDN Innovation Fund.

5. Holley quotation: June Holley, *Network Weaver Handbook: A Guide to Transformational Networks* (Athens, OH: Network Weaver Publishing, 2012), 45.

6. "A sliding scale that progressed . . .": In addition to these three relationship descriptors, USDN's survey uses a fourth descriptor of a minimal relationship: "I have been introduced to this person but do not exchange info with them on a regular basis."

7. "In 2004, Valdis Krebs . . . southeastern Ohio": Valdis Krebs and June Holley, "Building Sustainable Communities Through Social Networks," *Nonprofit Quarterly*, Spring 2004, 46–53. In 1985, Holley started to build ACEnet, the Appalachian Center for Economic Networks, a network of food, wood, and technology entrepreneurs in 29 counties in southeastern Ohio. She had noticed that the region "was home to many small, uncoordinated food clusters"—sets of related small businesses. "There was the Farmer's Market crowd, the natural bakery, a worker-owned Mexican restaurant, and a few other entrepreneurs creating unique food products," Holley recalls (p. 49). To help these clusters link to each other, ACEnet designed a kitchen incubator—a state-of-the-art facility for preparing and packaging foods. For one design session, people from the town's restaurants came together with small farmers who wanted to turn their produce into value-added products. Farmers learned about food-production safety from the restaurateurs, who explained how these procedures could be incorporated into the incubator. Some of the farmers also used the opportunity to sell their produce to the restaurants. Gradually, the unconnected business clusters became linked to each other; a new structure of relationships emerged. This was the first change in the evolution in ACEnet's connectivity structure.

8. Creech and Willard quotation: Heather Creech and Terri Willard, "Strategic Intentions: Managing Knowledge Networks for Sustainable Development," International Institute for Sustainable Development (2001), 67–68, www.iisd.com/pdf/2001 /networks_strategic_intentions.pdf.

9. Krebs and Holley quotation: Krebs and Holley, "Building Sustainable Communities," 46–53.

10. Network researcher quotation: J. D. Lewis, *Partnerships for Profit: Structuring and Managing Strategic Alliances* (New York: MacMillan, 1990).

Chapter 5

1. Waldrop quotation: Mitchell Waldrop, *Complexity: The Emerging Science at the Edge of Order and Chaos* (New York: Simon and Schuster, 1993), 12.

2. "Heather Creech . . . concrete work": Heather Creech and Terri Willard, "Strategic Intentions: Managing Knowledge Networks for Sustainable Development," International Institute for Sustainable Development (2001), 88–89, www.iisd.com.

3. Creech and Willard quotation: Ibid., 58.

4. Waldrop quotation: Waldrop, *Complexity*, 12.

5. Bridgespan Group quotation: Michele Jolin, Paul Schmitz, and Willa Seldon,

"Needle-Moving Community Collaboratives: A Promising Approach to Addressing America's Biggest Challenges," Bridgespan Group, 2012, 8, www.bridgespan.org/Publications
-and-Tools/Revitalizing-Communities/Community-Collaboratives/Needle-Moving
-Community-Collaborative-s-A-Promisin.aspx#.Urbzbs-A02E.

6. "As the West Michigan Manufacturers Council . . .": John Cleveland, "West Michigan Manufacturers Council: A Case Study of Inter-Firm Collaboration" (Regional Technology Services, 1995), 21.

7. Holley quotation: June Holley, *Network Weaver Handbook: A Guide to Transformational Networks* (Athens, OH: Network Weaver Publishing, 2012), 175.

8. Kanter and Fine quotation: Beth Kanter and Allison H. Fine, *The Networked Nonprofit: Connecting with Social Media to Drive Change* (San Francisco: Jossey-Bass, 2010), 2.

9. Holley quotation: Holley, *Network Weaver Handbook*, 135.

10. "For instance, the Shape Up Somerville community collaborative . . . all participating members": FSG, "Collective Impact Case Study: Opportunity Chicago," www.fsg.org /tabid/191/ArticleId/980/Default.aspx?srpush=true, accessed December 1, 2013.

11. Traynor quotation: Bill Traynor, "Vertigo and the Intentional Inhabitant: Leadership in a Connected World," *Nonprofit Quarterly*, August 5, 2009, www.nonprofitquarterly.org /management/1454-vertigo-and-the-intentional-inhabitant-leadership-in-a-connected -world.html.

12. FSG case study quotation: FSG, "Collective Impact Case Study: Opportunity Chicago."

13. Kania and Kramer quotation: John Kania and Mark Kramer, "Embracing Emergence: How Collective Impact Addresses Complexity," *Stanford Social Innovation Review*, blog, January 21, 2013, www.ssireview.org/blog/entry/embracing_emergence_how _collective_impact_addresses_complexity.

14. Eisenhower quotation: See www.quotationspage.com/quotes/Dwight_D. _Eisenhower.

15. West Michigan Manufacturers Council study: Cleveland, "West Michigan Manufacturers Council," 22.

16. Kania and Kramer quotation ("solutions and resources . . . over time"): Kania and Kramer, "Embracing Emergence."

17. Traynor quotation: Traynor, "Vertigo."

18. Kania and Kramer quotation ("openness to unanticipated . . ."): Kania and Kramer, "Embracing Emergence."

19. Holley quotation: Holley, *Network Weaver Handbook*, 45.

20. Bridgespan Group quotation: Jolin, Schmitz, and Seldon, "Needle-Moving Collaboratives," 7.

21. Shepard quotation ("Part of . . . credit for it"): Bonnie L. Shepard, "NGO Advocacy Networks in Latin America: Lessons from Experience in Promoting Women's and Reproductive Rights," North-South Agenda Paper No. 61, Dante B. Fascell North-South Center at the University of Miami, 2003, 73.

22. Shepard quotation ("This exclusion set off . . . network"): Ibid., 74.

23. Taylor quotation: FSG, "Collective Impact Case Study: Opportunity Chicago."

24. Bridgespan Group quotation: Jolin, Schmitz, and Seldon, "Needle-Moving Collaboratives," 12–13.

25. MomsRising purpose quotation: MomsRising.org, www.momsrising.org/page/moms /aboutmomsrising, accessed December 1, 2013.

26. Kanter and Fine quotation: Kanter and Fine, *The Networked Nonprofit*, 89.

27. Holley quotation: Holley, *Network Weaver Handbook*, 266.

28. Report about Vibrant Communities quotation: "Collective Impact Case Study: Vibrant Communities," www.fsg.org/tabid/191/ArticleId/979/Default.aspx?srpush=true, accessed December 1, 2013.

Chapter 6

1. Imai quotation: Wikipedia, Masaaki Imai, http://en.wikipedia.org/wiki/Masaaki_Imai, accessed April 24, 2014.
2. "She wanted to understand . . . increase impact": "Network Evaluation Summary Report" (Reboot and Jim Joseph Foundation, 2012), a summary of the Reboot 2012 evaluation, conducted by Madeleine Taylor and Peter Plastrik, and published online by the Jim Joseph Foundation, http://jimjosephfoundation.org/evaluations/reboot-inc-network-evaluation-summary-report/.
3. Decker quotation: "The Fire Learning Network Goes Under the Microscope," *Science Chronicles*, February 2011, 23.
4. "As a 2012 report . . .": Heather Creech, Michelle Laurie, Leslie Paas, and J-Ellen Parry, "Performance Improvement and Assessment of Collaboration: Starting Points for Networks and Communities of Practice" (International Institute for Sustainable Development, August 2012), 3, www.iisd.org.
5. "The Reboot maps revealed . . .": "Network Evaluation Summary Report," 15.
6. "Consultant Stephanie Lowell . . . steps (from 6.0 steps)": Stephanie Lowell, "Building the Field of Dreams: Social Networks as a Source of Sector-Level Capacity in the After-School World," Barr Foundation, 2006, www.barrfoundation.org/news/building-the-field-of-dreams/.
7. NetKAL mapping exercise: Authors Plastrik and Taylor conducted the exercise.
8. "A map of nearly 500 . . . at the center": Barr Foundation, "Mapping the Arts and Culture OST Network: A Learning Session," report, June 12, 2006.
9. Burt and Ronchi research: Ronald S. Burt and Don Ronchi, "Teaching Executives to See Social Capital," *Social Science Research* 36 (2007), 1156–83, http://faculty.chicagobooth.edu/ronald.burt/research/files/TESSC.pdf.
10. "In Boston . . . weavers and hubs": Stephanie Lowell, "Building the Field of Dreams: Social Networks as a Source of Sector-Level Capacity in the After-School World," Barr Foundation, 2006, www.barrfoundation.org/news/building-the-field-of-dreams/.
11. "When we developed . . . the network's collective capacities": Network Health Scorecard, http://networkimpact.org/downloads/NH_Scorecard.pdf, accessed December 1, 2013.
12. "In USDN's 2013 survey . . . was a priority": Julia Parzen, "2013 State of the Network," presentation to the Urban Sustainability Directors Network, September 16, 2013.
13. "When we conducted . . .": Coauthors Cleveland and Taylor conducted this network evaluation, results of which are included in: Massachusetts Interagency Council on Housing and Homelessness, "Regional Networks to End Homelessness: Pilot Project; Final Evaluation Report," February 15, 2011, www.ppffound.org/documents/ichh_final_report.pdf.
14. "The evaluation survey asked . . . relate to": "Network Evaluation Summary Report." 11.
15. "At USDN, most members reported . . .": Parzen, "2013 State of the Network."
16. "In a 2011 evaluation . . . funding decisions": Heather McLeod Grant and Rick Reed, "Leadership in Networks: Lessons from the RE-AMP Network," presentation to Leadership Learning Community, December 6, 2011, www.slideshare.net/leadershipera/llc-webinar-presentation-slidesfinal-0.

17. "In 2013, according to the USDN annual report . . .": Parzen, "2013 State of the Network."
18. "Rebooters are leading . . . young Jews": "Network Evaluation Summary Report," 13.
19. "A September 2013 USDN report . . .": Peter Plastrik with Julia Parzen, "Toward a Sustainable City: The State of Innovation in Urban Sustainability," Urban Sustainability Directors Network, September 2013, 12–13.
20. ICHH evaluation quotations: Massachusetts Interagency Council on Housing and Homelessness, "Regional Networks to End Homelessness."
21. Holley quotation: June Holley, *Network Weaver Handbook: A Guide to Transformational Networks* (Athens, OH: Network Weaver Publishing, 2012), 37.

Chapter 7

1. Einstein quotation: Goodreads, "Einstein," www.goodreads.com/quotes, accessed April 24, 2014.
2. Kanter and Fine quotation: Beth Kanter and Allison H. Fine, *The Networked Nonprofit: Connecting with Social Media to Drive Change* (San Francisco: Jossey-Bass, 2010), 29.
3. Holley quotation: June Holley, *Network Weaver Handbook: A Guide to Transformational Networks* (Athens, OH: Network Weaver Publishing, 2012), 246.

Chapter 8

1. Lao Tzu quotation: Stephen Mitchell, trans., *Tao Te Ching* (New York: Harper & Row, 1988), 66.
2. Senge quotation: Peter Senge, *The Fifth Discipline: The Art and Practice of the Learning Organization* (New York: Doubleday, 1990), 340.
3. Greenleaf quotation: "Servant leadership," http://en.wikipedia.org/wiki/Servant_leadership, accessed December 1, 2013.
4. Kanter and Fine quotation: Beth Kanter and Allison H. Fine, *The Networked Nonprofit: Connecting with Social Media to Drive Change* (San Francisco: Jossey-Bass, 2010), 164.
5. Decker quotation: "The Fire Learning Network Goes Under the Microscope," *Science Chronicles*, February 2011, 24.
6. Traynor quotation ("starve bad ideas . . ."): Bill Traynor, "Vertigo and the Intentional Inhabitant: Leadership in a Connected World," *Nonprofit Quarterly*, August 5, 2009, www.nonprofitquarterly.org/management/1454-vertigo-and-the-intentional-inhabitant-leadership-in-a-connected-world.html.
7. Traynor quotation ("Moving from a traditional environment . . ."): Ibid.
8. Traynor quotation ("the emotional energy . . . rule the day"): Ibid.
9. Traynor quotation ("I am lucky . . . to be human"): Ibid.
10. Petit background and policeman quotation: "Philippe Petit," http://en.wikipedia.org/wiki/Philippe_Petit, accessed December 1, 2013. A 2008 documentary with footage of Petit's walk, *Man on Wire*, won an Academy Award for filmmaker James Marsh.

Afterword

1. Gleichmann quotation: Gabi Gleichmann, *The Elixir of Immortality* (New York: Other Press, 2012), 411. In the text, novelist Gleichmann attributes the quotation to Voltaire, but in an e-mail to the authors, January 16, 2014, he acknowledged it was fictional.

Resources for Network Builders

Google the word *network* and you end up with 1.7 billion results. Leading the list are various services for computer networks; *Network*, the 1976 movie about television networks; and things that call themselves networks: the Food Network, Cartoon Network, Dish Network, Big Data Storage Network, Earth Day Network, and more.

Among the possibilities, there's a robust literature about networks and network building—books, articles, studies, online manifestos, websites, and more. Much of this writing focuses on particular kinds of networks: nets of commercial innovators and businesses, NGO advocacy networks in Latin America and Africa, networks of environmental organizations, government agencies in collaboration. Below we identify a range of websites, books, articles, and case studies that we found quite useful in learning to understand network building.

Websites

http://monitorinstitute.com/. The Monitor Institute is the source of a handful of excellent reports about collaboration and network building, especially for funders, and for using social-media technology to support collaborative efforts. Under the heading "Aligned Action," Monitor offers articles about "aligning for action in new ways."

http://www.geofunders.org/. Grantmakers for Effective Organizations—a community of 400 grantmakers—increasingly considers networks and collaborations as a way to achieve greater impact. Although it's focused on grantmakers, much of the information in GEO reports is useful to any network builder.

http://www.pattianklam.com. Patti Anklam is a network consultant, blogger, and author of *Net Work: A Practical Guide to Creating and Sustaining*

Networks at Work and in the World (Oxford: Elsevier, 2007). Her website offers workshops and a four-part course on network analysis. We turn to Patti to map some of our clients' networks. Her review of network-mapping software and other tools appears at http://www.pattianklam.com/net-work-tools.

www.bethkanter.org/. Beth Kanter's blog focuses on how nonprofit organizations can leverage networks; it is a source of great information about using social media to build networks.

www.networkimpact.net. Led by the authors of this book—Madeleine Taylor, an anthropologist and network consultant in Boston, and Peter Plastrik and John Cleveland, of the Innovation Network for Communities—Network Impact accelerates and spreads the use of networks to achieve increased social impact. Working with a variety of real-world advocacy networks and policy-change networks; social-service production networks (e.g., homelessness prevention); regional networks of innovators; community networks for grassroots leadership development—while studying network theory and best practice, the principals offer online tools and consulting services for start-up and ongoing networks. The site contains the Network Health Scorecard (www.networkimpact.org/downloads/NH_Scorecard.pdf).

Books and Articles

Barabasi, Albert-László. *Linked: The New Science of Networks.* Cambridge, MA: Perseus Publishing, 2002.

> For the lay reader, a book-length, illuminating exploration of the science of networks by a participant in the research. Especially strong in its explanation of how networks do what they do.

Creech, Heather, and Aly Ramji. "Knowledge Networks: Guidelines for Assessment." International Institute for Sustainable Development, 2004. www.issd.org.

> This article contains guidelines for evaluating network effectiveness, structure, governance, efficiency, resources, sustainability, and life cycle. It distills Creech and Ramji's experience with knowledge networks and international NGOs, and includes some sample interview protocols for assessing network effectiveness and efficiency.

Creech, Heather, and Terri Willard. "Strategic Intentions: Managing Knowledge Networks for Sustainable Development." International Institute for Sustainable Development, 2001. www.iisd.com.

> A longer article that provides an enormously useful analysis of the many tasks in organizing networks—with clear frameworks and advice. It is somewhat limited because it is based exclusively on Creech and Willard's

experiences with knowledge creation and innovation networks, but is well worth the attention. They provide excellent chapters on network management and governance, forming and working within virtual teams, and network monitoring and evaluation.

Goldsmith, Stephen, and William D. Eggers. *Governing by Network: The New Shape of the Public Sector.* Washington, DC: Brookings Institution, 2004.

Goldsmith, a former mayor of Indianapolis, and Eggers use a network framework to examine collaborations and partnerships in government—and the breakdown of traditional public bureaucracies.

Granovetter, Mark. "The Strength of Weak Ties: A Network Theory Revisited." *Sociological Theory* 1 (1983): 201–33.

The original article in which Granovetter argued that "weak ties" are critical for innovation and development, because they provide people with access to information and resources beyond those available in their immediate circles.

Hagel III, John, and John Seeley Brown. "Creation Nets: Harnessing the Potential of Open Innovation," April 2006. www.edgeperspectives.com.

Hagel and Brown explore the far-flung "open innovation" networks emerging in the commercial sector, and identify a "distinctive set of management techniques" that the organizers of these networks use to ensure focus and value creation. This is a conceptual treatment, worthwhile because it focuses on challenges of managing a type of network—open innovation—that social-change agents should be thinking about.

Holley, June. *Network Weaver Handbook: A Guide to Transformational Networks.* Athens, OH: Network Weaver Publishing, 2012.

Holley uses her experiences in network building to fill a self-published workbook with many useful insights and exercises for network builders, especially about building connections among members. May be purchased at http://www.networkweaver.com/shop/.

Holley, June, and Valdis Krebs. "Building Smart Communities by Network Weaving." Orgnet LLC, 2002–2006. www.orgnet.com.

Basic network concepts are explained in this accessible introduction to mapping and analyzing inter-organizational and community networks. Research is based on work with the Appalachian Center for Economic Networks. Easy-to-interpret maps describing a typical network's evolution illustrate the advantages of "knowing your network" and "knitting your network."

Jolin, Michele, Paul Schmitz, and Willa Seldon, "Needle-Moving Community Collaboratives: A Promising Approach to Addressing America's Biggest Challenges." Bridgespan Group, 2012. http://www.bridgespan.org/Pub

lications-and-Tools/Revitalizing-Communities/Community-Collabor
atives/Needle-Moving-Community-Collaborative-s-A-Promisin.aspx#
.Urbzbs-A02E.

> The authors identify the success factors for a wide range of community-based collaborations among organizations that have had measurable social impact. Offers important insights into the development of local collaborations.

Kelly, Kevin. *New Rules for the New Economy: 10 Radical Strategies for a Connected World*. New York: Viking, 1998.

> By the cofounder and former editor of *WIRED* magazine, this classic, thought-provoking primer explains network rules and principles that underlie the networked economy.

Miller, Jed, and Rob Stuart. "Network-Centric Thinking: The Internet's Challenge to Ego-Centric Institutions," www.compasspoint.org/sites/default/files/images/NonprofitDay/NetworkCentricThinking.pdf.

> Arguing that the new "tools of digital democracy"—online petitions, blogs, and meet-ups, for instance—are strengthening network-centric approaches, Miller and Stuart detail in plain language the forces that keep civil society organizations stuck in the "egocentric" thinking of "old power" organizations.

Network Impact and Center for Evaluation Innovation, "The State of Network Evaluation: A Framing Paper" and "Casebook." Network Impact, April 2014. www.networkimpact.org.

> These two papers, commissioned by several funders, provide a first deep look at the practice of evaluating a social-impact network's performance. The framework describes the key elements in evaluating a network, while the casebook provides 10 cases of network evaluations. Coauthors include Madeleine Taylor and Peter Plastrik.

Plastrik, Peter, and Madeleine Taylor. "Network Power for Philanthropy and Nonprofits." Barr Foundation, 2004. www.barrfoundation.org.

> Drawing on cases of nonprofit networks, this article makes a case for expanding the use of networks in the civil sector and examines the practical uses of the knowledge developed by "network science."

Robinson, Andy. "The Less Visible Leader: Emerging Leadership Models for Environmental Networks, Coalitions, and Collaboratives." Institute for Conservation Leadership, 2012. https://www.icl.org/resources/publications.

> An insightful article about the capabilities and attitudes of successful network leaders.

Scearce, Diana, Gabriel Kasper, and Heather McLeod Grant. "Working Wikily: How Networks Are Changing Social Change." *Stanford Social Innovation*

Review (2010): 31–37. http://monitorinstitute.com/?c=what-we-think &item=working-wikily#working-wikily.
An excellent article, based on research with the Packard Foundation, that explores how social-media tools are driving more connected ways of working, characterized by principles of greater openness, transparency, distributed effort, and collective action.

Scott, John. *Social Network Analysis: A Handbook*. London: Sage, 2000.
An accessible introduction to the theory and practice of social network analysis (SNA) in the social sciences. Scott explains basic concepts, uses, and methods in language that is technical but easier to interpret than most textbooks on the subject. Helpful for understanding network metrics and mapping tools.

Skidmore, Paul. "Leading Between: Six Characteristics of Network Leaders." In *Network Logic: Who Governs in an Interconnected World?*, edited by Helen McCarthy, Paul Miller, and Paul Skidmore. London: Demos, 2004.
Skidmore outlines key leadership skills and approaches adapted to a networked world in one of several articles in this volume by leading thinkers in networks across a range of disciplines.

Surowiecki, James. *The Wisdom of Crowds: Why the Many Are Smarter than the Few and How Collective Wisdom Shapes Business, Economies, Societies, and Nations*. New York: Doubleday, 2004.
Surowiecki, a staff writer for the *New Yorker*, brilliantly describes the ways that decentralized processes—from betting on sports to identifying the SARS virus—aggregate into unexpected patterns of "collective intelligence."

Taschereau, Suzanne, and Joe Bolger, "Networks and Capacity: A Theme Paper Prepared for the Study 'Capacity, Change, and Performance.'" European Centre for Development Policy Management, September 2006. http://lencd.com /data/docs/119-Networks%20and%20capacity.pdf.
Using the lens of complex, adaptive systems, the authors provide a clear, relatively simple framework for understanding the capacities and effectiveness of social networks, based on international examples.

Traynor, William J., and Jessica Andors. "Network Organizing." *ShelterForce* (March/April 2005). http://www.nhi.org/online/issues/140/LCW.html.
Drawing on their experiences building the Lawrence CommunityWorks network, Traynor and Andors offer important advice for developing large-scale, grassroots networks that connect community residents to opportunities and each other.

Vandeventer, Paul, and Myrna Mandell. *Networks That Work*. Los Angeles: Community Partners, 2007.

A useful overview of what's involved in building collaborations among organizations.

Watts, Duncan. *Six Degrees: The Science of a Connected Age.* New York: W. W. Norton and Company, 2003.

One of the most reader-friendly of the books explaining network science, filled with fascinating stories about a wide range of networks and clear explanations about the scientific analysis of network phenomena.

Wei-Skillern, Jane, Nora Silver, and Eric Heitz. "Cracking the Network Code: Four Principles for Grantmakers." Washington, DC: Grantmakers for Effective Organizations, 2013. www.geofunders.org.

Aimed at helping philanthropic foundations understand how to support network building, this relatively short article clearly describes four essential ways of thinking about networks and how funding them is different from funding organizations. The authors provide excellent general advice for funders.

Network Case Studies

Fire Learning Network:

Bruce Evan Goldstein and William Hale Butler have written six articles for various publications about the Fire Learning Network. These can be downloaded at http://conservationlearningnetworks.weebly.com/fire-learning-networks.html.

Lawrence CommunityWorks:

Plastrik, Peter, and Madeleine Taylor. "Lawrence CommunityWorks: Using the Power of Networks to Restore a City." Barr Foundation, 2004. www.barrfoundation.org. A companion article to "Network Power," provides a detailed look at a remarkable early-stage grassroots network growing in Lawrence, Massachusetts.

Preer, Robert. "Lawrence CommunityWorks Expands the Definition of a CDC." *CommonWealth* (Summer 2005). http://www.commonwealthmagazine.org/Departments/Innovations/2005/Summer/Lawrence-CommunityWorks-expands-the-definition-of-a-CDC.aspx.

Partnership Fund for New York:

Wylde, Kathryn, and Peter Plastrik. "The New York City Investment Fund: An Emerging Model for Corporate Engagement in Urban Development." Brookings Institution, October 2001. http://www.brookings.edu/research/articles/2001/10/metropolitanpolicy-wylde.

RE-AMP:

Grant, Heather McLeod. "Transformer: How to Build a Network to Change a System: A Case Study of the RE-AMP Energy Network." Monitor Institute, Fall 2010. http://www.garfieldfoundation.org/resources/Monitor%20Institute%20RE-AMP%20Case%20Study.pdf.

Reboot:

"Network Evaluation Summary Report." Reboot and Jim Joseph Foundation, 2012. This is a summary of the Reboot 2012 evaluation conducted by Madeleine Taylor and Peter Plastrik and published by the Jim Joseph Foundation at http://jimjosephfoundation.org/evaluations/reboot-inc-network-evaluation-summary-report/.

Urban Sustainability Directors Network:

Lippitz, Mike. "Exploring the Urban Sustainability Director's Network." Blog at Innovation Excellence website, posted April 16, 2012. www.innovationexcellence.com/blog/2012/04/16/exploring-the-urban-sustainability-director's-network-usdn/.

Network Membership Model

The Central Appalachia Regional Network (CARN) of about 20 organizations promotes policies and actions to improve quality of life in a six-state region: Kentucky, Maryland, Ohio, Tennessee, Virginia, and West Virginia. A part of the Kellogg Foundation's "Rural People, Rural Policy" initiative, CARN developed a comprehensive, detailed membership structure that spells out benefits and expectations for three categories of members. New members must be nominated by a current member and approved by the CARN Membership Committee, and must have participated in the network for six months as an affiliate member.

See table on next page.

Central Appalachia Regional Network

Members: Organizations active in both a policy work group and sustainability of the network. Members have a one-vote decision-making ability.*

Benefits

Receive financial support for meeting attendance if needed

Access to network infrastructure (extranet, coordinator, conference calls, etc.)

Oversees vision and objectives of the network

Use of CARN logo on organizational materials

Has decision-making capacity (one vote)

May apply to serve as a TA (technical assistance) provider and receive financial support for services

Working relationships with other rural advocates throughout the country (other Rural Policy Networks, National Rural Assembly, etc.)

Access to research, policy advocates, and connections relevant to issues of concern to Central Appalachia

Opportunity to share ideas, research, and connections in support of policy goals

Opportunity to seek and sign on in support of agreed upon network policy goals with the option to "opt out"

Expectations

Must commit two participants to the network activities (with decision-making abilities on behalf of their organization)

Must attend quarterly network meetings (minimum one participant)

Must attend monthly network conference calls (minimum one participant)

Must participate on both a policy work group and a network committee (Marketing Committee, Sustainability Committee)

Respond in a timely manner to input requests for feedback, information, decision, etc. (two days via e-mail)

Promote the work of the network through own connections, and activate their networks when appropriate action is deemed necessary

Commit funds or resources needed for participation (time, travel, etc.)

Participate in the development, approval, and implementation of annual work plan, including fundraising and other network sustainability initiatives

Central Appalachia Regional Network

Founding Members: Original CARN member organizations who started the network through the Kellogg Initiative.

Expectations

Same as Network Members

Benefits

Same as Members, but Founding
  Members have veto power
  with regard to admitting new
  membership and determining network policy positions

Affiliate Members: Participate in a policy work group or general activities of the network. Not required to participate at the Members level, but support the network and share relevant work through network contacts.

Expectations

Must participate on either a policy
  work group or a network
  committee
Respond to input requests in a timely
  manner
Promote the work of the network
  through own connections, and
  activate their networks
Commit funds or resources needed
  for participation

Benefits

Access to network infrastructure
May be recommended to serve as a
  TA provider and receive financial
  support for services
Working relationships with other
  rural advocates throughout the
  country
Access to research, policy advocates,
  and connections
Opportunity to share ideas, research, and connections

A Guide to Collaboration Software

Cause Communications produced a report that identified different uses for collaborative communications tools in an effort to help potential users figure out which tools were right for them. A portion of this analysis and advice is provided here, with additional details available at www.idealware.org/articles/options_collaboration_software.php.*

What Types of Software Exist?

First off, let's run through the types of collaboration tools that might be helpful to you depending on the different working scenarios your situation may present.

For Informal Conversations and Presentations

1. *Conference Calls*—tools that connect multiple callers on one phone line, for example, Freeconferencecall.com or Freeconference.com.

2. *Video Conferencing*—conference calls that also display video of one or all callers, such as Google Hangouts, WebEx, and some hardware solutions.

3. *Online Conferencing*—conference calls with an online component, such as shared slides, documents, videos, and/or screen sharing. GoToMeeting, Yugma, and WebEx, among others, provide this functionality.

For Information Sharing

1. *E-mail Discussion Lists*—e-mail groups, facilitated by tools like Yahoo! Groups or Electric Embers, that let participants easily e-mail everyone in the group.

2. *Existing Social Networking Sites*—online networking sites, like Facebook or LinkedIn, where users can create profiles and connect with others.

3. *Collaborative Documents*—users share and edit documents online, either over time or in real time, in a tool like Google Docs.

4. *Message Board*—online forums focused around questions and answers, such as tools like vBulletin and phpBB.

For Longer-Term Structured Collaborations

If your group is going to be working together over a period of time, it can be worthwhile to set up more-sophisticated collaboration environments. These tools will take more time to set up and to learn to use, but provide more structured functionality to help team members work together effectively.

- *Online Project Management Tools*—users share documents, calendars, tasks, and structured conversations, using software like Basecamp or Central Desktop.

- *Online Community*—users share profiles, documents, calendars, message boards, and more. Online applications like Ning or Kick-Apps let you build this type of custom community.

- *Wiki*—a collaborative website, where all who can view can also edit, using a tool like Confluence or MediaWiki.

- *Blog Network*—a community of linked blogs where users interact with posts and comments. Any blog tool, like WordPress or Type-Pad, will support this.

How Do You Choose?

These options come with trade-offs that aren't always clear. Easy-to-use tools often don't allow for easy documentation and archiving of conversations, for instance, while more-structured tools generally require significant up-front time to set up and define the processes that will help your group succeed. Before you decide, it's important to think through some key considerations about what will work best for your group. The following criteria can help you narrow down your options:

- *Software Cost.* Cost is always a factor, but less so in this area than most. Many options are free; others start at less than $20 or so per month.

- *Discussions in Real Time.* For some conversations, it's critical to have everyone together at once. But in other situations—for instance, to accommodate different schedules or time zones—it can be useful to let participants think and weigh in at their convenience.
- *Ease of Setup.* Some of these collaboration methods require almost no setup—just pick up a phone or fill out a quick screen and you're ready to go. Others require days or weeks of planning, especially to define the processes needed to ensure successful collaboration.
- *Participant Ease-of-Use.* The easier a system and process is for your participants, the more likely they'll actually use it. Don't underestimate the work needed to train users and get them to buy in on software that requires them to use unfamiliar tools or change their current processes.
- *Central Document Storage.* If you want to create or share documents across your team, it can be useful to have a central place to store them all. A number of methods let you post links or share files, but fewer help you organize or find them again later.
- *Conversation Archive.* A year from now, will you have any idea why you made a certain decision? A tool with solid archiving and documentation features lets you store conversations and then find them again later.
- *Structured Conversations.* The ability to collect all discussion about a particular topic in one place, or to break down a discussion into component parts, can be useful to those looking for tools to help in gathering input and making decisions.
- *Support for Personal Relationships.* Some methods help you share relevant background information and hold discussions that really feel like conversations. Others prioritize process over relationships, and make it harder to get to know your fellow participants.

Outline for a Network Work Plan

Although a network work plan looks much like an organization strategic plan, some elements are unique to the nature of a network. Below is the outline of a work plan developed for eight regional networks of urban sustainability directors.

1. Background about Network

    1.1.   Start Date

    1.2.   Purpose / Mission

    1.3.   Accomplishments to Date

    1.4.   Member History (number by year)

    1.5.   Major Activities in Past Year

    1.6.   Regular Activities (e.g., annual F2F meeting, monthly calls)

    1.7.   Existing Infrastructure (e.g., communications, coordination)

    1.8.   Current Members (Name, Title, Community)

        1.8.1.   Identify past and present leaders

    1.9.   Membership Rules (e.g., eligibility, participation)

    1.10. Governance Model / Processes

    1.11. Budget History

    1.12. History of Sources of Funding and Partners by Year

    1.13. What Is Known about Member Interests / Value Propositions for Being in Network

    1.14. SWOT Analysis of the Network

        1.14.1. Strengths and Weaknesses

        1.14.2. Opportunities and Threats

2. Goals/Objectives for Next Two Years
    2.1.   Network Impacts (on urban sustainability)
        2.1.1. Learning (e.g., about specific urban-sustainability topics)
        2.1.2. Activities (e.g., collaboration projects)
        2.1.3. Others?
    2.2.   Network Condition
        2.2.1. Number of Members
        2.2.2. Degree of Connectivity and Participation
        2.2.3. Others?

3. Network Partners

4. Network Activities to Achieve Goals/Objectives (Network Impacts and Network Condition)
    4.1.   Learning Processes
    4.2.   Collaborative Projects
    4.3.   Others?

5. Network Management to Achieve Condition Goals
    5.1.   Leadership
    5.2.   Member Management (Recruiting, Onboarding, Relationship Building)
    5.3.   Others?

6. Network Infrastructure
    6.1.   Communications
    6.2.   Coordination
    6.3.   Funding
    6.4.   Network Assessment Processes

7. Quarter-by-Quarter Activities/Management for Next Year

8. Milestone Indicators for Quarterly Progress

APPENDIX D

Network Health Scorecard

The Scorecard contains four diagnostic categories—purpose, performance, operations, and capacity—with many subtopics. Ask network members to score each topic on a scale of 1–5, with 1 = Not so much and 5 = Totally! Aggregate and analyze the scores, then have members consider them together, asking: What patterns do you see? What results need further discussion and/or action?

We suggest doing this exercise quarterly and seeing what changes over time. Add questions of your own to the Scorecard. Download available at www.networkimpact.org/downloads/NH_Scorecard.pdf.

SCORING

NETWORK PURPOSE
All members share a common purpose for the network.
Together, members have identified strategic goals and
    objectives for the network.
Network plans reflect network goals.

NETWORK PERFORMANCE
Members are working jointly to advance network goals.
Members are adding value to each other's work.
Members are creating new knowledge or insight together.
The way the network communicates with stakeholders builds
    support for the network.
The network is creating value for the constituents it serves.
The network is able to attract additional network funds,
    as needed.
Members honor their commitments to the network.

SCORING

The network is meeting its strategic goals and objectives.

Members are achieving more together than they could alone.

NETWORK OPERATIONS

Decision-making processes encourage members to contribute
and collaborate.

The network anticipates, surfaces, and addresses conflict when
it arises.

The network's internal communications systems are serving
it well.

All members are contributing time and resources to the
network.

The work of the network is attuned to the comfort and energy
levels of members.

Members reflect on network experience and adjust network
practice accordingly.

The network has mechanisms in place to promote accountability
among members (e.g., agreements, understandings).

NETWORK CAPACITY

As a network, members have the material resources needed to
advance network goals.

As a network, members have the skills they need to advance
network goals.

As a network, members have the connections they need to
advance goals.

Network-Centric Leadership

Many lists have been produced that seek to describe what network leadership is all about and how it's different from organization leadership. The Institute for Conservation Leadership, in its publication, Robinson, Andy, "The Less Visible Leader" (see Resources section), offers one of the most insightful and useful descriptions of network leadership attributes:

Catalyzes a Culture of Spirited Cooperation

1. Listens deeply to fully appreciate and understand the diversity of perspectives and motivations held by all involved.
2. Shows gratitude and encourages mutual appreciation for the ideas and contributions of all.
3. Regularly uses "both/and" thinking to identify solutions that meet both shared and individual goals and needs.
4. Communicates openly and clearly, matching the medium to the message.
5. Fosters opportunities (at all levels of the system) to develop camaraderie and trust.

Shares Power and Generates Momentum

6. Creates space for others to step up and contribute.
7. Embraces ambiguity and encourages experiments and innovations.
8. Helps the group to develop enough infrastructure to effectively make decisions and keep everyone moving forward.
9. Pays attention to conflicts in values and beliefs and productively orchestrates resolution.

Stays True to the Long-Term Vision while Navigating Frequent Twists and Turns

10. Persistently holds a clear picture of the purpose for working together.

11. Helps those inside and outside the collaborative effort understand the progress that is being made as well as the roots of that success.

12. Courageously continues to adapt in an effort to successfully achieve the long-term vision.

Personality Traits

Among other tools for assessing candidates for jobs, Stang Decision Systems uses a framework of five general personality traits, further divided into 29 facets or sub-traits, in order to screen candidates for jobs. Below is the list, with definitions for each facet. More at www.stangdecision systems.com.

EXTROVERSION

Extroversion is a measurement of how socially active or engaged a person is. Extroverts will usually be described as social, assertive, talkative, and active people who enjoy others and readily seek out large groups or gatherings. They will generally be comfortable in social situations and may prefer to work in teams, and are likely to take on a leadership position when doing so. Introverts, on the other hand, are typically described as quiet, reserved, and willing to let others take the spotlight. They may be viewed as "shy," but, in reality, they simply prefer to be alone or in the company of smaller groups of individuals. In work situations, they may prefer working alone to participating in team projects.

Friendliness   Friendly people enjoy the company of others and readily seek them out. They will typically make friends easily, feel comfortable in social situations, and appear open and approachable. People with low scores on this facet should not be perceived as unfriendly, but they may have a tendency to be more withdrawn and are not likely to approach other people without encouragement.

Gregariousness   People scoring high on this scale find being around other people exciting and fun. They enjoy large crowds and big parties. People scoring low on this scale will tend to find big groups overwhelming and usually prefer smaller gatherings.

Assertiveness   A high score on the Assertiveness scale indicates both a willingness and a desire to assume leadership positions or to take charge of situations. Assertive people will tend to be vocal, directive, and forward. Unassertive people are usually described as quiet, unassuming, and willing to let others take control.

Activity Level   High scorers on this scale tend to be busy, on-the-go people who take on multiple activities or responsibilities. Low scorers will tend to adopt a more relaxed, laid-back pace, and are likely to have fewer irons in the fire.

Excitement Seeking   Excitement seekers crave thrills and are often bored without a high level of stimulation. They are likely to be described as fast moving, and tend to enjoy being the center of attention. Low scorers will not seek out the spotlight and will possibly be overwhelmed by excessive hustle and bustle.

Cheerfulness   The Cheerfulness scale is a measurement of a person's tendency toward feeling and expressing a wide range of positive emotions. High scorers will generally be described as happy, optimistic, and outgoing. Low scorers do not necessarily experience negative emotions, but they are far less likely to appear outgoing or upbeat from day to day.

AGREEABLENESS

Agreeableness is largely a measure of a person's interpersonal skills. Highly agreeable people will tend to place a greater value on getting along with others. They will tend to be sympathetic and helpful, and fully expect that others will be as well. Agreeable individuals tend to get along well with others and usually achieve a certain degree of popularity; however, they may value cooperation so much that they are unwilling to take a stance that will portray them in a negative light or damage their popularity. Disagreeable people are usually viewed as being focused on themselves. They are often dubious about other people's intentions and therefore less likely to reveal information about themselves that might be used against them.

Trust   Individuals with high levels of Trust assume that most people are honest and forthright, whereas individuals with low levels of trust are more likely to believe that other people are deceptive or have ulterior motives. People with low levels of trust can be difficult to win over. People with high levels of trust may be naive, but are generally likable.

Forthrightness   People with high Forthrightness scores are sincere and genuine. They see no reason for deceptive behavior and believe the same to be true of others. They will tend to be open, frank, and honest. People at the opposite end of the spectrum could be referred to as "covert." They may be concerned that others will use information against them and will, therefore, disclose less. Covert people are likely to misrepresent themselves if it serves a purpose.

Caring   A high score on the Caring scale indicates a person is genuinely concerned with the needs of others and gets a sense of satisfaction out of helping out. While this may be viewed positively, it also comes at a price if priorities are not carefully evaluated. High scorers on caring are likely to be viewed as considerate and helpful. Low scorers on this scale are less interested in helping others and are likely to view requests for help as impositions. Low scorers will have less trouble doing difficult but necessary tasks such as cutting staff members who are not performing effectively.

Cooperation   Highly cooperative people will tend to value getting along with others more than being right or getting their way. They will usually avoid conflict and are likely to defer to others rather than engage in arguments. Low scorers are more likely to be seen as forceful or aggressive.

Modesty   Modest people are generally viewed as humble and self-effacing. This is not necessarily due to a lack of self-esteem; in fact, it is just as likely to be a result of the person thinking it is unbecoming to be boastful. Those people scoring low on the modesty scale are more likely to be viewed as immodest or even arrogant.

Sympathy   Highly sympathetic people are concerned for the well-being of others and feel genuine pain over human suffering. They will generally be viewed as kindhearted and generous. People scoring low on the sympathy scale consider themselves more rational and objective. Low scorers may be viewed incorrectly as callous or uncaring.

CONSCIENTIOUSNESS

Conscientiousness is largely a measure of self-control. Highly conscientious people are organized, strong-willed, determined, and resourceful. Sometimes called "prudent," conscientious people will tend to be viewed as cautious, wise, and intelligent. They will generally be reliable and easy to supervise, but they may also be stiff, overly rule-oriented, and resistant to change. Low scorers on the Conscientiousness scale are more likely to act on impulse, put off planning, and take a more laid-back approach to work and goals. They may be viewed as unreliable or lacking in ambition, but they will also tend to be more flexible and able to roll with the changes.

Self-Efficacy   People high in Self-Efficacy have confidence in their ability to get things done. They believe they have the skills and dedication to accomplish tasks effectively and to excel in their endeavors. People scoring low on this scale are less confident and generally do not believe that there is a strong correlation between effort and success.

Orderliness   A highly orderly person is well organized and tidy. They will tend to keep lists, make plans, and have a clear place for each of their possessions. Low scorers are more likely to be disorganized and messy.

Dutifulness   Persons scoring high on the Dutifulness scale are scrupulous rule followers and feel morally obligated to fulfill promises. They are likely to be viewed as ethical and will almost always do what is expected of them. Low scorers are more likely to feel confined by regulations and may be viewed as irresponsible and unreliable.

Achievement-Striving   Achievement-Striving individuals have a desire to set and meet difficult goals. They are likely to have a strong sense of direction. Extremely high scorers may be viewed as single-minded or obsessed with their jobs. Low scorers may be viewed as lazy or willing to do just enough to get by.

Self-Discipline   Self-Discipline is a measure of determination and persistence. People scoring high in this area have the ability to begin and finish even the most mundane tasks. Low scorers are more apt to procrastinate and become distracted, and may fail to complete projects they do not find interesting.

Cautiousness   Cautious people will plan their actions and carefully plot out their courses. They will tend to act deliberately and thoughtfully. They are likely to be described as reliable and steady but may also be viewed as fearful. Low scorers will often do or say whatever comes to mind without considering the outcome. They are likely to be described as direct and unfiltered. Low scorers may also be viewed as unreliable.

NEUROTICISM

Neuroticism identifies individuals who are prone to some form of distress. High scorers may have a tendency toward feelings of anxiety, anger, self-consciousness, or even hostility. High scorers are more likely than most to have a negative outlook and will have difficulty dealing with pressure or adversity. While this may make them difficult to work with, at times it can also be motivating if their worries are centered on getting work done. Low scorers are more likely to be even-keeled and positive from day to day. They are not likely to become frustrated by most situations. In some cases a low-scoring person's calmness can be viewed as apathy.

Anxiety   People who score high on the Anxiety scale tend to be fearful, nervous, and pessimistic. They are more likely than most to feel as though something bad is about to happen. Conversely, people with a low score on the Anxiety scale are more likely to be calm and unafraid.

Anger   High scorers on the Anger scale are easily annoyed or irritated and will have a tendency to lose their temper more quickly than low scorers. A high score on the anger scale is not necessarily an indication that the person will express their annoyance; rather it is a measure of how likely they are to feel angry. Assertiveness, agreeableness, emotionality, and self-discipline all play a part in how anger is expressed (or whether or not it is expressed at all).

Depression   A measure of a person's tendency to feel sad, uncomfortable, or blue, high scorers on the Depression scale may have difficulty feeling inspired. Low scorers are generally free from depressive feelings.

Self-Consciousness   People scoring high on the Self-Consciousness scale are highly sensitive to the opinions of others. They will have a tendency to feel uncomfortable as the center of attention and will prefer the company of close friends to a party full of strangers. Low scorers will usually be unaffected by situations a self-conscious person would consider uncomfortable. They will generally be at ease in most social or business situations.

Immoderation   High scorers on the Immoderation scale have a relatively difficult time controlling cravings and resisting temptations. They will often be described as having a well-developed capacity for enjoyment, but taken to an extreme it can also be self-destructive. Low scorers are better able to control their urges and will rarely over-indulge.

Vulnerability   A high score on the Vulnerability scale indicates a general susceptibility to stress. High scorers will often describe themselves as easily overwhelmed, unable to deal with stress, and prone to panic. Low scorers are more likely to remain composed and confident, even in high-stress situations. Low scores will also bounce back more quickly after failure or rejection.

OPENNESS TO EXPERIENCE

Openness to experience measures a person's interest in seeking out experiences for their own sake rather than for financial gain or getting ahead in the workplace. High scorers will tend to be curious and creative. They will usually have a deep appreciation for art and music, will care deeply about the aesthetics of their surroundings and their work products, and will often adopt an intellectual style. Other people are likely to describe the Open individual as creative, free-thinking, and "smart" (regardless of their true problem-solving skills). Low scorers will tend to have less abstract interests. Their thinking will generally be more straightforward and to the point. They are more likely to be described by others as practical and down-to-earth. Their curiosity is typically centered on areas that have near-term applicability.

Reverie   High scorers on the Reverie scale have vivid imaginations. They may find the real world too ordinary and boring, and will therefore spend a good deal of time lost in fantasy or daydreaming. Low scorers are more inclined to be satisfied by the things going on around them. While at work, low scorers are relatively more likely to be focused on the work at hand.

Artistic Interests   Individuals with high Artistic Interests have affection for art and a keen appreciation for aesthetics. They enjoy museums, poetry, music, and looking for beauty in everyday structures. In the workplace, they are likely to be concerned with the appearance of their office space and with their work products. Low scorers are generally not as sensitive to appearance and will spend more time worrying about content.

Emotionality   People with high scores on the Emotionality scale are aware of their own feelings and empathetic toward others. They will tend to express themselves openly. Low scorers are less likely to expose their feelings.

Adventurousness   Adventurous people are excited about new challenges and enjoy a variety of activities. They are not likely to do something in a particular way simply because it is the conventional method. High scorers may also become easily bored and often perform best in fluid, changeable work places. Low scorers will prefer familiarity to change and will have a tendency to stick to traditional, "proven" methods.

Intellect   Intellect is a cognitive style, not an indication of intelligence. Highly intellectual people will tend to be creative, enjoy abstract thoughts and ideas, appreciate the arts, and involve themselves in philosophical and theoretical discussions. Although Intellect is not a measure of cognitive ability, others usually perceive intellectuals as being bright. Low scorers, on the other hand, will prefer more-concrete and practical ideas.

About the Authors

Peter Plastrik is a cofounder of the Innovation Network for Communities (INC), a nonprofit national network that develops and spreads scalable innovations that transform the performance of community systems. Before founding INC with John Cleveland, Peter served as a partner in Integral Assets Consulting, a firm that specialized in strategic planning, innovation development, and organizational development with nonprofits, foundations, networks, and social enterprises. He was also CEO of New Urban Learning, a nonprofit that started and managed innovative schools in Detroit. He served as a senior executive of the Michigan Partnership for New Education, a public–private partnership seeking reform of the state education system. Before that, he served in a number of public-service positions, including chief deputy director of the Michigan Department of Commerce, president of the Michigan Strategic Fund, and executive director of Michigan Governor James Blanchard's Jobs and Economic Development Cabinet Council. A prolific author, Peter wrote *Banishing Bureaucracy: The Five Strategies for Reinventing Government* and *The Reinventor's Fieldbook: Tools for Transforming Your Government* with coauthor David Osborne. He is also a veteran newspaper reporter, having worked for Booth Newspapers in the State Capitol (Lansing, Michigan) Bureau and the *Kalamazoo Gazette*. Peter lives on Beaver Island in Lake Michigan. More information is available at www.in4c.net.

Madeleine Beaubien Taylor is the CEO and a cofounder with Peter Plastrik of Network Impact, which provides social-change agents with strategies, tools, research, and consulting expertise to design and use networks for increased impact. Madeleine is also a cofounder and principal of Arbor Consulting Partners, a social science research and evaluation consultancy located in Boston, Massachusetts. For more than 20 years, Madeleine has worked with public and nonprofit organizations and national foundations on strategy, program development, and assessment, most recently with a focus on social-impact networks. Over the last decade, she has contributed to the design, implementation, and evaluation of a wide range of network initiatives in the United States, including place-based efforts to increase civic engagement, cross-sector initiatives to promote immigrant integration, network organizing to support policies that benefit rural people and places, and regional collaborations to end homelessness. Madeleine has led the development of innovative tools and approaches for network assessment and works to provide grantmakers and others with practical up-to-date information about effective network evaluation. Madeleine received her PhD in anthropology from Brandeis University and spent her early professional career working in southern Africa. She currently consults in the United States, Brazil, and in her native Canada. More information is available at www.networkimpact.org.

John Cleveland is a cofounder and president of the Innovation Network for Communities (INC), a national nonprofit that develops and spreads scalable innovations that transform the performance of community systems. John also serves on a part-time basis as the executive director for the Boston Green Ribbon Commission, a group of 33 business and civic leaders supporting the implementation of the City of Boston Climate Action Plan. John has more than 30 years' experience spanning the public, education, nonprofit, and private sectors. He has done extensive work across the country in sustainable development, green building design, organizational learning, socially responsible businesses, school reform, and economic development. Prior to founding INC, John served as vice president of IRN, Inc., a market intelligence firm located in Grand Rapids, Michigan, that provided strategic planning, market research, automotive forecasting, and merger-and-acquisition due diligence to midsized manufacturing companies. Prior to joining IRN, John worked as a private consultant; as director of continuous improvement for Grand Rapids Community College; and as director of the State of Michigan's industrial extension service. John graduated Magna Cum Laude with a degree in City Planning from Yale University. More information is available at www.in4c.net.

Index

Note: page numbers followed by "n" refer to endnotes.

ACEnet (Appalachian Center for Economic Networks), 113, 115–16, 197n7, 203
adaptation planning, 105–6
adaptive management: about, 120–21; communication challenges, 134–35; drivers of adaptation, 122–24; edge of chaos and the balance point, 121–22, 183; governance model and, 128–32; member engagement and, 124–28; periphery relationships, 139–44; provisional planning, 135–39; routines and, 144–45; staffing model and, 132–34
adaptive problems, 193n16
Advanced Energy Economy (AEE), 6–7, 69–70, 98
affinity and membership, 47–48
The Age of the Network (Lipnack and Stamps), 2
Agreeableness, 180–81, 224–25
alignment networks, 35, 36
alignment phase, 104, 106–7, 170–71
alliances and coalitions, 29, 30–31, 105, 169
Andors, Jessica, 72, 205
Anklam, Patti, 155, 201–2
Appalachian Center for Economic Networks (ACEnet), 113, 115–16, 197n7, 203
Aristotle, 26
Armstrong, Michael, 177–79, 182, 184
Arter, Mia, 95
assessment. See evaluation and

assessment of networks
associations vs. networks, 29

balance point, 119, 121–22, 183
Barabasi, Albert-László, 1, 202
Barr Foundation, 152, 157
Bartsch, Laura, 69–70, 97–98
Beckstrom, Rod, 33, 193n18
Benkler, Yochai, 3–4
Bennett, Roger, 16
Bennett, Vicki, 106
Block, Peter, 1–2
board members and evaluation, 163–64
Bolger, Joe, 58, 205
Bornstein, David, 5
Brafman, Ori, 33, 193n18
Branding a network, 140–42
bridgers, 96, 116
Bridgespan Group, 67, 122, 140, 142
Brown, John Seeley, 41, 203
"Building Smart Communities by Network Weaving" (Holley and Krebs), 203
Burt, Ron, 154
business models, 59–65
Butler, William Hale, 21

C40 Cities Climate Leadership Group, 17, 142
Cascade Engineering, Inc., 15
"Casebook" (Network Impact and Center for Evaluation Innovation), 204
Central Appalachia Regional Network (CARN), 209–11
centralization and decentralization, 1–2, 58, 134, 179
chaos, edge of, 119, 121–22, 136, 183–84

Chicago Jobs Council, 133
Chung, Patrick, 54
Climate Change Knowledge Network, 50
Clinton, Bill, 26
closed networks, 46
"closing the triangle," 95
clusters, 96, 116, 118
cluster structure, 111–13
coalitions and alliances, 29, 30–31, 105, 169
Colbert, Stephen, 2, 29
Colbert Nation, 29
collective action, 71
collective impact model, 45
communication costs, 60
communication infrastructure, 58–59. *See also* information and communications technology (ICT); information flows and exchange
communications, customized, 134–35
community decision making, 67–68
competencies value, 52–53
complex social problems, 27, 193n16
conference calls, 94, 213
connect-align-produce ("C-A-P") sequence, 36, 104–09
connection phase, 104, 170–71
connection value, 52–53
connectivity: adaptive management and, 121; assessment and mapping of, 69–70, 149, 150–56; beyond connected core, 101; core building, 87–89; customized weaving, 95–101; importance of, 36; introductions, 83–85; levels of intensity of, 85–86; mass weaving, 92–94; shape or structure of, 109–17; value and, 71–72; weaving, art of, 89–92
connectivity networks, 34–35, 37
"connectors," 8
Conscientiousness, 226–27
consensus governance, 67–68
consultation and openness, 77
convening costs, 60
coordination roles and design, 54–57
core-periphery structure, 116–17
costs, operational and project, 60
Covey, Steven, 103

"Cracking the Network Code" (Wei-Skillern, Silver, and Heitz), 13, 75–76, 79, 206
"Creation Nets" (Hagel and Brown), 41, 203
credit, sharing, 140–42
Creech, Heather, 41, 48, 50, 51, 58, 65, 80, 115, 120, 202–3
crowdfunding, 63
culture and operating principles, 70–73, 175
Curtis, Jennie, 19–20, 35, 76–82

Daley, Richard, 13–14
Dean, Howard, 2
decentralization and centralization, 1–2, 58, 134, 179
decision making: adaptive, 122; governance models and, 65–69; transparent, 72, 131
Decker, Lynn, 20–21, 23, 119–20, 121, 123, 142, 148, 182
democracy decision making, 68
De Pree, Max, 1–2
design of networks: assessment and, 69–70; as balancing act, 73; coordination, facilitation, and communication, 54–59; funding models, 59–65; governance models, 65–69; key elements and issues, 40–43; membership, 46–51; operating principles and network culture, 70–73; purpose, 43–46; value propositions, 51–54. *See also* resetting network design
directories, 93–94, 135
domination, 81–82, 115, 118, 174
dues, 48, 62

earned income, 63
edge of chaos, 119, 121–22, 136, 183–84
Eggers, William D., 203
Eichel, Amanda, 87
Einstein, Albert, 167
Eisenhower, Dwight D., 136
email, 94, 213
emergence decision making, 68
engineers and engineered networks, 43, 75–82, 98

Ethen, Leslie, 168–69
evaluation and assessment of networks:
connectivity and mapping, 69–70,
150–56; engineers and, 81; framework
for, 149–50; health assessment, 156–60;
impact assessment, 160–63; initial
assessment, 69–70; lessons about, 163–
65; organizations compared to, 148–49
evolution of networks: adaptation
and, 120; C-A-P (connect-to-align-to-
produce) sequence, 104–9, 170–71;
connectivity structure and, 109–17;
core of connectivity and, 89; defined,
103–4; foresight and, 117–18; health
assessment and, 157–58; impact
sequence and, 162; intentional guiding
of, 103; mapping and, 153–54; staffing
and, 133
exclusion as governance problem, 174
Extroversion, 223–24

Facebook, 28
facilitation, 57–58
feedback and planning, 138
Fine, Allison, 3, 34, 63, 92, 126, 143, 174,
180
Fire Learning Network: about, 7;
adaptation and, 119–20, 121, 123;
assessment and, 148, 182; beginnings,
20–21, 23; branding, 142; case study,
206; as generative social-impact
network, 25–28; information flows
and, 34; legal model, 64; as production
network, 35; value propositions, 54
flexible capacity, 32–33
focus groups, 158–59
Friedman, Thomas, 2–3
funders: advice for, 75–82; educating,
163–64; evaluation and, 162, 164;
as partners, 144; philanthropic, 62;
questions of, 63; value and, 61, 64
Funders' Network for Smart Growth and
Livable Communities, 62
funding models, 59–65
fundraising, 61–65

Garfield Foundation, 19–20, 22–23, 32,
35, 76–82

generalized reciprocity, 38
generative problems, 27–28, 193n16
generative social-impact networks:
advantages of, 31–34; characteristics
of, 25–28; closed membership and, 46;
command-and-control and, 193n18;
defined, 5–6; distinctions, 28–29;
generosity and identity as forces
in, 37–38; starting, 13–24. *See also*
networks
generosity, 37–38
Gephi, 154–55
"gift economy," 37–38
Gladwell, Malcolm, 2, 8, 83
Gleichmann, Gabi, 187
Global Warming Strategic Action Fund
(RE-AMP), 23
Godin, Seth, 2
Goldsmith, Stephen, 193n16, 203
Goldstein, Bruce Evan, 21
Gospel of the Network, 4
Gotsch, Maria, 123
governance structures: adaptation and,
122–23, 128–32; design of, 65–69;
engineers and, 80; resetting and, 174
Governing by Network (Goldsmith and
Eggers), 203
government grants and contracts, 63
Granovetter, Mark, 203
Grant, Heather McLeod, 204–5
Grantmakers for Effective Organizations,
80, 201
grants, government, 63
Greenleaf, Robert, 179–80
Green Media Toolshed, 58

Hagel, John III, 41, 203
Hais, Michael D., 3
Hazard, Bruce, 70–71
health assessment, 149–50, 156–60
Health Care Without Harm (HCWH),
30–31
Heartland Local Government
Sustainability Network, 46–47
Heifitz, Ronald, 193n16
Heitz, Eric, 13, 206
Hershey/Cause Communications, 59
holes, structural, 154

Holley, June: ACEnet and, 113, 197n7; assessment and, 165; "Building Smart Communities by Network Weaving" (Holley and Krebs), 203; connectivity and, 87, 89, 90, 96, 99; design and, 71, 72; management and, 126, 127–28, 138, 143; network evolution and, 109, 117; resetting design and, 174; start-up and, 29; on uncertainty, 183
hub-and-spoke structure, 111–16
hubs, 95–96, 114–15, 118

ice breakers, 94
identity, shared, 37–38
Imai, Masaaki, 147
impact assessment, 150, 160–63
imposition, decisions by, 68
InFlow, 155
information and communications technology (ICT), 58–59, 135, 213–15
information flows and exchange: on activities, 130; alignment and, 35; connectivity networks and, 34–35; methods, variety of, 94; as network advantage, 33–34; news and updates, 94; online tools, 213–14; in person, 91; stock of information, 135; transparent, 72
In Search of Excellence (Peters and Waterman), 1–2
International Institute for Sustainable Development (IISD), 48, 115, 149
Internet, 58–59, 92, 213–14
interviews of members, 158–59

Jewish-American community. *See* Reboot
Jim Joseph Foundation, 147–48
Johnston, Sadhu, 13–14, 15, 17, 26–27, 66, 87
Jolin, Michelle, 203–4

Kahane, Adam, 27
Kalamazoo Community Foundation, 24
Kalamazoo Promise, 21–22, 24. *See also* Learning Network of Greater Kalamazoo
Kania, John, 5, 28, 32, 45, 135–37, 193n16

Kanter, Beth, 3, 34, 63, 92, 126, 143, 174, 180, 202
Karliner, Josh, 30–31
Kasper, Gabriel, 3, 204–5
Kearns, Marty, 58
Keller, Fred, 14–19
Kellogg, Foundation, 22, 24, 33, 92–93
Kelly, Kevin, 2, 37, 73, 204
"Knowledge Networks" (Creech and Ramji), 202
knowledge value, 52–53
Kramer, Mark, 5, 28, 32, 45, 135–37, 193n16
Kravis, Henry, 6, 32–33, 52, 108
Krebs, Valdis, 113, 117, 155, 203

Lao Tzu, 177
Law of Increasing Returns, 33
Lawrence CommunityWorks (LCW): about, 7; assessment and, 156–57; beginnings, 39–40; case studies, 206; connectivity and, 90; flexible planning and, 72; governance, 66; leadership development, 131; legal model, 64; membership and sizing, 46, 49; online information, 135; planning, 136; purpose, 44; value propositions, 51, 52, 71–72; working groups, 108–9
leadership: network-centric, 181, 221–22; personality traits for, 180–81; servant, 179–80; serving but not waiting, 182–83; steering committees, 50, 66, 80; trusting the network, 182; vertigo, embracing, 183–84; walking the talk and balancing acts, 184–85
"Leading Between" (Skidmore), 205
learning members, 50
Learning Network of Greater Kalamazoo: about, 7; alignment and, 35, 106; beginnings, 21–22, 24; branding, 141; capacity building and, 32; connectivity and, 88; governance adjustments, 122–23, 183; leadership and, 180; staff decentralization, 134
Lee, Je Hoon, 34–35, 51–52
legal entity models, 64
"The Less Visible Leader" (Robinson), 204

Levin, Rachel, 14, 16, 18, 32, 121
Linked: The New Science of Networks
    (Barabasi), 3, 202
links, in networks, 26
Lipnack, Jessica, 2
logistics coordination, 55
Lowell, Stephanie, 152

management. *See* adaptive management;
    evaluation and assessment of
    networks
Mandell, Myrna, 88, 205–6
many-channels structure, 111–13, 115–17
mapping of connectivity, 150–56
market test, 48
Massachusetts Interagency Council on
    Housing and Homelessness (ICHH), 7,
    35–36, 159, 163
Massachusetts Smart Growth Alliance,
    65–68, 195n20
Mead, Margaret, 4
measurement, shared, 45
meetings, 91, 97–101
membership: balance of core and non-
    core, 170–71; benefits of, 51–54;
    CARN model, 209–11; design, 42,
    46–51; directories of, 93–94, 135;
    disconnection and resetting, 171–72;
    documentation and observation,
    159–60; dues, 48, 62; enabling of,
    122; engagement, variation in,
    124–28; interviews of, 158–59; natural
    expansion of, 79–80; news and updates
    for, 94. *See also* connectivity
Memphis Fast Forward, 141–42
Millennial Generation, 3
Miller, Jed, 41, 204
mission statements, 44–45
modesty, 180–81, 182, 225
MomsRising.org, 142–43
monitoring. *See* evaluation and
    assessment of networks
Monitor Institute, 201
morphing, 29, 30–31
Moxon, Kathy, 83–85, 89, 92–93, 104
multiple-hubs and multiple-clusters
    structures, 111–13, 115–17

National Day of Unplugging, 18
National Fire Roundtable, 21
National Rural Assembly, 142
The Nature Conservancy, 20, 23, 64, 142,
    148. *See also* Fire Learning Network
"Needle-Moving Community
    Collaboratives" (Jolin, Schmitz, and
    Seldon), 203–4
net-centric approach: birth of, 2–4;
    leadership and, 181, 221–22; staff and,
    133
NetKAL (Network for Korean American
    Leaders), 7, 51–52, 54, 152–53
network builders. See *specific topics and
    networks*
"Network-Centric Thinking" (Miller and
    Stuart), 41, 204
network design. *See* design of networks;
    resetting network design
network evolution: capabilities, 104–09;
    structure, 109–17
The Networked Nonprofit (Kanter and
    Fine), 3, 126, 143
Network for Korean American Leaders
    (NetKAL), 7, 51–52, 54, 152–53
Network Health Scorecard, 157, 158–59,
    163, 164, 202, 219–20
Network Impact website, 202
network maps, 152–56
"Network Organizing" (Traynor and
    Andors), 205
"Network Power for Philanthropy and
    Nonprofits" (Plastrik and Taylor), 204
network readiness, 41
networks: advantages of, 31–34;
    distinctions, 28–29; history of social-
    impact networks, 4–5; nodes and links
    in, 26; serving but not waiting for,
    182–83; serving the network, 179–81;
    trusting, 182; types of, 34–36. *See also*
    generative social-impact networks;
    specific networks
"Networks and Capacity" (Taschereau
    and Bolger), 205
Networks That Work (Vandeventer and
    Mandell), 205–6
Networks United for a Rural Voice

(NURV), 84–85, 89, 92–93, 101, 104–5
Network Weaver Handbook (Holley), 29, 126, 203
network work plans, 217–18
Neuroticism, 227–28
New England Municipal Sustainability Network, 47
New Rules for the New Economy (Kelly), 2, 204
news updates, 94
New York City Investment Fund. *See* Partnership Fund for New York
nodes, 26
NodeXL, 154
Noveck, Beth, 4
NURV (Networks United for a Rural Voice), 84–85, 89, 92–93, 101, 104–5

Olivarez, Juan, 21–22, 24
online conferencing, 213
online tools. *See* information and communications technology (ICT)
"open innovation" networks, 203
Openness to Experience, 181, 228–29
open networks, 46
operating principles for network culture, 70–73, 175
operational costs, 60
Operation Ceasefire, 140–41
operations coordination, 55
Opportunity Chicago, 133
organization-centric view, 1–2, 5, 41, 133
orientation, 127, 131–32

participation standards, 128
Partnership Fund for New York: about, 6; case study, 206; evolution of, 108; FinTech Innovation Lab, 123–24; flexible capacity and, 32–33; value propositions, 52
partnerships, 62, 132–33, 142–44
Parzen, Julia: assessment and, 147–52, 165; connectivity and, 87, 89, 94, 95, 97–100; design and, 56, 57, 71, 72; management and, 125, 131, 132–33, 140; on network-building roles, 182–83; network evolution and, 109, 111;

search for replacement for, 180; start-up and, 15
patience, 82
performance measurement, shared, 45. *See also* evaluation and assessment of networks
periphery and core, 116–17
periphery relationships, 138–44
personality traits, 180–81, 223–29
Peters, Tom, 1–2
Petit, Philippe, 185
philanthropic funders, 62. *See also* funders
Pickett-Erway, Carrie, 24, 88, 123, 134–35, 141, 180, 183
pilots, 169–70
planning, flexible, 72
planning, provisional, 135–39
Plastrik, Peter, 204
political campaigns, 2
practice, network building as a, 8–9
production networks, 35–37
production phase, 104–5, 107–9, 170–71
project costs, 60
project management tools, online, 214
purpose, 43–46, 76–77, 120, 169–71
"pyramid" of engagement, 125–26

Ramji, Aly, 202
RE-AMP (Renewable Energy Alignment Mapping Project): about, 7; alignment and, 35, 106; assessment and, 159–60, 161; beginnings, 19–20, 22–23; capacity building and, 32; case study, 207; connectivity and, 88; engineers and, 76–82; funds, internal, 144; as generative social-impact network, 25–28; Global Warming Strategic Action Fund, 23; legal model, 64; membership and sizing, 49, 50; orientation to networks, 132; partnerships, 142, 143; shared measurement and, 45; staff decentralization, 134; Steering Committee, 50, 80, 129–30; strategic management, 56 57; working groups, 108
Reboot: about, 7; adaptive management and, 121; affinity and, 47–48;

assessment and, 147–48, 150, 151, 155, 161–62, 163–64; beginnings, 14, 16, 17–18; branding, 140; bridging and, 116; capacity building and, 32; case study, 207; connectivity mapping, 153; as generative social-impact network, 25; legal model, 64; membership, 42, 49; as production network, 35; production phase and, 105; staffing, 133
reciprocity, 92
Redwood Coastal Rural Action, 83
Reed, Rick, 71, 88, 132, 138
relationship building. *See* connectivity
Renewable Energy Alignment Mapping Project. *See* RE-AMP
resetting network design: governance issues, 174; membership issues, 171–72; network builders and, 167–69; operating principles and, 175; purpose issues, 169–71; value proposition issues, 172–74
resources value, 52–53
The Right Place, 64
rightsizing, 48–49, 122
Robinson, Andy, 204
Ronchi, Don, 154
Rural People, Rural Policy, 7, 33, 83, 142

Sacks, Adene, 147, 148, 151, 163–64
Savage, Lois, 80
scattered emergence structure, 114
Scearce, Diana, 3, 204–5
Schmitz, Paul, 203–4
Scott, John, 205
Seldon, Willa, 203–4
self-discipline, 184–85, 226
Senger, Peter, 179
servant leadership, 179–81
Shape Up Somerville, 128
Shepard, Bonnie, 50, 91, 141
Silver, Nora, 13, 206
Six Degrees (Watts), 3, 206
sizing, 48–49, 122
Skidmore, Paul, 205
small-world reach, 33
social-impact networks, history of, 4–5. *See also* generative social-impact

networks; networks
social media, 3, 28–29, 214
social movements vs. networks, 29
social network analysis (SNA), 152, 205
Social Network Analysis (Scott), 205
software for collaboration, 213–15
Southeast Sustainability Directors Network, 40, 45–46, 47
Southwest Rural Policy Network, 158, 164
Speirn, Sterling, 22
SPIN (State Policy Innovation Network), 97–98
sponsorships, 62
staff decentralization, 58
staffing costs, 60
staffing models, 132–34
Stamps, Jeffrey, 2
Stang, Spencer, 180–81
Stang Decision Systems, 223–29
The Starfish and the Spider (Brafman and Beckstrom), 33, 73
start-ups: engineered, 43, 75–82; managed, 19–24; mash-up, 13–19; morphing, 29, 30–31; types of networks, 34–36. *See also* design of networks
"The State of Network Evaluation" (Network Impact and Center for Evaluation Innovation), 204
steering committees, 50, 66, 80
Stevenson, Karen, 92
steward leadership, 179–80
Steyer, Tom, 6–7
"Strategic Intentions" (Creech and Willard), 202–3
strategic management, 55–57
"The Strength of Weak Ties" (Granovetter), 203
Strive, 45, 106
Stuart, Rob, 41, 204
success as driver of adaptation, 123–24
succession, lack of, 174
"Sukkah City" design competition, 18
Surfrider Foundation, 126
Surowiecki, James, 2, 205
surprises, 78, 138–39

surveys, 158–59

Sustainable Development Communications Network (SDCN), 80, 115

Sutherland, Susanna, 45–46, 47

Talent 2025, 19

Tamarack Institute, 144

Taschereau, Suzanne, 58, 205

Taylor, Blair, 141–42

Taylor, Madeleine, 204

term limits, 130–31

The World Is Flat (Friedman), 2–3

The Tipping Point (Gladwell), 2

Trade Knowledge Network, 115

transparency, 72

Traynor, William J. (Bill), 39–40, 51, 52, 72, 90, 131, 136, 182, 183–84, 205

triads, 95

Trippi, Joe, 2, 4

trust, 86, 90–92, 143–44, 182, 224–25

Ullman, Maggie, 40, 45–46, 47

Unleashing the Ideavirus (Godin), 2

Urban Sustainability Directors Network (USDN): about, 6; Armstrong and, 177–79; assessment and, 147–48, 155, 157, 160–62, 164; beginnings, 13–14, 17; branding, 140; case study, 207; connectivity and, 87, 89, 93–101, 110, 111, 116; connectivity mapping, 153; dues, 62; funds, internal, 144; as generative social-impact network, 25–28; governance, 66; Innovation Fund, 45, 89, 107–8, 109, 143; leadership and, 180–81; legal model, 64; membership, 42, 46–47, 49–50; membership dues, 48; mission statement, 44–45; network advantage and, 33, 34; participation options, 126; partnerships, 142; planning, yearly, 136; Planning Committee, 17, 56, 66, 89, 96–97, 130–31, 137, 178; purpose, 78; regional networks, 40, 46–47; staff and, 132–33;

strategic manager roles, 56, 57; value propositions, 52–53, 54, 72, 173; working groups, 107–9, 125

value propositions: adaptation and, 122; assessment of, 69; connections flowing to value, 71–72; design of, 51–54; engineers and, 77–78; network weaving and, 88; resetting and, 172–74

Vandeventer, Paul, 88, 205–6

vertigo, embracing, 183–84

Vibrant Communities, 136–37, 144

video conferencing, 213

volunteer efforts, valuation of, 64

voting, 68

Waldrop, Mitchell, 119, 121–22

Watts, Duncan, 3, 4, 206

The Wealth of Networks (Benkler), 3–4

weaving. *See* connectivity

Wei-Skillern, Jane, 13, 206

Western Adaptation Alliance (WAA), 105–6, 168–69

West Michigan Manufacturer's Council: about, 7; alignment and, 106–7; beginnings, 14–19; legal model, 64; member engagement, 125; membership, 42; network type and, 37; planning, 136; value propositions, 53

Wikipedia, 4

Wikis, 214

Willard, Terri, 115, 120, 202–3

Winograd, Morley, 3

The Wisdom of Crowds (Surowiecki), 2, 205

working groups, 71, 107–9, 125

"Working Wikily" (Scearce, Kasper, and Grant), 204–5

workshops, 94

Wylde, Kathryn, 108

Zero Mercury Working Group, 30

Zuckerberg, Randi, 28